Village Voices

Village Voices

a memoir of the
Village Voice Bookshop

PARIS, 1982–2012

ODILE HELLIER

foreword by
C. K. WILLIAMS

7

SEVEN STORIES PRESS

New York · Oakland · London

SEVEN STORIES PRESS
140 Watts Street, New York, NY 10013
www.sevenstories.com

LIBRARY OF CONGRESS CATALOGING-IN-PUBLICATION DATA

Names: Hellier, Odile, author.
Title: Village voices : a memoir of the Village Voice Bookshop, Paris,
1982-2012 / Odile Hellier.
Description: New York : Seven Stories Press, [2024] | Includes
bibliographical references.
Identifiers: LCCN 2024013703 | ISBN 9781644213797 (trade paperback) |
ISBN 9781644213803 (ebook)
Subjects: LCSH: Village Voice Bookshop (Paris, France) | Hellier, Odile. |
Bookstores--Paris--France. | Booksellers and bookselling--Paris--France.
| Expatriate authors--Paris--France. | Paris (France)--Intellectual
life--20th century.
Classification: LCC Z310.6.P37 H45 2024 | DDC
381/.450020944361--dc23/eng/20240710
LC record available at https://lccn.loc.gov/2024013703

College professors and high school and middle school teachers
may order free examination copies of Seven Stories Press titles.
Visit https://www.sevenstories.com/pg/resources-academics
or email academic@sevenstories.com.

Printed in the United States of America

9 8 7 6 5 4 3 2 1

For Gloria, who made it happen.
With gratitude and love.

Village Voice

Anglo-American

Bookshop

Village

Finishing touches.
© Martine Lafon

CONTENTS

FOREWORD

I've been fascinated for a long time by the way the shape of the city can change one's experience of it. When I first lived in Paris in 1957 when I was twenty, I knew no one, met no one, was very lonely, and the hotel I stayed in became my refuge and my sanctuary. When I went out, it was as though a string was attached to me, so my solitary wanderings through the streets, my quick visits to American Express to pick up my (usually nonexistent) mail, my trips to somewhere in the thirteenth to buy francs on the black market, were always brief excursions, never real voyages.

In the fifty years or so since then, I've lived in many neighborhoods in the city, and with each move the center of the city would shift, the shape of the whole alter, my access to it enlarge. There would always be various loci, the swimming pools where I exercised, the cafés I frequented, the museums I most often visited, and for the longest period in those years—this is the point I've been getting to—the Village Voice, and Odile.

This is what most struck me when I heard the sad news about the closing of our great bookstore, because when I left Paris with Catherine to move to the country, Paris had one single center for me—the Voice. When I come to the city now, it's almost always the first place I go; when I'm to meet someone, it's at the Voice; when literary friends who don't know Paris arrive, I tell them about the Voice, so that they, too, will have a firm center to their experience of the city.

I don't want this keepsake for Odile to be too much of a lament, though I suppose it will at least partly have to be that. So many years now since the day I wandered into what at first seemed as much a tearoom as a bookstore, and became part of a lively and growing community of resident readers and of visitors, of writers who live in the city, and writers passing through, who, as the Voice evolved into the singular bookstore it became, would read from their work in that wonderfully intimate upstairs room, in which each person in the audience seems a close friend. I've heard so many great writers up there, from Ray Carver, to Grace Paley, to Michael Ondaatje, to Mavis Gallant . . . on and on.

We each have our memories of those splendid evenings, so I think I should stop here, because this has surely now become a lament, not so much for the past as for the sad future which will have this benevolent home place missing from it.

Instead, I'll offer warm thanks to Odile, for all the years we did have of a bookstore, the brilliant and passionate selection of books which matched any I've known anywhere, and forever welcoming, ever warm, ever enthusiastic presence . . .

—C. K. WILLIAMS
Farewell Day
Paris, June 16, 2012

PROLOGUE

This desire for voice is physical: talk to me,
tell me a story.[1]
—ERICA WARNER

Bloomsday, June 16, commemorates the multifaceted life in exile and internationally lauded modernism of the Irish writer James Joyce. On this day, in 2012, hundreds of friends, writers, and patrons gathered at the Village Voice Bookshop for a farewell to their "home away from home" as American expatriates affectionately called our bookshop. Crammed inside and spilling out onto the narrow rue Princesse, the festive crowd celebrated three decades of Anglophone literatures and kinship forged around books and author readings they remembered as "raucous fun" and "deeply personal" in "a place of words and ideas where literature was not just a pastime but the very stuff of life," and "one felt oneself a guest rather than a customer." Here was "a community of writers and readers," and everyone had a story to tell, or to write down in the farewell guest book,* to convey what the Village Voice had meant to them over the years.

Author events set the tempo of its life, and apart from a few exceptions, took place in that "intimate upstairs room where elbow to

---

* All these quoted snippets are from the farewell guest book.

elbow, huddled in their chair," regulars and visitors from different corners of the world engaged in spontaneous and informal exchanges with guest writers who gave them a unique opportunity to participate in a discussion of their recently published texts. It stands to reason that enthusiasts of these literary events expressed the hope that we would make the record of our readings available to them.

When the bookstore closed, my plan was to ensure the safety of our audio and videotapes in an archival foundation. Yet, before shipping them all off, I had to sort them out, that is, go through twenty years of obsolete-looking audio cassettes and ten more years of videotapes packed away in a plethora of boxes.

Fortunately, while listening to these recordings, I realized that, besides summoning up a good number of our shared moments, each tape revived its author's specific voice, their work, and the special ambience of their reading that was a story in itself, a fragment of a whole. Brought together, they provided a vast and rich literary panorama wherein often starkly different worlds complemented one another.

It was inconceivable that such precious material be forgotten, or worse yet, relegated to relative oblivion. Each reading had to be restored within its own context and given in the author's authentic voice, keeping in mind that this particular voice is their signature. Wary of the uninterrupted and sometimes deafening brouhaha of our digital era, I felt the need to revive our author readings through a somewhat selective but coherent narrative in the form of a collective written memoir that would modestly conjure up "the very rich hours"* of the Village Voice Bookshop.

I have borrowed this expression from the literary memoirs of Adrienne Monnier, the owner of La Maison des Amis des Livres

---

* Originally the title of an "illuminated and illuminating" medieval manuscript, here this expression refers to *The Very Rich Hours of Adrienne Monnier*, translated and presented by Richard McDougall in *The Very Rich Hours of Adrienne Monnier: An Intimate Portrait of the Literary and Artistic Life in Paris between the Wars* (New York: Scribner's, 1976).

on the rue de l'Odéon, just across from Shakespeare and Company where Sylvia Beach boldly published James Joyce's *Ulysses* in 1922.

Through their dedication to literature, these partners made the rue de l'Odéon the buoyant interwar scene of a literary vanguard that attracted so many American, British, French, and other European writers and their readers.

Adrienne Monnier's and Sylvia Beach's respective and anecdotal memoirs are a mine of precious details that highlight their collaborative activities, including their friendships with many of the most innovative writers of the early twentieth century. Those writers came to their salon-bookshops to launch their works, engaging in debates around the current modernist trends in literature, the subtleties of translation, and other artistic pursuits of the audacious 1920s and '30s.

In the same spirit, our Village Voice Bookshop was firmly rooted in its own epoch—a thirty-year transitional period that prompted our authors to question the past while fully embracing a new century with the promises and immense challenges of the societal, ecological, and geopolitical upheavals that now called for adequate expression.

Though conducted in English, our events came to life in a French-owned bookstore located in the heart of Saint-Germain-des-Prés with its centuries-old stone buildings still bearing the imprint of prestigious French, American, and British writers from a historical past. The constant interplay between the two languages continued to enhance our lively question-and-answer sessions with its complex cultural and linguistic layering.

Hundreds of writers launched their works at the Village Voice, but for obvious reasons I could not give all of them their due here. It is my hope that everyone who read at our bookstore may find accents of their own voices in those of the authors who have been included in our chronicle of a specific time and place.

Announcement of the official opening of the Village Voice Bookshop, October 1982. © Le Prince Esspé

INTRODUCTION

I was forty years old when I opened the Village Voice Bookshop in July 1982. Oddly enough, at no moment in my previous careers did I consider selling books as a plausible profession. This surprising leap of faith would undoubtedly put me out on a limb once again. But hadn't I always listened to my instincts and taken the road not traveled when it came to choosing one direction over another in my earlier adult life? What mattered to me was the feeling that I was going forward, even tentatively, just out of reach of some elusive, ever-beckoning elsewhere.

In the immediate postwar years, children's books were rare, yet there were plenty of stories floating around, and I enjoyed eavesdropping on adult conversations that intrigued me and teased my imagination. Recalling my early childhood, I see myself and my younger brother exploring our large garden in Nancy, my mother's native city, or running through fields and farmlands during our summers in Brittany.

I was nine years old when we moved from Nancy to Saint-Brieuc, settling permanently in this small but lively port city on the northern coast of Brittany. We lived two steps away from our public high school, named after the author Ernest Renan, also close to the picturesque cemetery overlooking two valleys and the sea in the distance where Albert Camus's father was buried. He was

not even a year old when his father was killed in 1914 at the start of
the First World War. Forty years later, accompanied by his friend,
the writer Louis Guilloux, a native of our city, Camus visited his
father's grave. In his posthumously published last novel, *Le premier
homme*, the author recalls how shaken he was at discovering his
father's birth date inscribed on his tombstone, realizing that the
man lying in this grave was younger than his own son.

Mostly attracted to nature and outdoor activities as a child, I
turned to music and dance in my adolescence, but it was books
that truly filled my life. I never sought out stories written primarily for a young adult audience; rather, I was fond of documentaries
shown in our ciné-club, and I dreamed about exotic ways of jour-
neying in the real world. In my quest to live a life more intense
than my own and even become another person, I read the books
we had at home, mainly twentieth-century contemporary French
authors. Among my favorites: Alain-Fournier's *Le grand Meaulnes*,
Marguerite Yourcenar's *Memoirs of Hadrian*, Vercors's *The Silence of
the Sea*, and Rilke's *Letters to a Young Poet*. Jean-Paul Sartre's *La nausée*
put a name on what I felt to be my own existential malaise while
Simone de Beauvoir's autobiographical writings strengthened my
resolve to be free, independent, and travel the world.

One day during my last year of high school, I had an unlikely
encounter with a woman named Natacha that changed the course
of my studies and the future I had envisioned. Born in Russia,
Natacha had grown up amid the circles of the Russian immigration in Paris in the twenties and thirties. Perhaps intrigued by my
curiosity, she offered to teach me her native tongue.

The Russian language was totally alien to me and not even
taught in our public high school; however, as ancient Greek was
part of my lycée curriculum, the Russian alphabet already seemed
fairly familiar. On Saturday afternoons, I would walk across town
to get to her place, excited by the prospect of learning her language
by reading excerpts from Russian classics she had carefully chosen

for our session. She would receive me in her living room gloriously walled in by shelves of books by Pushkin, Gogol, and the like, and we would sit at her table facing the bow window with a cup of hot tea, ready to dive into another world. Encouraged by her and the promise of the unknown, I decided to take up advanced Russian studies at the University of Rennes. Our Saturday afternoon ritual continued, and before long, I was speaking Natacha's language.

In 1962, Solzhenitsyn's *One Day in the Life of Ivan Denisovich* was published in the literary review *Novy Mir*—the first hint of Stalin's gulags in postwar Soviet literature. It was a breakthrough moment that generated hope for a further easing of censorship. Khrushchev's relative relaxation of repressive measures had made it possible for Natacha to trace family members left behind in Moscow more than thirty years beforehand. They became a surrogate family for me when I was completing my junior year abroad at the Moscow State University (1964–1965), inviting me to spend my weekends with them, a rare opportunity for a foreign student to experience their daily life from the inside.

Yet hardly a month after my arrival, Khrushchev was overthrown by Brezhnev, who immediately halted the attempts of his predecessor to open up the country. Repression of writers resumed with even greater intensity. This was not good news even at my modest level as before I left for Moscow, my professor of Russian literature had entrusted me with a letter for his friend, the writer Andrei Sinyavsky, to be delivered to him in person.

In January 1965, unable to reach him by phone for an appointment, I showed up at his door and was told the author "would not be available for a while." Aware of his satirical critiques of Soviet society, I understood what this cryptic message really meant: Khrushchev's Thaw was definitely over. Only when I was back in France would I learn about the trials of Andrei Sinyavsky and other writers of his generation, including the poet Joseph Brodsky. All of them had been sentenced to labor camps during my own stay in Moscow.

In 1966, now certified as a teacher, I taught Russian in Paris and Vannes. Yet the stagnation, repression, and nuclear threats of the Soviet Union during this ongoing Cold War period did little to encourage French students to embrace its language. Two years later, in August 1968, Soviet tanks invaded Prague. I found myself comparing this offensive with the 1940 brutal Nazi occupation of France. A year afterwards, I resigned my tenured position as a lycée teacher of Russian studies.

My experiences in the Soviet Union had only deepened my understanding of the complexities of the Cold War with its ever-growing tensions. Just as strongly, it had awakened in me a new interest in world affairs. I enrolled at the École des Hautes Études Commerciales that, back in the 1960s, trained translators and interpreters for international organizations. I was now looking at world events from a different angle, and given this new professional challenge, I decided that the time had come for me to discover the United States, the reigning world power and major rival of the Soviet Union.

In the fall of 1969, at the height of the Vietnam anti-war demonstrations, racial and feminist protests, and the recent landing of the first man on the moon, the eyes of the world were turned toward the US. In due time I left Paris for the university city of Amherst in Massachusetts where I had secured a small job, one of several to follow in the States.

It was, however, my Greyhound bus trips that led me to discover the diversity of this wide country. I took in breathtaking natural scenery from the East Coast shores to the stunning bays of California. But it was the scenes of desolation I stumbled on that marked me most, calling up passages from Richard Wright in *Twelve Million Black Voices*[1] written thirty years earlier. One of these encounters took place just outside Baton Rouge, Louisiana.

Straying from city limits, and quite by chance, I ran into a group of impassive Black men sitting on cinder blocks in front of a row of shacks. They seemed to be staring into a void; suddenly, a big, tough white guy with a rifle on his shoulder appeared out of nowhere. Shouting loud threats at me, he started to chase me away.

Such a foray into the heart of the country only increased my interest in racial justice, inspiring me to translate one of Michael Thelwell's stories, "Fish Are Jumping an' the Cotton Is High: Notes from the Mississippi Delta" (*The Massachusetts Review*, 1966). It describes a trip to the heart of "Dixieland" in the mid-sixties that revealed the huge gaps between the stark realities of the lives of disenfranchised Black peoples and the lingering image of the mythologized "Old South." I sent my unsolicited French translation to Sartre's review *Les Temps Modernes*, which published my work in 1971.

During this same period, a friend of mine, a French social worker versed in the successful methodology of the community activist Saul Alinsky (later a model for the young Barack Obama) asked me if I would help him translate Alinsky's *Rules for Radicals*.[2] Our *Manuel de l'animateur social* that included Jean Gouriou's preface about his Chicago/Alinsky experience would come out with Éditions du Seuil in 1976.

As planned, I went back to France at the end of 1970 to complete the second and last year of business school. Then, out of the blue, I received an invitation to work as a translator for the major Algerian oil and gas company Sonatrach that had just opened an office in Washington, D.C. Its director was none other than the scholar who had led the Frantz Fanon seminar I had attended at U. Mass in Amherst. He had also been the first ambassador of independent Algeria to Washington, but, following his country's diplomatic break with the US over a political disagreement, had stayed on in the capital to continue to work out a rapprochement between the two countries.

Algeria had an enormous potential of natural resources waiting to be fully developed, but in 1971 its relations with France were at their lowest. Sonatrach turned to North America to set up a working commercial and industrial collaboration: Algeria would sell the US its liquefied natural gas while the latter's highly experienced industrial companies would participate in Sonatrach's ambitious, large-scale development projects. I immediately accepted the unexpected but attractive offer this promising company held out to me, not unaware that Algeria was now enjoying leadership status among other aspiring developing countries. In fact, the seventies proved to be years of intense activity between our Sonatrach office and its host country. Riding the headwinds of international politics, the Algerian company had managed to set up a working partnership with the US. By the end of 1979, having met our original goals, Sonatrach closed its D.C. office.

The previous year, a family tragedy had awakened in me memories of childhood events I had been able to hold at a distance all this time abroad. Now, I was ready to go back home where I felt I was needed. Strangely enough, once there, these flashbacks continued to haunt me, including one in particular from my early years.

On August 3, 1944, I had just turned two in the small town of Corlay in the heart of rural Brittany. I clearly remember lying on the floor face down, squeezed between my elder sister and my baby brother. My mother was stretched out on top of us, her arms enfolding all three children. At eye level I could just about make out the sunbeams filtering through the shutters being hit by stray bullets coming from the fight outside between local Resistance fighters and occupying German soldiers. All of a sudden, there was a walloping bang at the door, and precipitously my mother stood up. I have no memory of what came next. Some time later, I was told that my grandmother Françoise had died that morning, but I must have been three or so before I began to grasp what had actually happened.

On that fatal day in August, after breaking through a Resistance defense line, a Gestapo division operating in the region forced two villagers to reveal the names of active partisans. Under death threats, they indicated the road to my grandmother's café-restaurant called À la Descente des Courses ("Where the Races Meet"), a friendly gathering point for fans of Corlay's famous horse races.

In fact, this much beloved woman had not hesitated to turn its basement into the clandestine meeting place of our nearby Resistance members. When the two hostages were brought there they blurted out, "C'est là que ça se passe" ("This is the place"). By noon, the Nazi soldiers had stormed and shelled the café.

Fighting in an area close by, my father did not arrive in time. When he did manage to get there, he had to face the utter chaos of the fierce battle that had just occurred. He was to discover two bodies on the café floor: those of his mother and her young friend, the pregnant wife of a fellow Resistance fighter. They were lying in a pool of blood, their faces riddled with bullets. The German officer who had ordered the assault was likewise dead. In an effort to check his identity papers, my father searched through the breast pocket of his uniform. There, he found the photo of a wife and child. At such a moment, he must have felt despair, but also a good measure of guilt. Be that as it may, he vowed to go and visit the officer's family in Germany once the war was over. Three months later, my father was blown up on a land mine at la Pointe de la Varde (Saint-Malo). He never accomplished this journey.

These two dramatic events have always stayed with me, but buried inside. Yet I was never able to articulate how the loss of my father had actually shaped my values in life, including my deep and continued love of books.

One day, years later, in the middle of an interview I was giving, I had a vision of books burning in the middle of the street. This image jolted my mind as I immediately understood that these books set afire by the Gestapo had belonged to my father. Straight away I remembered my mother's description to me of this very auto-da-fé in Strasbourg. This startling reminder would bring me face to face with the reality that my starting up a bookshop was not at all a random decision.

Rather, it was a way of bringing a luminous quality to the darkened piles of books once brutally tossed into the street. I could thus continue my silent dialogue with the father I had never known.

Throughout my thirty years at the Village Voice Bookshop, I realized that I had never felt more at home than among its books, each one with its own story to tell.

Well after the Village Voice Bookshop had closed, I found myself looking through hundreds of author transcripts and listening to just as many tapes. These voices were witty, jocular, even outrageous—a sign of the times that could only make me smile. They were testimonies to brilliant writings, steadfast friendships, beguiling loves, and bold, stylistic strands of beauty.

Nevertheless, I was unable to dismiss that these very voices also recreated in me a sense of loss and stirred the memory of losses suffered—be it through an exile or the erasure of personal history and identity; the estrangement from one's native tongue and culture; the plundering of the natural world; the seemingly irreparable separation from loved ones. Inscrutably, these same voices gave me hope for three decades and continually reinvigorated the raison d'être of our long journey together in their affirmation of life.

When I close my eyes, I still hear them rising in ever-widening circles from our small, but cozy niche in the neighborhood of Saint-Germain-des-Prés.

PART ONE

"Paris, Paris, Above All, Paris!"[1]

Village Voice Bookshop poster, 1982. © Rollin

It Takes a Village
A TIME AND A PLACE

"A stroll from rue de l'Odéon, Les Deux Magots or
the Luxembourg Gardens, the hanging sign reads
Village Voice: Anglo-American Bookshop. The narrow
door and window frames are painted Greek island
blue.... Lingering a while in front of the window display, you'll want to dive inside, into an ocean of story."[1]

—HAZEL ROWLEY

When I returned to France at the end of 1979, contrary to
my expectations, the country had not changed much.
Living in different continents, in widely different
capacities as I had done, was not seen as a sign of curiosity, let
alone entrepreneurial spirit. Rather, it was labeled sheer instability.
I quickly realized I would have to reinvent my life by inventing
my own job.

One day, as I was browsing in a bookstore, recalling the
stimulating literary gatherings at Kramerbooks & Afterwords
in D.C., and Three Lives in New York, the idea of opening my
own bookshop crossed my mind, but of course it was a mere
fantasy: I didn't have the capital to undertake such an endeavor.
Yet the thought was a nagging one, and I finally mentioned it in

passing to friends and close family who, to my surprise, reacted positively. Encouraged, I set out to work on this project by first enrolling in a professional school for booksellers, all the while looking for funds and a promising location.

From the start, I knew that the bookshop had to be in Saint-Germain-des-Prés, in the sixth arrondissement, the postwar sanctuary of existentialism though no longer, as author Edmund White ironically remarked, "the Intelligence Central for the whole world, as it once claimed to be."[2] Nevertheless, it was the prestigious "Golden Triangle" of the major French publishing houses and famous bookstores and, with the Sorbonne at the end of the boulevard Saint-Germain, it still flaunted an air of heady bohemia. Its legendary literary cafés continued to attract tourists from all over the world, and luxury boutiques—traditionally found on the Right Bank—were slowly crossing over the Seine to the Left Bank, setting up shops and bringing a lively international crowd to the neighborhood.

I had already visited a number of sites when I stumbled upon a "To Let" sign at number 6, rue Princesse, a quiet narrow street just off the busy boulevard Saint-Germain. The place was in a sorry state of disrepair, abandoned by a restaurant owner who had fled abroad, in the hope of outdistancing President Mitterrand's new socialist policies that had brought so-called "leftists to dance in the streets and French capitalists to leave the country."[3]

A close acquaintance of mine expressed an interest in buying the two-story location with the specific purpose of renting it out as a future bookshop. The owner at that time, Madame Grès, a leading figure in French haute couture, and seemingly relieved by my friend's offer, agreed to sell it and received us in her imposing office overlooking the Place Vendôme. A gracious woman with a commanding presence, Madame wore a distinctive pearl-gray silk turban wrapped around her head, reminiscent of her signature draped gowns. The dignified document signed that day of

September 1981 was to be the breakthrough moment that would turn the hoped-for bookstore into reality.

The space had excellent potential, according to my brother, an architect, who had already reworked it in his imagination, but its strong point was its location: tucked between two historical churches—Saint-Germain-des-Prés with its sober Romanesque architecture and the Baroque mammoth of Saint-Sulpice. The rue Princesse also stood at the center of a magical circle of American literary landmarks that conjured up the names of famous writers who had made Paris their home and epicenter of their very lives: the rue Cardinal Lemoine was once the address of a young Ernest Hemingway; on the rue de l'Odéon, Sylvia Beach had presided over her mythical bookshop Shakespeare and Company; around the corner from the Luxembourg Gardens, the rue Fleurus had been the home of Gertrude Stein's salon, that "charmed circle"[4] of global writers and artists, while Natalie Clifford Barney, the muse of the rue Jacob, gathered into her Temple of Friendship the many talented American women who had crossed the Atlantic in search of freedom and self-expression.

In the 1950s, Richard Wright lived on the rue Monsieur-le-Prince and, two streets away, the Café Tournon became his head-quarters where, together with his African American friends, all expatriates like him, he used to engage in heated debates. In the 1960s, Henry Miller had briefly stayed at 4 rue Princesse, next door to our future bookstore, and closer to la Place Saint-Michel, Allen Ginsberg and his Beat friends hung out in a small, seedy hotel on the rue Gît-le-Cœur. All boded well for us, as the Village Voice was to be within walking distance of these streets, peopled with these invisible presences.

Compared to these prestigious landmarks, the rue Princesse looked like a modest village street. Built upon the ruins of a royal mansion, it became the rue Révolution before recovering its orig-inal name under Napoleon I. Yet la rue Princesse had nothing

princely about it: its sixteenth- and seventeenth-century buildings were plain looking, and the walls of my future bookshop
were not even straight. However, just across from number 6, the
Bordas Gallery continued to display the stone on which Picasso,
Chagall, Miró, and other artists had printed their lithographs. A
few doors up, the exclusive night club Chez Castel would welcome
both Parisian and international jetsetters, offering early risers
the eerie spectacle of glamorous stars tipsily searching for their
chauffeur-driven limousines after a long "Nuit Princesse" party.[5]

Designed by my brother, the two-story bookstore-cum-café and
gallery with its decor of light wood and old beams painted pastel
blue looked like a high loft, where "its unusual atmosphere encompassing bookstore, café, and art welcome customers who, at the
immaculate blond wood tables, nurse their cappuccinos and espres-
sos while engaged in conversation or scribbling in wire notebooks."[6]

Given its cool look and its ambience of intellectual bohemia,
it came naturally to me to call the bookstore the "Village Voice
Bookshop," harkening back to the emblematic newsweekly the
Village Voice, born in downtown Manhattan in 1955. As a precious
alternative source of information during my American years on
the politics of the time (Vietnam and protest movements) and
vanguard arts, it was an indispensable guide to my New York weekends. And there was the added lure of its no-holds-barred classified ads. I couldn't imagine a better choice for the kind of place I
had in mind. We contacted the Village Voice office, and within three
days, its legal department gave us the green light to use its name
"exclusively for a bookshop."

In response to our invitation to its official opening in October
1982, the newsweekly sent us a number of mementos, including
the traditional blue aprons of its town criers, together with car-
toons and among them, a Gallic rooster perched on top of the
Eiffel Tower with its "cocorico" announcing the opening of the
Paris Village Voice. These charmingly inventive wishes for success

really made for a warm welcome. In the years to come, from time to time, a couple of their jazz critics would burst into the bookshop with a resounding "Hi everyone, Nous voilà!" to check if the store was honoring its appellation. After a look around and a few joking asides, they would leave, ready to pursue other Parisian adventures, satisfied that their own *Village Voice*[7] was popular and selling well in its aptly named new home. A few months after its opening, this "new home of American expats," started to spark the curiosity of the French, and mostly the Anglophone press. In fact, the former wondered if it made sense to open yet another English-language bookshop in a city with more than half a dozen. On the other hand, the Anglophone press welcomed this new venture, seeing it in the continuum of the rich and memorable tradition of expatriate writers in the Paris of the interwar years. Indeed, these same writers had launched the rich and varied literature of the twentieth century.

In the following chapters, we will listen to such numerous and talented expatriate and visiting writers who gravitated to the Village Voice Bookshop, delighting us with lively and memorable readings from their most emblematic works. All questions are asked by members of the audience, unless specified otherwise.

Odile with Shari Benstock. © C. Deudon

The Lost and Found Generation
PARIS WAS A WOMAN[1]
Noël Riley Fitch, Shari Benstock, Joan Schenkar

"In the rue Princesse, a few streets away from the rue
de l'Odéon where Sylvia Beach nurtured the careers
for James Joyce and Hemingway, a French woman has
created a legitimate haven for books and writers."[2]

—BARRY GIFFORD

As soon as the bookstore opened, browsers and customers started to compare it with Sylvia Beach's mythical Shakespeare and Company. It was a flattering but specious observation. Thanks to her literary intuition and against all odds, Beach had made history by publishing James Joyce's *Ulysses*, the emblematic novel of the modernist movement, censored for obscenity in Great Britain and the United States. However, between 1922, the year of *Ulysses's* first printing, and the opening of our bookshop in 1982, the world had changed and censorship was no longer what it had been.

Likewise, quite unexpectedly, successive waves of young American writers and artists, disenchanted with Ronald Reagan's conservative economic policies, were looking for new horizons and started to converge in Paris. The recently opened Village

Voice Bookshop became the venue of their literary and artistic production. The allusion to Beach took on added significance as the Anglophone press began to describe our shop as "the center of gravity for a shifting population of artists and writers in the expatriate colony . . . and, in the tradition of Sylvia Beach, its owner has made bookselling into the art of cultural entrepreneurship."[3]

As it happened, this so-called "Third Wave" of American expatriates awakened keen interest in the literature of the 1920s "Lost Generation" and its avant-garde authors, with Ernest Hemingway leading the way. Soon, our shelves were overflowing with reprints of memoirs from that period, along with a flurry of original publications recounting the American expatriate experience of that decade and then on into the 1930s. One of the most striking aspects of this revival was the rediscovery of forgotten women writers and artists who had greatly contributed to the fame of the Lost Generation. Given the increasing number of women's studies departments around the US, a diligent generation of female scholars started to unearth their findings from dusty archives and give them life through critical works and detailed biographies.

Noël Riley Fitch

On July 31, 1983, the first anniversary of the bookshop, Noël Riley Fitch, a vivacious American woman radiating a definite joie de vivre, presented her biography of Sylvia Beach, *Sylvia Beach and the Lost Generation: A History of Literary Paris in the Twenties and Thirties.*[4]

In addition to her research at the Sylvia Beach archives of Princeton University, Fitch had tracked down friends who had been close to Sylvia and were able to provide new insights into the bookseller and publisher's life and her Parisian bookstore, Shakespeare and Company. A couple of older people in the audience that night recalled Beach as a bookseller, making her presence almost palpable.

At the start of her talk, Fitch introduced the central issue of the book—James Joyce's *Ulysses* and the sad end of the mythical friendship between Beach and the author, alluded to in the famous photograph reprinted on the book cover: the two friends are standing apart and looking in different directions, Beach tentatively glancing at Joyce who is sternly fixed on the camera. They are not talking to each other. Fitch gave a fascinating and precise account of their close but contentious collaboration in the fastidious editing and final printing of *Ulysses*. After long months spent together poring over commas and semicolons in the novel, their friendship turned sour as Joyce pressed Beach to renounce her rights to the work, bringing their long working relationship to a close.*

Jim Haynes, a most popular figure of the American expatriate community in Paris, was at the reading and later that evening added a personal anecdote: in 1959, as the owner of the Paperback Bookshop in Edinburgh, he had invited Sylvia Beach to visit him. She graciously thanked him for his kind gesture and "especially for not mentioning the name of James Joyce, whom every one of her correspondents felt obliged to cite." [laughter]

Joyce was not the only indelicate friend of Shakespeare and Company, Fitch told us: according to a certain Eleanor, Beach's assistant, Hemingway, also a regular visitor, would pick up books and reviews and go out without paying. Aware of their constant cash flow problem, Eleanor would conscientiously but discreetly write down in a notebook the titles taken away and the sums owed for them.

One day, in the absence of Sylvia and alone in the bookshop with Hemingway, she presented him with the bill. Taken aback, he took a twenty-dollar bill from his wallet and, without a word,

---

* Noël Riley Fitch explains the reasons for the falling-out between the two: Joyce's loans and other advances from Beach were to be compensated by rights to the book, but he never honored his debts or his promise.

walked out. Briefed by Hemingway about the incident, Sylvia had a word with Eleanor, warning her against such initiatives in the future and insisting that the friends of Shakespeare and Company had the right not to pay if they did not wish to. The latter was flabbergasted and even felt humiliated, but Sylvia did not heed the young author's boorish advice "to get rid of that female" and refused to fire her. He continued to do as he pleased and paid for only three of the twenty copies of his new book For Whom the Bell Tolls, ordered as gifts for his friends.[5]

As this episode intimates, Sylvia Beach had a strong personality put to the test more than once in her life, especially during the Nazi occupation of Paris, when, in 1941, she firmly refused to sell a Nazi officer her last remaining copy of Finnegan's Wake.[6] Rather than give in to his threats, she chose to close her bookshop that same day, however vital it was to her survival. After the war, she would never have the chance to reopen it.

Among the questions asked by the audience that night, the most frequent one concerned the current Shakespeare & Co: "Was it Sylvia Beach's bookshop that moved from Odéon to the quays?" Fitch reminded us that, upon Sylvia's death in 1962, her sister Holly collected the store's archives and sold them to Princeton University. The name Shakespeare & Co. had since been freely used by some seven bookshops in Europe and the United States. "Their owners," Fitch told us, "had taken up the appellation as a way of placing themselves in the literary tradition of Sylvia Beach's original Shakespeare and Company."[7]

Shari Benstock

Sylvia Beach is, naturally, one of the women cited at length by Shari Benstock in her seminal work, Women of the Left Bank, Paris, 1900-1940, that explores the life and writing of some twenty extraordinary female writers and cultural icons of the era.[8] Through their literary achievements, they contributed to the unique cultural scene of the Lost Generation, usually associated with male writers such as Ernest Hemingway and F. Scott Fitzgerald.

An elegant woman with a gentle face and striking presence, Benstock presented *Women of the Left Bank* at the Village Voice on January 15, 1987. Her friend, Isabelle de Courtivron, a professor of French studies at MIT and author of several works on feminism, introduced her, stressing the unique and essential role of the Paris American literary salons of Sylvia Beach, Gertrude Stein, and Natalie Clifford Barney "as scenes of intense literary and artistic creativity, enhanced by mutual support and friendship." Benstock went on to add that "these salons created the ideal conditions for this unique and historical convergence in Paris of so many American women's talents at one specific time . . ."[9]

Out of the twenty women in her book, our guest speaker chose to highlight Djuna Barnes, the author of the novel *Nightwood* (1936), decried by some as a work of lesbian perversion and depravity, but seen by Benstock as a meticulous exploration of "women's existential torment."[10] This bold novel that portrayed lesbianism in all its complexities is also representative of the modernist narrative form of the time: "not a shadow to Joyce's *Ulysses*, but a singular undertaking that addresses woman's place in the patriarchal construct."[11]

Q: "Why did these women from moneyed backgrounds choose to abandon their American privileges for a hazardous life in Paris?" (a recurring question)

Benstock: "To these women, France meant freedom. In America, they transgressed the rules of their class. To write poetry was okay, but fiction was considered too risky, and besides, as a woman, you couldn't sign your own books. American old-money rules were strict, but behind the decorum and beyond the reproach, gossip reigned and could be dangerous and even destroy a reputation. If you were a woman, a secret, private life was impossible. Paris offered these women a release from American Puritan ethics."[12]

Q: "Sapphic love played a major role in these women's lives and creativity. Could that be the reason why they disappeared from sight until the women's movement of the '70s?"

Benstock: "These women adamantly rejected patriarchal values, and they found inspiration in Paris women's communities. It was not accidental that the city's three main salons were established by women, and the three of them were lesbians. However, such women were not just pursuing sexual freedom, they were also seeking a stimulating intellectual climate. Admiring the European cultural tradition, they were looking for the company of the great European minds and artists of the time."[13]

Natalie Barney's Temple of Friendship was perhaps the most diversified and cosmopolitan assemblage of talents at that time. In her recollections *Aventures de l'esprit*, Barney details her conversations and correspondence with such artists as Gide, Proust, D'Annunzio, Valéry, T.S. Eliot, and many others who had immense admiration for this woman of letters.[14] Her closest friend was Remy de Gourmont, "the greatest humanistic intelligence of pre-war Europe"[15] whose own correspondence with Barney (*Lettres à l'Amazone*),[16] musings on love, absence, pleasure, boredom, memories, and forgetfulness, invites us to imagine their exchanges infused with brilliance, sincerity, and wit.

If intellectual ebullience, together with creative, playful entertainment, was the ferment of Barney's Temple, sapphic love was its credo. One of Barney's great loves was Dolly Wilde,[17] "the niece of Oscar Wilde, playing the impertinent, frolicking role of puppy Wilde" and whose obscured and extravagant but doomed life is brought to us by Joan Schenkar in her singular biography *Truly Wilde*.

Joan Schenkar

Quite an original person, sporting a signature crimson red flower in her tousled black hair, Joan Schenkar was an American playwright and biographer who divided her life between New York and Paris, once nesting around the corner from our bookshop. On October 10, 2000, Schenkar conjured up the ghost of Dolly Wilde through the story of her consuming passion for Natalie Barney who, since childhood, had been fascinated by Dolly's uncle, Oscar Wilde.[18] Barney had met him during his triumphant lecture-tour in America in 1882, and her early and lasting admiration for the Irish poet and dramatist may have played a role in their love affair, especially since Dolly dressed like her uncle, often impersonating him.[19]

The author of *Signs of Life: six Comedies of Menace* and a lauded biography of Patricia Highsmith, Schenkar is a writer who probes the inner demons of her characters. In her singular biography *Truly Wilde: The Unsettling Story of Dolly Wilde, Oscar's Unusual Niece*, Joan Schenkar powerfully conveys the tortured life of Dolly Wilde, a woman entangled in her very talents and shortcomings.[20] Yet given her beauty and dazzling mind, she was able to attract the most interesting men and women of her generation, including Natalie Barney, her longest love affair. Through a dire combination of drug abuse and irrational behavior, the gifted Dolly, promised to great achievement, ended up destroying herself. "Nevertheless," Schenkar reminded the audience, "their reciprocal love was inspired by their recognition of each other as women of their time—free, complex, talented, and ambitious."[21]

In the context of this fateful passion, our author shows Natalie Barney to be "the radical sustainer of an unprecedented community of art-making women who formed by their work and their relations with each other the only serious critique of Modernism as it was practiced by male artists in the twentieth century."[22]

(*right*) Flyer for small press fair, June 1, 1985.

(*below*) John Crombie, Michael Lynch, Carol Pratl, Odile, Jim Haynes, 1985.

© Village Voice archives

small press fair

saturday june 1st

village voice bookshop

6. rue princesse

paris 75006

noon-7 pm

with: handshake, SPHINX, frank, paris exiles, moving letters, paris atlantic...

3

The Third Wave of American Expatriates and Literary Magazines

John Strand, Kathy Acker, Eduard Limonov, Ricardo Mosner,
Carol Pratl, David Applefield, Edouard Roditi, Jim Haynes

"There can be no innovation without tradition.
We gratefully acknowledge the great Paris expatriate
traditions, but we won't sink into nostalgia for the
still-swirling ghosts. . . . Instead we will keep in mind
how tradition can serve creativity."[1]

—JOHN STRAND

As I was working on my project of an Anglo-American bookstore in 1981, I never anticipated the sudden arrival of so many young Americans in Paris, coinciding with the future opening of the Village Voice, and so a stroke of luck for us. Yet there was nothing surprising in this new influx of expatriates from the US.

Reminiscing about his youth in 1930s Paris and his joint reading with Hemingway at Beach's Shakespeare and Company (1937), the English poet Stephen Spender remarked at his Village Voice reading in 1988 that the new wave of Americans had the same economic basis as the massive immigration of the Lost Generation. In both cases, they could live in Paris on a "far traveling dollar." Barely worth four francs in 1979, the dollar value rose to ten francs in 1983, given France's inflationary economy. Sheer happiness for our fledgling bookshop, as it meant more American customers and a larger audience for our readings! On the other hand, importing books from the States cost more than anticipated, cutting into our inventory resources. Fortunately, the attractiveness of our café steadily brought in the necessary funds to continue to import a wide range of American titles, the distinctive feature of our bookstore.*

I first became aware of the growing number of Anglophone expatriates in and around Paris through the discovery of the English-language *Paris Passion*, a large-format magazine with eye-catching covers.[2] It primarily targeted American expats, providing them with precious information on French ways of life and culture, and, by a happy coincidence, the first issue we carried featured an article called "French Intellectuals and the Left Bank."

Started in 1980 by Robert Sarner, a young entrepreneurial Toronto journalist, *Paris Passion* was the forerunner of a flurry of small American literary magazines that popped up in Paris, following the great tradition of the glorious 1920s.

Alongside various poetry booklets, literary magazines appeared in the winter of 1984 and '85, among them *Paris Exiles*, *Frank: An International Journal of Contemporary Writing & Art*, and *Sphinx: Women's International Literary Review*. Each was launched at the Village Voice, creating a continuing dialogue between contributors and their readers, coming mostly from the community of American transplants.

John Strand

The founder of *Paris Exiles*, John Strand, a young American playwright, clarified its title in his first editorial note, writing that "exile has many shades of meaning of which political exile is

---

* The café and monthly art exhibits had created a specific ambience, but five years later I took the risk of dedicating all the space to books, my first priority.

only the most visible . . . exile could be self-imposed, spiritual and artistic." Whether physical or emotional, the feeling of exile is an experience common to people living away from their familiar environment. This complex theme led Strand to conceive his review as an open forum wherein writers and artists from all countries could meet and exchange their works.

Consistent with his mission, on January 25, 1985, he launched the first issue of *Paris Exiles* at the Village Voice, along with three emblematic young authors of the eighties: the American iconoclast Kathy Acker, the Soviet dissident Eduard Limonov, and the '68 French "New Philosopher" Bernard-Henri Lévy.[3]

Kathy Acker cut a dashing figure, sporting her punk haircut, ear piercings, and tattoos on her muscular arms. She looked like an intrepid tomboy, but New York literary circles considered her to be the heir to William Burroughs. Like Burroughs, she was a subversive writer ready to break all taboos and an adept of his Dadaist technique

Kathy Acker and Eduard Limonov at the Village Voice Bookshop, January 25, 1985. © Leigh Miller

of the "cut-up." Acker read an excerpt from her work-in-progress *Don Quixote, Which Was a Dream*, a conversation between a dog called Nixon and its bitch, Mrs. Nixon. Herein she ignored the politically correct and turned her invective against American politics and its purveyors into the most extravagantly tall stories. The piece was later performed at the American Center, which closed in 1994 after fifty years of showcasing the French-American avant-garde arts.[4]

Another one of Acker's novels, *My Death My Life by Pier Paolo Pasolini*, was staged at the Théâtre de la Bastille by the American playwright and stage director Richard Foreman who, at one of Kathy's readings, described her to us as "the wildest writer going.... Originality. Sheer voice. Guts."

Eduard Limonov, a Soviet dissident, was another writer who loved to provoke a scandal. Like Acker, Limonov was a hellion, even calling himself "the Russian punk." Taking advantage of the timid stirrings of the perestroika, in 1974 he moved to New York, the long dreamed-of destination of Russian youth. Disenchanted with "the New World," he then lived in Paris from 1980 to 1991, enjoying fame and a pleasant lifestyle provided by the sale of his books in the US and France.

That same evening of January 25, 1985, Limonov read passages from *It's Me, Eddie* (1976) and *His Butler's Story* (1981), comical stories based on his picaresque adventures in New York. Looking like a scraggy tomcat with piercing eyes magnified by thick-rimmed glasses, Limonov, the Soviet "refusenik," had become the pet writer of the Western publishing world.* In the excerpt he chose, the language he used to describe his trysts with Jewish girls was shocking, but strangely enough, did not seem to offend our American audience, so accustomed to the rule of the politically correct back home. In this first month of 1985, the world celebration of Orwell's classic *1984* was still in the air, a reminder of the propagandist

---

* That night, it was impossible to imagine Limonov posing later in the Serbian-Bosnian war with a Kalashnikov pointed at Sarajevo, or setting up the National Bolshevik Party in 1993, in the wake of the collapse of the Soviet Union.

language that continued to prevail in the Soviet Union. The dissident Limonov seemed to embody the aspirations of a whole country to free speech, and his audience gracefully tolerated the extravagant writer's repeated verbal excesses.

Following these two mavericks, Bernard-Henri Lévy appeared somewhat aloof, certainly not the forthcoming personality we were used to seeing on our TV screens. He was the star of the "Nouveaux Philosophes," that circle of young, fervent philosophers in vogue in the 1980s who, engaged in a critical reflection on totalitarianism, broke away from the tenets of the Marxist-Leninist as well as Maoist currents of the 1970s.

With his distinctive white shirt casually opened on his chest, Lévy read an excerpt from his first novel, *Le diable en tête*, translated into English in *Paris Exiles*. It described Jerusalem, a city close to his heart, appearing here as "the very symbol epitomizing the cosmopolitan city . . . the only city that preserves in its very stone the impalpable foundation of its origin." An eloquent and passionate man in his opinions and ongoing struggle for human rights, he actually spoke very little, seemingly out of place as he addressed an audience not fully aware of his aura in France.

Ricardo Mosner

"To present, as we do, the painters alongside the poets is simply to acknowledge a truth of our time, that the written word is no longer and will never again be superior to the image."[5] These words of the editor of *Paris Exiles* were a reference to the other vocation of the review which was to promote the visual arts. Designed by graphic artist Scott Minick, its second issue featured pen and ink drawings by Ricardo Mosner, an Argentine artist exiled in Paris.[6]

On the afternoon of its launch, July 17, 1985, a young man entered the bookshop carrying a large roll of canvas under his arm and a huge bag of paints. He introduced himself as Ricardo Mosner, the artist who was to work on a painting during the event. It was a big surprise to me, but used to the unexpected, I fetched the tacks he needed to stretch his canvas on the one empty wall of the room upstairs where the readings took place. I was a little bit nervous, wondering how Ricardo would be able to paint anything at all, squeezed as he would be between the wall and an anticipated big crowd.

As the place had quickly filled up, a woman yelled out in a high-pitched voice: "An intimate audience, indeed; an inch closer, it would have been adultery," triggering peals of laughter. Her protest was apparently a Dorothy Parker witticism.

This new issue of *Paris Exiles* introduced the French writer Pierre Guyotat to American readers. He was the author of *A Tomb for Five Hundred Thousand Soldiers*, a grueling piece denouncing the French army's acts of torture during the Algerian War which, for a time, had been censored in France. Pierre Joris, eminent poet and translator, told us of the difficulties he had encountered while translating an extract for *Paris Exiles*. As the language and syntax were so strange, it read like a dialect. It was a difficult, time-consuming job, and literary magazines were "great devourers of time," Joris lamented. On the other hand, his "was a work of love," he admitted, "but also a huge drain on your own creative energy since the time you spend on the magazine you don't spend on your own work."*

In the meantime, precariously perched on a ladder, Mosner had been splashing colors onto his canvas for an hour and a half; his "action painting" performance stopped the minute the reading ended, revealing figures in motion, drinking to life, as celebrated in a tango, all of them reeling under a brandished knife. It was a street art mural on canvas, bursting with energy, movement, and vibrancy. Named by the artist *Serie Tremenda*, the title called to mind both "tremendous" enjoyment of life, and "tremors," perhaps a metaphor for a country

---

* At that reading, Joris explained the reasons for the short life-span of these reviews and magazines, including *Paris Exiles* which disappeared after this second issue. The only one to survive a few more years was *Frank* magazine.

known for its vitality, but recently shattered by violent political repression. Hanging over the staircase that connected the two open floors, this work became the silent witness of all our readings and the guardian angel of the bookstore, opening its wings to the world.

Carol Pratl

The first issue of Sphinx: *Women's International Literary Review* was launched at the Village Voice on December 7, 1984, the brain-child of Carol Pratl, a young American poet who had moved from Chicago to Paris in the late 1970s, by now speaking fluent French. Though described as a "women's review," "Sphinx had no feminist vocation,"* Pratl explained that evening. "It was meant to publish male writers and artists beyond the stereotypes found in stan-dard women's publications." Even if she looked like an elf with her braided blond hair right out of Longfellow's tale of Rapunzel, Carol was a ball of fire, a dynamo who organized literary events and wrote poetry as well as articles on contemporary dance.

A student of Russian at the Sorbonne, she attended the lectures of Andrei Sinyavsky, an author censored in Russia and living then in exile in France.[7] Later on, taking advantage of Gorbachev's per-estroika, Carol made several trips to Moscow and Saint Petersburg (then Leningrad). There, she befriended artists involved in the avant-garde theater movement started in the 1960s as well as dancers, former students of Isadora Duncan, the American cho-reographer who had revolutionized the art of dance at the turn of the twentieth century. Duncan's choreographed works contin-ued to be performed underground by her adepts throughout the worst years of the Soviet period. During her Moscow stays, Carol

---

* Journalist Alexandra Tuttle declared that evening, not without a touch of humor, that she was the "token misogynist" on the editorial board of Sphinx. In 1993, she was tragically killed during her coverage of the Georgian-Abkhazian war for the *Wall Street Journal*, a shock for us all.

gathered new information about Duncan's life and dance creations in the Soviet Union in the 1920s, inspiring her to write a book on Isadora Duncan along with her grandniece, Dorée Duncan.* At the same time, acquainted with many writers in the Soviet Union, she embarked on the bold project of gathering female writers together from America, France, and the Soviet Union.

The First International Women's Conference took place in Paris from January 30 to February 3, 1989, with about forty female writers from these countries. This landmark event included round-table debates, public appearances, and readings in various venues, including the Village Voice Bookshop. However, as the Canadian writer Nancy Huston observed, these three groups of writers— American, French, and Soviet—voiced very different approaches to feminism and women's literature, leaving the prospect of a future International Women Writers Forum rather bleak.[8]

David Applefield

David Applefield left his native Boston for Paris in 1984 with the first issue of his newly born literary journal *Frank: An International Journal of Contemporary Writing & Art* in his suitcase. His was a warm, outgoing personality as he was curious about people and open to innovative ideas. A cosmopolitan at heart, and feeling at home in his adopted city, he was asked in an interview what it meant to be an expatriate living in our city. David replied: "Krakow, Kiev, Perth, New Jersey, Montreuil, Cotonou, Tripoli. I like street corners in fifty nations, and I have friends in Istanbul, Bamako, Amherst, and feel equally comfortable in a café in Dakar, Paris, or Boston."[9] For him, Paris was the place where these four corners converged

---

* Carol Pratl, Dorée Duncan, and Cynthia Splatt, *Life into Art: Isadora Duncan and Her World* (New York: W.W. Norton, 1993), presented by Carol at the Village Voice October 11, 1993, in the presence of Dorée Duncan's mother, Ligoa Duncan, niece of Raymond Duncan, artist and owner of a famous art gallery in Paris that closed at his death in 1966.

Anglophone Writing in Paris Today

(*above*) Ligoa Duncan, novelist Catherine Rihoit, and Carol Pratl at the Village Voice Bookshop, October 11, 1993. © C. Deudon

(*left*) Publisher John Calder and David Applefield, Frank: An International Journal of Contemporary Writing and Art, 1998. © John Minihan

and the starting point for new cosmopolitan adventures. Given the international vocation of *Frank*, a special section in each issue, called "Foreign Dossier," was dedicated to a chosen country's cultures and literatures. A few examples are "The Philippines" (1987), "Pakistani Writing" (1988), "Contemporary Chinese Poetry" (1990), and "Anglophone Writing in Paris Today! Updating the Myth."

In the summer of 1985, Applefield launched the fourth issue of his magazine, dedicated to **Edouard Roditi,** the highly respected senior member of the Anglophone community in Paris, at the Village Voice. He introduced him to us as the author of art essays, adding that Roditi was fluent in more than eight languages. Of Turkish Sephardic Jewish origin, Roditi was raised in France, educated in England and the United States, and "could boast of an address book containing 613 entries—like the Talmud," he said with a big smile.

Applefield had also invited the French poet Alain Bosquet to participate in this homage. The two men met in Berlin in 1948 at the start of the Cold War. Bosquet was part of the Allied Control Commissions while Roditi was working as a translator at the Nuremberg trials. Yet it was their love of literature that cemented their friendship. On July 4, 1985, he introduced his friend Roditi as "a self-appointed ambassador of every possible culture to every other possible culture."[10]

Invited to recall an event that had marked his life, Roditi spoke of a particular moment in London in the 1930s. He had just turned twenty and was writing surrealist poetry, but the political and social context created by the Great Depression of 1929 was a matter of concern to him. He happened to befriend a certain Eric Blair: they were both enamored by literature and had a shared empathy for the down-and-outs. "We would take walks," Roditi reminisced, "and I remember a particular night at Trafalgar Square: homeless men were gathered together sleeping outside in the cold. Sometime later, I happened to read a book by a George Orwell, *A Clergyman's Daughter*, and, stunned, I realized that one of its scenes was precisely the one my friend and I had witnessed together. Eric Blair was none other than George Orwell."[11]

Another great admirer and close acquaintance of Roditi was Michael Neal, our dear associate at the Village Voice and a "bibliomaniac." He passionately read and reread Orwell, his hero. At Roditi's death, Michael was entrusted with this friend's papers and memoirs.

Jim Haynes

Handshake Editions was a title that fully reflected the personality of its editor—friendly, open, and a most popular figure in the American expat community in Paris. Jim's background included the cultural and sexual revolution of the 1960s in Edinburgh, where he owned the Paperback Bookshop and staged avant-garde plays at his famous Traverse Theatre.

On November 23, 2005, Haynes arrived at the bookshop with his Scottish friend, John Calder, the main publisher of Beckett in Britain, to share memories of the prestigious writers they had invited to participate in the first Edinburgh International Writers' Conference[12] back in 1962. Over the following fifty years, they attended the annual Edinburgh Festival, still organizing literary events, never missing a single season.

Haynes came from the wide-open spaces of North and South America and had lived in many other countries, never actually stepping out of the sixties. He taught Media and Sexual Politics at the University of Vincennes, an offshoot of the 1968 student protest movement. Hearing about the Village Voice Bookshop, a name redolent of the turbulent New York scene, he appeared at the door one day and offered his help. Soon, the store became one of his favorite spots to hobnob with his friends from around the world—all writers and artists—a blessing for an emerging bookstore.

His catalogue of *Handshake Editions*, a small kitchen-table literary publication, as he called it, listed forty titles that resonated with the free spirit of the time: *Workers of the World, Unite and Stop Working* (Jim Haynes), *Weird Fucks* (Lynne Tillman),[13] and *In Praise of Henry: A Homage to Henry Miller* (Jim Haynes). However, what sparked Jim's ongoing popularity in the American community here and just about everywhere were his traditional Sunday dinners in his fourteenth arrondissement atelier, once Henry Miller's neighborhood. This venue was a beehive of comings and goings: artistic activities with video screenings, photo shows, and a real base in Paris for people to meet, exchange views, cook, and share meals. The two-story studio was often too small and too crowded, so the patio with its colorful flowerbeds and shady trees soon became the perfect Left Bank setting for a budding romance. Sunday dinners "Chez Jim" have been featured in dozens of international articles, and his aptly named autobiography, *Thanks for Coming*, is a who's who of the guests who at one time or another attended his weekly "happenings" over the years: John Lennon, Yoko Ono, Germaine Greer, Mick Jagger, and other stars. What a time we had![14]

Jim Haynes and Lynne Tillman, Village Voice reading, 1992. © C. Deudon

4

Black America in Paris
UPDATING THE MYTH[1]

"Remember Me"[*]
The Legacy of James Baldwin and Richard Wright
Gordon Heath, Julia Wright, Ernest Gaines, James Emanuel, Jake Lamar

"The tradition of Richard Wright and Baldwin is
obvious, but it is not just that. One day you simply
say: Ah! That's Paris."

—JAKE LAMAR,
  Village Voice reading, January 15, 1995.

I met James Baldwin in the spring of 1986 at a conference of
American and French writers in Aix-en-Provence. The adopted
son of the region of Provence,[2] Baldwin was the guest of honor,
with its roll call also including a number of other American friends
and writers: Grace Paley, Robert Coover, Jerome Charyn, John
Ashbery, Robert Creeley, Lawrence Ferlinghetti . . . all of whom
had read or would do so at the Village Voice.

I had been invited to this conference by Kenton Keith, the
American cultural attaché in Paris and a close friend of Baldwin's

---

[*] In Shakespeare's *Hamlet*. "Remember me," some of the final words of Hamlet's father
to his son. Another relevant reference here is *Remember Me to Harlem: The Letters of Langston
Hughes and Carl Van Vechten* (New York: Vintage, 2002).

from the 1960s in Turkey. It was in this capacity that Keith had collaborated with him on various theater projects. One of them was a play based on Baldwin's *Giovanni's Room*. A young Turkish actor, whom the author had befriended at the Actors Studio in New York, took on the central role. Sexually explicit, in line with the spirit of the times, the piece was quite daring for a Muslim country. As it was received with enthusiasm, Kenton later commented that "Turkey was ready for Baldwin and needed his message. The place was bursting at the seams with cultural fervor . . . there was music, there was jazz, there was theater."[3]

Now, one late afternoon, after a day of roundtables and debates, Keith invited me to meet his friend "Jimmy," as he called Baldwin. It was a delightfully privileged moment to be sitting with them on the terrace of the hotel rooftop, overlooking the old city of Aix and its surrounding hills in the dimming light. The two friends called up memories of their past in Istanbul, regularly breaking out into loud laughter. Trying to follow their conversation, but feeling intimidated, I did not say much. I just managed to ask Baldwin about his stay in Amherst where he had taught the year before at the University of Massachusetts, invited by Mike Thelwell, already the head of the Department of African American Studies back in 1969-1970, the year I lived in Amherst.

The next day, Baldwin closed the conference with a talk on the Atlanta child murders that involved twenty-eight African American boys and young men who had disappeared or been killed between 1979 and 1981. On stage, he was not the relaxed and jovial man I had previously met; he looked tired and grief-stricken as he recollected his recent trip to Atlanta to further investigate those crimes left unpunished. He had just published a book-long essay, *The Evidence of Things Not Seen*, a revised and enlarged version of his original 1981 coverage of the subject in *Playboy* magazine.

James Baldwin had arrived in Paris in 1948, two years after his mentor and friend Richard Wright. His postwar city had little to do with the bright lights of the Paris of Gertrude Stein, Ernest Hemingway, Natalie Barney, and F. Scott Fitzgerald. In fact, Nazi-occupied Paris had chased many Americans away, but after the war, the liberated city once again welcomed a wave of expatriates from the US. Among them were African American victims of continued racial discrimination at home and often pursued by Senator McCarthy's witch hunts at the onset of the Cold War. They formed part of a community that Baldwin called "the New Lost Generation."[4]

More than thirty years later, when the Village Voice opened, Baldwin was still part of the collective memory in Paris, but I met only one man who actually remembered him. It was **Gordon Heath**: tall and handsome with a charismatic presence, he used to drop by the bookshop, silently browse in the quiet opening hours, and then leave. Little by little, we got to know this mysterious visitor who had also arrived in Paris in 1948, and whom Baldwin referred to in his "Encounter on the Seine: Black Meets Brown": "Gordon Heath, who will be remembered for his performances in Broadway's *Deep Are the Roots* some seasons back, sings ballads nightly in his own nightclub on the Rue de l'Abbaye."[5] Commenting on a superb recording of Baldwin's I had given him, Heath praised his style in this way": Jimmy's mastery of the language, his nuance, his musicality makes everyone else sound illiterate."[6]

Heath gave three major readings at the Village Voice: the first one on February 12, 1986, was an homage to Langston Hughes, the African American poet of the Harlem Renaissance. His poems were recited by Heath himself, the jazz poet Ted Joans, and James Emanuel, an African American poet living in Paris and author of a book on Langston Hughes. Yet, it was Heath's stage reading of Shakespeare's *Macbeth* with five other actors on March 9, 1987, that gave the full measure of his acting talent and awe-inspiring presence. His last evening at the Village Voice was a warmly applauded concert of folksongs and spirituals from his Abbaye repertoire on New Year's Day, 1989. He sadly died in August 1991, the month his book, *Deep Are the Roots: Memoirs of a Black Expatriate*, came out in the States, somewhat bringing new life to his eventful and artistic career, long ignored in his native country.

In January 1986, *Paris Passion* published an article on this burgeoning community in Paris, featuring a dozen portraits of African Americans interviewed on their choice of a new home, their activities, and their concerns while living here. Their answers varied widely, but most of them agreed that they had come "not in a spirit of protest like their elders, but as people eager to try their hand at making a living and expressing their capabilities abroad." They were not the New Lost Generation of Baldwin, but a post–civil rights movement youth who belonged to the third wave of expatriates who had moved to Paris to enlarge their horizons and enjoy the experience of a different culture in an unfamiliar country.

The front cover of the magazine featured **Ted Joans**, the seasoned and still emblematic figure of this new generation, though he had been around since the 1960s. He described himself as a Beat and jazz poet, having played jazz with John Coltrane, and, in the early '60s, joined his Beat friends—Ginsberg, Corso, Orlovsky—in their Paris haunt on rue Gît-le-Cœur, just around the corner from the student quarter of the Place Saint-Michel. After getting to know the surrealist poet André Breton, Joans made collages in this fashionable vein and loved to call himself "the Black Surrealist." An eternal nomad, he would disappear for months at a time, roaming the world—he had friends everywhere. Once back in Paris, he would show up at the bookshop to perform a reading that would turn into a jazz session, "swinging" the words of his poems. His tenor voice filled up the space, chanting his trademark poem: "If you should see / a man / walking down a crowded street / talking to himself / don't run / in the opposite direction / but run toward him / for he is a poet! You have nothing to fear / from the poet / but the truth."[7]

Julia Wright

The daughter of Richard Wright,* the legendary author who rev-olutionized African American literature with *Native Son* (1940) and *Black Boy* (1945), Julia organized several readings at the Village Voice. We had a friendly relationship, but she never brought up anything personal about her life, much less about her father. Our casual conversations with Julia always seemed to concern him— new publications, conferences, reprints, translations, all endeavors to keep his memory alive.

One day, she dropped by the bookstore and handed me a small paperback entitled *Rites of Passage*, a story by her father about a Black child taken in and then abandoned by his foster family. He eventually runs away, trying to survive on his own. Somewhat amazed by her gift, I opened the book and read Julia's entry: "If my father were still alive, your bookshop—a haven for writers like him—would be one of his favorite haunts, Paris, March 29/96." Seeming to have a personal resonance for her, these words were all the more precious to me.

Out of loyalty to her father, but also stemming from strong personal conviction, in the early 1990s, she had taken to heart the plight of Mumia Abu-Jamal, the African American journalist and political activist caught in a melee of shots during which he was accused of killing a white Philadelphia policeman. His death sentence in 1982 gave rise to controversial investigations, and in 1995, Julia invited Mumia's defense lawyer, Leonard Weinglass, to

---

* Richard Wright was closely watched by Senator Joseph McCarthy. Given his po-litical positions and his works, he was deemed subversive. In 1947, great admirers of Wright, Sartre and Beauvoir helped him and his family settle in Paris where he lived in exile until his mysterious death in 1960.

speak at our bookstore. He was to present his defense conclusions detailed in his work *Race for Justice: Mumia Abu-Jamal's Fight against the Death Penalty.*[8]

That same year, Mumia Abu Jamal's first book *Live from Death Row,*[9] was published in the US and in French translation with a foreword by the French philosopher Jacques Derrida, making the Mumia case a cause célèbre in France. To highlight this double success, Julia set up a second reading with two eminent American literary figures, **Ernest Gaines** and **James Emanuel.** The former is the author of *A Lesson Before Dying,*[10] a novel set in the Deep South during Jim Crow. It tells the story of a young man with the symbolic name of Jefferson, sentenced to death for a crime he has not committed. Waiting in his cell to be executed, he learns how to read and write to prove his own lawyer wrong for describing him as "an animal without words." Jefferson gains his dignity as a full human being, able to speak for himself in court and thus nobly face the death sentence imposed on him by a white judge. We had often recommended this book to French school teachers who, reading it with their students, brought up a topic rarely discussed in class at the time.

The poet **James Emanuel** followed with haikus he had especially written for this occasion, grouped under the title *Reaching for Mumia.*[11] Emanuel's support of Mumia was all the more moving since his only son had committed suicide in the aftermath of a beating by "three cowardly cops," in the poet's words.

Determined never to return to the United States, he had moved to Paris in 1984, leaving behind a prestigious academic career, yet continuing to write and publish poetry and autobiographical essays. The last work he read that evening was "Deadly James," his exemplary poem dedicated to his son and "to all the victims of police brutality."[12] His *Haikus for Mumia* recited in the presence of Julia Wright were also a tribute to her father, who had written hundreds of haikus himself in the dark hours of his life. Rejected at the time by his publisher, Wright's *Haikus* were now being taught in American classrooms, Julia reminded the audience.

The Mumia evenings had rallied big audiences, but Julia's most personal and significant event at the Village Voice was the launching of her father's last, unfinished novel, *A Father's Law*, on May 29, 2008.[13] After Wright's sudden death at fifty-two, his publisher had rejected the work, considering it not on par with his previous writings, but Julia felt emotionally closest to it. After her visit to the mortuary, she went to her father's studio where a page of his unfinished novel lay on his Underwood. She considered it to be her "father's last letter to her."[14]

With Wright's centennial birthday approaching in 2008, Julia wrote a detailed letter to his publisher, asking him to mark the date with the publishing of *A Father's Law*. She told us that evening that this unfinished novel was "sketchy and faulty," but nevertheless written at a most difficult time when "free to speak out in France, not mincing his words, and openly speaking against the death penalty, he was put back on the US National Security Index." Those times were over, and Julia saw nothing "provocative" in this novel that could hamper its publication. Finally, she triumphed, and her letter became the introduction to *A Father's Law*, published in February 2008 to coincide with Black History Month. "It was the birthday gift to my father," she told us.[15]

A thriller with singular interest in the psychology of the murderer, a motif running throughout Wright's work, *A Father's Law* is also about a conflicted relationship between a father, a policeman, and his son, a university graduate who he feared would eventually betray him. Oddly enough, a few weeks before his own death, as he was endorsing his daughter's university choice, Wright warned her "not to forget or leave behind the world where your father comes from."[16] A sensitive subject to him.

Indeed, Wright's painful experience of his broken friendship with Baldwin, his young protégé back in New York, had never healed. Upon arriving in Paris, the latter wrote two essays critical of his mentor's iconic novel *Native Son*, an act that Wright felt to be a betrayal. The two never came to an understanding.

Yet Julia did not believe that Baldwin's criticism of her father's work was the cause of the fallout between these two influential African American writers of the twentieth century. With a few remaining qualms about their quarrel, in 1987, hearing that Baldwin was dying in Saint Paul-de-Vence, she rushed there to see him, hopeful there would be some kind of reconciliation. "That's where the test took place," she told us. "Isn't it true, Jimmy, that there was not enough room for two stars up there?" Lying in pain, he laughed out loud and begged her: "Stop making me laugh, Julia, it hurts."

Whatever Baldwin's enigmatic answer meant, in *Alas, Poor Richard*, his essay written after Wright's death, he admitted that the older man's work had been "an immense liberation and revelation," but to him, then a young man of twenty-six, "a carnivorous age," Wright had also been "a road-block, the sphinx, really, whose riddles I had to answer before I could become myself."[17]

It is also true that they had different approaches to the issue of racism in America and its tenacious roots. The day of the publication of Baldwin's controversial essay "Everybody's Protest Novel" (1949), the confrontation at the famed Brasserie Lipp between the two friends was so "ghastly," Baldwin recalled that "even though [he] never forgot it, [he] doubted that [he] would ever be able to re-create it."[18] In 2012, more than sixty years after this violent scene that left an indelible trace on the new lost generation," Jake Lamar, a young African American novelist living in Paris, wrote and staged *Brothers in Exile*, a vivid evocation of the African American community in the postwar city, fraught with tensions and rivalries among figures caught in the larger context of Cold War ideological dissension.

Jake Lamar

Lamar arrived in Paris in 1993, the rising author of *Bourgeois Blues*, published in the United States to critical acclaim two years beforehand.[19] It is a memoir that tells the story of the writer born at the beginning of the civil rights movement, who grew up in a lower middle-class Black family and emerged as a Harvard graduate and journalist for *Time* magazine. In it he recognized that he belonged to the first generation of African Americans able to reap the rewards of the struggles of their parents and other elders.

Jake's recollections are not so much about his accomplishments as about his bitter disenchantment with the failed promises of this protest era in the States. Blatant racism was not as open as before, but stealthily continued to hold sway under cover of the politically correct, facilitating the apparition of more subtle and pernicious forms, such as "power-plays," "innuendoes," "disguised humiliations," often encountered in his own professional experience and personal life.

An endearing person with a contagious laugh and big heart, Jake became the darling of the eclectic crowd gravitating around the Village Voice and part of the circle of writers at the forefront of its literary life, among them Diane Johnson, Edmund White, Mavis Gallant, Ellen Hinsey, Denis Hirson, and the poet C. K. Williams, whom he considered a mentor.

Through his fiction, he would continue his reflections on race relations, but not just in the States. Living in the eighteenth arrondissement, one of the city's ebullient multicultural neighborhoods at the foot of Montmartre, he had just the right material to animate his two works in progress that centered on African American characters: *Rendezvous Eighteenth*[20] and *Ghosts of Saint-Michel*.[21]

In the first novel, which came out in 2003, the central protagonist, Ricky Jenks, is an African American jazz pianist in Montmartre who shares his life with a Muslim woman of Moroccan descent. Suddenly, he finds himself under investigation for two crimes he has nothing to do with. At a loss and looking for some comfort, he turns to his community of African American compatriots "who feel the need to seek each other out to share their lives and experiences in ways that they couldn't with people of other backgrounds." With him, we penetrate this community, a mix of "old timers" going back to the '40s and '50s and the next generations of "all-around non-conformists . . . who saw expatriation to France as one of a variety of alternative lifestyle choices." Now, in the 1990s, the new generation of expats "tended to be more careerist" with professionals sent to Paris by their corporations back in the States. They were "lawyers, chefs, artists, translators, academics, computer programmers . . ." Whoever they were and whatever they did, hanging together gave them "a powerful sense of inter-connectedness that might be called brotherhood."[22]

In *Ghosts of Saint-Michel*, published in 2006, Lamar continues to focus on the issues of race and identity in a multicultural society. Already present in his novels set in the US, this thorny question, traditionally deemed by the French to be a specifically American issue, had now reared its ugly head in their own society. In the three years separating these two Parisian novels, immigrant riots had erupted in the suburbs, spilling into the very center of the capital. The country was painfully awakened to the reality of the aftermath of its long-ignored colonial past.

Like all of Lamar's thrillers, this novel, haunted by the ghosts of a recent terrorist attack on Place Saint-Michel, the very heart of Paris, is driven by its characters. Marva Dobbs is a charismatic African American woman who owns a successful soul food restaurant in Montmartre. Her French husband, Loic Rose, embodies the political and social predicament of a sector of France struggling to accept the growing immigrant populations from its former colonies. An ex-communist who, in his youth, fought for the independence of Algeria and the cause of immigrants, Rose becomes a CIA informant.

With malicious delight, the author stirs up even more confusion: Marva seems to have disappeared with her lover who could very well be the Algerian terrorist sought by the police—an ironic turn of events that speaks volumes.

This fast-moving novel, full of details about recent French history, provides pertinent insights into the societal predicament of France, the result, according to the author, of the government's determination to cling to a unifying approach to the political, historical, cultural, religious, and social problems of its multiethnic populations—an approach inherited from its colonial past. For this keen observer, the old adage "We are all French and One Republic" is a tall challenge in a divided society like France.

Jake Lamar, November 20, 2003. © Dorli Lamar

David Sedaris reading at the Village Voice Bookshop, February 9, 2006, Village Voice Bookshop archive.

5

Emergence of a Literary Force[1]

Diane Johnson, Steven Barclay, David Downie, David Sedaris,
Adam Gopnik, Edmund White, René de Ceccatty

"A great voice on the Paris scene, the Village Voice has
reawakened a sense of literary community that has
been dormant in Paris for many years."[2]

—JEFF GREENWALD

The "Lost Generation" of the '20s and the "New Lost Generation" of the '40s undoubtedly left their mark on American literature. For the aspiring young writers of the 1980s Third Wave, the literary achievements of these two predecessors were an incentive, but just as much a daunting task. In fact, there were doubts within the Paris community and the Anglophone press as to whether the Third Wave would be able to claim either a Hemingway or a Baldwin. In an article entitled "Making Waves: A Letter from Paris," Virginia Larner, who taught literature at the American School of Paris and was a regular of the Village Voice, wondered too whether "Paris could sustain a vibrant literary community of expatriate writers that continued to draw inspiration from its historical Muse."[3]

This "Muse," the Paris of the interwar and postwar years, was no longer the fertile ground for a vanguard renewal. At the start of the 1980s, the world's eyes were turned to New York, the hub of buzzing artistic creativity and literary inventiveness. At the same time, there was no denying that Americans were back in Paris, and the cultural and literary effervescence generated by the fresh talents of the Third Wave, busy writing and launching their magazines, started to attract even established authors from the States. Together, they formed the core of a strong literary presence within the walls of the Village Voice.

"Americans have always loved Paris," Edmund White writes in *The Flâneur: A Stroll Through the Paradoxes of Paris*,[4] but we might add that they only saw the city through the lens of their own eyes and time. The Paris of Hemingway's *A Moveable Feast* was not the Paris of the 1980s. Drawn into a more cosmopolitan world, our city was entering the era of postmodernity, balanced between tradition and innovation, a city of "paradoxes" as White aptly perceived.[5]

TO EACH WRITER THEIR OWN PARIS

Diane Johnson

Already a bestselling author[6] when she settled in Paris in the early '80s, Johnson fell in love with the city in 1967 as she was passing through, with only a couple of hours to look around between trains. In a much later interview, she recalled that precise moment: "Place de la Concorde, at dusk, a light snow-fall. The lights going on all around the Place . . . And that was it."[7]

She lived near the Romanesque church of Saint-Germain-des-Prés, one of the oldest landmarks in the neighborhood, and the city, for that matter. From her kitchen window she discovered "a rounded structure" in the yard of the building next door. Intrigued, Johnson came to learn that it was the remnant of a chapel built in 1608 by Marguerite de France, aka Queen Margot, whose reign was darkened by the sixteenth-century French Wars of Religion. Transplanting the story of this unrest to her book *Into* a Paris Quartier,[8] she also included the boisterous life of her neighborhood at the turn of the seventeenth century, the central stage of political intrigues, bravura adventures, and alcove romances brilliantly portrayed by Alexandre Dumas in The Three Musketeers (1844). While the ever-present architecture of her neighborhood called up a much-distant past, shadows of the postwar artists and writers were likewise haunting its streets and literary cafés.

Steven Barclay

The founder of the San Francisco Steven Barclay Agency for Lectures and Readings, Steven Barclay is part and parcel of this chapter as he brought some of the greatest American literary voices of the 1980s and '90s to our bookstore. During this period, he divided his time between the West Coast and Paris, the latter a kind of haven for him. Steven had grown up in our city and confided in his memoir that "in the same way childhood experiences imprint themselves on your emotional power, what Paris had to offer remained engraved in my memories and emotions." His collection of pieces, A Place in the World Called Paris, is indeed an impressionistic portrait of the capital, made up of more than one hundred and seventy fresh and often startling excerpts from world authors that call to mind their own personal experience here, from Kafka and Rilke to Henry Miller and Vladimir Nabokov.[9]

Presenting his work at the Village Voice on June 29, 1995, Steven insisted that it was not an anthology of quotes. He had specifically chosen each selection as a reflection of his own Paris and the emotions it evoked in him: "There is me in this book; it is a book of the heart, in which I meant to convey my own sensorial and sensual experience of Paris." He further confided that walking through the city, he found "isolated moments of great beauty, a sort of symphony of grays: this is the Paris I love." To illustrate this point, Steven quotes Vladimir Nabokov, who "regarded Paris with its gray-toned days and charcoal nights, merely as the chance setting for the most authentic and faithful joys" of his life, and Henry Miller contemplating Paris with its "range of grays . . . seemingly infinite . . ."[10]

In her introduction to his memoir, Susan Sontag, another fervent lover of Paris and Steven's lifelong friend and former mentor, made the connection between him and Chekhov's *Three Sisters* and their longing for Moscow. Like the young women distraught at being away from Moscow, Steven continued to yearn for the city of his imagination and barely concealed aspirations.[11]

Charcoal illustrations by the artist Miles Hyman emphasize this subdued atmosphere of the skyline in soft gray shades.

David Downie

A writer of books about Paris as the city of culinary art and lovers, but also of intrigue and night crime, Downie was at the Village Voice on October 20, 2005, to launch his new *Paris, Paris, Journey into the City of Light*[12] and to share with us his serendipitous wanderings through the city. He likened them to "the butterfly's irreverent, erratic fluttering from one place to another . . . alighting onto . . . those green, battered book boxes clinging to riverside parapets." These were the bookstalls of the Bouquinistes[13] along the riverbanks, an endless curiosity to tourists. Downie did not just browse through these multiple boxes, but engaged in conversations with their owners, learning about the long and fascinating history of this singular Parisian trade: "These quay-lifers were more than mongers of a mishmash of books; they were the inheritors of a five-hundred-year-old tradition of book lovers, possessed by an obsession they call 'la maladie des livres.' All day long and year around, rain or shine, they did not miss one day at their bookstalls despite meager takings."

Enhanced by Alison Harris's black and white photographs of unusual street scenes, Downie's book *Paris, Paris* is an invitation to brief but fortuitous encounters.

David Sedaris

For this *New Yorker* author of popular and witty stories, living in Paris meant the arduous job of learning French. The American humorist, who was in and out of the city through the 1990s, gave no fewer than five readings at the Village Voice over the years. Every American could identify with his stories grounded in US society and culture, but, as we know, humor does not always translate well. It is just amazing that his books have been translated and well-received all over the world, including France.

The top selling one here is *Me Talk Pretty One Day*[14] (*Je parler français*) that relates his comical experience of taking in French and coming out with gibberish, told with a healthy dose of self-derision. His bilingual audience at the Village Voice often asked him if he was popular in France. In the presence of his French publisher and his translator, he remained rather vague in his reply. His books had been published in twenty-six different languages and, he explained, their reception depended on the translation, over which he had no control. What surprised him were the enthusiastic crowds at his readings in some non-English-speaking countries whose cultures were so different. As Sedaris said, "a story really comes to life when read out loud with the necessary rhythm."[15] And to him, his success abroad remained a mystery.

"Your stories are universal!" someone shouted from the tightly packed rows of the standing crowd one evening. Perhaps "universal" was the right word. Behind the humor and mockery of his homegrown American culture, his short fiction caught on just about everywhere, perhaps because he was able to tap into the infinite range of human experience.

As a matter of fact, at each of his signing sessions that sometimes lasted until midnight, David took the time to listen to every single reader who came to him with a copy to sign and a life story to share. A certain detail would find its way into one of the small blue notebooks he often pulled out of his shirt pocket. Years later, he would open one at random, and a remark would jump out at him, becoming the seed for a new story.

Edmund White

This Paris "flaneur," as the author described himself, was the eminent literary figure of the Third Wave of American expatriates with an impressive number of fiction and nonfiction books set in Paris, his adopted city from 1983 to 1995. Edmund lived on the Île Saint-Louis in the shadow of Notre-Dame de Paris, one of the oldest and most elegant neighborhoods with stately seventeenth-century buildings gracing its riverbanks, illuminated at night by sightseeing cruises on the river Seine. Yet he was irresistibly drawn to the other Paris that did not figure on postcards, but was only waiting to be discovered.

An admirer of Baudelaire, the poet of the "Tableaux Parisiens"[16] that revealed the underside of a glittering nineteenth-century Paris of the time, Edmund followed in his footsteps, becoming "that aimless stroller who loses himself in the crowd, who has no destination and goes wherever caprice and curiosity direct his or her steps." His book *The Flâneur: A Stroll through the Paradoxes of Paris*[17] is a recollection of his wanderings through the twists and turns of Parisian streets and alleys and his discovery of other neighborhoods: not the classical "pearl-grey city" of Baron Haussmann with "its long vistas of leafless plane trees . . . and unbroken façades,"[18] but the peripheral "teeming districts of Belleville and Barbès where Arabs and Blacks lived and blended their respective cultures into new hybrids."[19] They embodied a changing Paris, "a landscape made of living people." Yet just around the corner, the "odd detail" caught his eye: "the weathered threshold . . . the burlap sandbags" in the gutter, or "the lace curtains in the concierge's window."

The Flâneur captured the contrasts of Paris and its paradoxes at a moment when the city was progressively absorbing the multiracial world at its margins. Identifying with the Baudelairian figure of the flaneur or, according to the poet, "the embodiment of the contemporary spirit," Edmund remarked, not without a touch of humor, that he "did so much aimless wandering that Baudelaire would have considered [him] thoroughly modern."[20]

THE CULTURAL DIVIDE

Adam Gopnik

A contributor to *The New Yorker*, Adam Gopnik was curious about the much-discussed cultural differences between France and the United States. In 1995, his review sent him to Paris to report on political, social, and cultural events. He was to put five years of observations into an informative and engaging chronicle of the nineties entitled *Paris to the Moon*,[21] presented at the Village Voice on May 3, 2001.

This intriguing title that seemed to call up Jules Verne and his extravagant adventures actually referred to a nineteenth-century print of a train climbing to the moon, a metaphor for a daring and inventive France on the move. It must be said that this reference was mostly ironic since, according to what Gopnik had seen and experienced, France remained "a country adamantly bent on its status-quo." It was not surprising that the largest and longest transport strike in the history of the country ended up halting the reforms initiated by Prime Minister Alain Juppé.

More strikes were to follow, one by university students asking for "smaller classes and more money," and another of high school students marching for "more classes and tougher teachers." For twenty years, the school system had tried national reforms, but a country that was unwilling to forgo its dependence on "rote learning" at the expense of creativity and individual thinking left him perplexed.

Another topic that confounded him was the "national craze" to retire early in hopes of a more promising and enjoyable life while our speaker recognized that "in the US, to stop working is, in a sense, to stop living." In a similar vein, the author's wife found that the French health system (coming from the family's brief experience with clinics and public hospitals) was "royal for the users, good for the doctors and expensive for the society"—a backhanded compliment at best. Her husband added that the level of care that the French have insisted on might prove to be "unsustainable."

Paris to the Moon is not just a window onto French politics and society, mostly observed with an amused look; "it is," Gopnik insisted, "the simple story of family life in Paris. We came to Paris for the pleasure of seeing our small son grow up in a foreign city and in a foreign language, and most of all, surrounded by beauty."[22]

One example of the latter is the culture of food so prominent in the French art of living that he, an amateur chef himself, greatly extols. We easily picture the writer browsing in open-air markets, eager to get friendly tips on where to find the freshest products. If he learned to cook true traditional recipes, he also enjoyed trying gourmet restaurants and local brasseries with family.

During the reading at the bookshop, Luke, his six-year-old son, stood beside his father, sharing center stage. After all, this book was supposed to be a fairy-tale journey to the moon, and Luke could claim to be its privileged passenger! However, reality is no fantasy, and it was the author's wife, Martha, sitting in the audience, who had this final word: "In Paris, we had a beautiful existence, but not a full life." Mais oui, matière à réflexion! (Food for thought!)

Diane Johnson

Before coming to Paris, Diane had lived in Iran, and her first reading at the Village Voice on April 21, 1988, was to launch her seventh novel, *Persian Nights*,[23] set in Iran at the turn of its Islamic Revolution. It focused on the radical cultural changes the new Iranian theocracy imposed on its citizens, including American expatriates, mostly scholars and scientists, like her husband engaged in medical research there.

Once settled in Paris, Diane wrote, among other works, a trilogy that takes place in contemporary France and presented its first volume, *Le divorce*,[24] at our bookstore on October 5, 2000. She was introduced by the poet C. K. Williams, a long-standing honorary Parisian who compared her to Edith Wharton and Henry James, adding "Diane is another sort, nothing to do with cunning or judgment, rather with good-heartedness. I always sense when I'm reading her works a genuine smile . . . one that manifests a quiet delight."[25]

Like these prestigious predecessors, Diane set her comedy of manners in a French aristocratic family, albeit one lacking the grand style of the past. Their son is divorcing a modern and bright young Californian woman, and a war is brewing between the two clans over the French family heirloom, an Old Master's painting. The Californian brood has landed in Paris to discuss the divorce, with each party firmly determined to win the battle over this valuable piece.

Under the smooth surface of false pretenses, both sides furbish their musty weapons: the French, their aristocratic superiority; the Californians, their pragmatism and sense of reality, silently noticing the telling state of the "decrepit château . . . in great need of repair and modern comfort."

Dotted with innuendoes that betray true positions, the Sunday lunch ritual turns into a hilarious parody of each family's cultural biases and deep-seated hang-ups, generously acknowledged by the laughter from our bicultural audience.

Q: "Had you lived longer in Paris, do you feel that you would have perceived those cultural differences with the same acuity?"

Johnson: "Mary McCarthy remarked that the longer she stayed in Paris, the better she understood the danger of being too long in one place, making you lose the perception of those differences. But so far, it has not happened to me because I feel a stranger in Paris, and it seems to me, I will always be one. [laughter] Confronted with my otherness, I feel more and more American in Paris. Yet I admit that moving from Illinois, my native place, to San Francisco, I felt more like an expatriate there than moving from San Francisco to Paris." [more laughter]

Q: "Why did you specifically situate the novel in the French upper class and not in the middle class?"

Johnson: "The upper class is more inclined to preserve ancient patterns of behavior, and the rigidity of the aristocratic class allows one to better examine this fact. Also, you observe what's around you, whom you feel at home with. Through my daughter who married a French architect, I'm exposed to their social milieu, but it is not my world. I write about people I know ... This being said, I was told by my French publishers that some French magazines would not write a review about my novel as it would be too tricky ... for their readers."[26]

Alan Riding, the new Paris correspondent of the *New York Times* at the time, had previously concluded in his own review that the Franco-American divorce in Johnson's novel "with its muted war between the two parties [was] a metaphor for the apparent hopelessness of an entente cordiale between the two cultures."[27]

Edmund White

On the other hand, moving to Paris in 1983 at the peak of the AIDS epidemic in America, Edmund White, a warm and outgoing

(*above*) Diane Johnson at the Village Voice Bookshop, October 5, 2000. © Roberta Fineberg

(*left*) Edmund White, reading at Village Voice Bookshop, April 24, 1997. © C. Deudon

personality, turned out to be as at ease in French society as in his own. His first reading at the Village Voice showcased A Boy's Own Story[28] in September 1983. At this point, he was one of America's rising literary voices, and in Sontag's words, "one of its outstanding writers of prose today."[29] Uncannily so, he was still virtually unknown in France. Notable exceptions were a few friends and intellectuals that included the novelist Gilles Barbedette, the French translator and publisher of this fictional memoir, just starting to be praised here for providing a new perspective on homosexuality.

White's growing circle in Paris also included Michel Foucault, whom he had met earlier in New York and who was a friend of Barbedette's. The American expressed to both men his amazement at the way they, and for that matter, French gay people in general, continued to live as usual, seemingly undisturbed and unconcerned by the ravages of the AIDS epidemic decimating his friends in New York. A longtime advocate for gay rights and the cofounder of Gay Men's Health Crisis in New York, White knew what he was talking about and vainly tried to caution his close circle about a pending health crisis in France.

In response to White's warning, Foucault laughed at him and retorted: "Don't you realize, Edmund, how puritanical you're being? You've invented a disease aimed just at gays to punish them for having unnatural sex." "Yes," Gilles chimed in, "that's a very American idea."[30]

A year later, Foucault was dead, and the left-wing newspaper Liberation, one of the most respected dailies in France at the time, "denied the real cause of death on the front page as though it were a calumny invented by his enemies."[31]

I myself vividly recall the mid-eighties at the Village Voice when young poets and writers became frantic upon discovering strange lesions on their bodies, undeniable signs of the brutal reality they suddenly had to face. Fourteen young men, friends of our bookstore, died of AIDS within months.

Always taking an active part in our author events, Edmund not only read from his own works, but introduced many other recognized authors that included Harry Mathews, Raymond Carver, Richard Ford, Diane Johnson, David Leavitt, Michael Ondaatje, C. K. Williams, as well as budding talents. He even wrote a generous article on the bookshop, published in *Vogue* magazine under the title "Paris's Movable Lunch,"[32] a nod to Hemingway's *A Moveable Feast*, that broadened the visibility of our bookshop in the States and even worldwide.

Speaking fluent French and a great connoisseur of its culture and literature, Edmund soon decided to embrace a project as vast and complex as the life of Jean Genet,[33] a social pariah who had managed to become a famous figure in French literature. He launched his biography at the Village Voice on October 22, 1993, with a reference to Genet's emblematic novel *Notre Dame-des-Fleurs* (1944), which he presented within the context of homosexual literature in France in the 1940s and '50s.

Edmund explained that, in those years, "homosexuality was treated as an illness that demanded sympathy and compassion from the reader." He went on to say that such a conception was alien to Genet, who deemed homosexuality "a sin and a crime."[34] In fact, Genet had a "gloomy view" of a "condition" that, contrary to Sartre's opinion, he had not chosen. Accordingly, Genet wrote to Sartre that "Homosexuality [. . .] has happened to me like the color of my eyes or the number of my teeth."[35]

After more than a decade in Paris, the city had become a ghost town to Edmund, and he was eager to return to his vibrant, "abrasive" New York.*

---

* As early as April 1987, Edmund had confided to Ray Carver his desire to return to New York "to write about things there." This is how Tess Gallagher sums up their conversation in her Paris Journal: "America is his workshop. Things are almost too perfect here in Paris. Edmund needs the abrasiveness of American life" in *Our Private Lives* (New York: Vintage, 1989).

Two years later, he came back to the Village Voice on September 12, 1998, to talk about his book *The Farewell Symphony*. The reading turned into an enlightening dialogue between White and **René de Ceccatty**, a renowned French novelist and literary critic, as it revealed more surprising cultural differences between the two countries.

de Ceccatty: "Was Genet an influence on you, Edmund?"

White: "Genet made his own life a legend, and, doing this, he lied a lot, and so what! What he has written is so beautiful. For Genet, homosexuality was something one could transcend only through artistic creation. He preferred beauty to truth while I do prefer truth to beauty. A gay writer, Genet was also a most original writer."

de Ceccatty: "Genet, a gay writer? Why this need for a label, Edmund? It would be unthinkable in France to categorize Proust, Gide, or Cocteau as homosexual or gay authors. It would be felt as a diminution of human freedom."

White: "I constantly come into conflict with the French over this subject of homosexuality and its naming, and many friends, including the openly homosexual intellectuals and writers, were afraid that I would present Genet as a gay writer who had a violent gay life. What I tried to do with Genet's homosexuality was to trace the truth, to trace his irreverent attitudes toward homosexuality. When you talk about this subject, French attitudes and reactions are different from those of Americans. The way bookshops are set up in the two countries is a good example. In America, everything is organized by subjects: African Americans, Feminism, Gay Studies . . . For us, there is no general reader as there is no general voter; there are only special interests, elements that do not melt in the melting pot."

de Ceccatty: "What is the end purpose of partitioning cultures in American bookstores?"

White: "If we think of literature as a great dialogue between all the literatures of the world, to separate them has no meaning, but in America, we do not think that way—we ghettoize everything. On the other hand, our system works in more than one way. It gives gay books a much longer life than general literature. The average life of a book on a shelf is three, four months while being labeled a gay writer has carried me through many years, and all my books are kept in print."

de Ceccatty: "The reception in America of *The Farewell Symphony* was mixed. Some readers were shocked by your straightforwardness in the way you show sex in these given times. They accused you of doing it from a distance, coldly, without emotion. I personally don't agree with this. It seems to me that distance can create emotion and that, throughout the book, we feel the constant presence of romance and love."

White: "Right now in America, a large Puritan movement is coming back with its usual focus on monogamy. Homosexuals are accused of not getting married and not having children. But we cannot be assimilated. There are gay writers, though, such as David Leavitt,* who reject being ghettoized, and whose fiction characters are integrated into the great human family. In my own books, the homosexual man's life is a life apart. You've mentioned that my straightforwardness in the book is shocking to some people, but Genet is genuinely shocking. Yet at the same time, there is in him a mix of crude sex and love: 'I've never lived my homosexuality in its purest form,' he wrote, and what he meant by it is that he had always mingled it with love. It's the same for me, but I do it in a furtive way. For me, there is always an element of love in the sexual act, if

---

* David Leavitt gave three readings at the Village Voice, including *While England Sleeps* (London: Viking UK, 1993) inspired by the life of Stephen Spender. Yet Leavitt's 1990s were not Spender's 1930s, and the depiction of homosexual love in his novel shocked Spender, who felt his private life had been intruded upon. The novel was withdrawn, edited, and reprinted.

not a fascination for the other, at least for his personality, for what makes him different."[36]

de Ceccatty: "Great writing stands on its own; no need to be specified by such an adjective as 'homosexual': *The Farewell Symphony* is a novel about life and death, but there is something else in it."

White: "In this book, I wished to recall the joy, the exaltation it had been to be gay in the 1970s, a decade of great expectations extinguished in no time by the catastrophic AIDS epidemics and infused with utter despair. It had been so exciting to be a writer then, for homosexuality had become an exciting subject, revitalizing the genre of the novel. The gay culture of the 1970s has been lost, and there is a whole new generation of young gays who have no idea of what we went through, and, like an anthropologist, I wanted to reconstitute that period from its roots to its boughs."

The Farewell Symphony was also "his adieu to Paris," and, though not the last one, White's reading was nevertheless an "au revoir" to our bookshop and his loyal audience. A talented, prolific, generous, magnanimous and witty person, Edmund White greatly contributed to the emergence of a literary force at the Village Voice and to its growing reputation.

6

From Home to Paris and Elsewhere

IRISH WRITERS AT THE VILLAGE VOICE BOOKSHOP

Želkjo Ivanjek, John Calder, Anne Atik, Harry Clifton, Deirdre Madden

S tarting in the 1990s, the Irish community in Paris was steadily growing as their resident American counterparts befriended young writers who, in turn, started to give their own readings in Paris. The Ulster conflict that dragged on at home may partially explain why they crossed the Irish Sea (hopping over England) in great numbers at this time, but Ireland's joining the European Union a decade beforehand certainly facilitated staying on in our city. In fact, the two countries' cultural ties went back to the sixteenth century, with the founding of the Irish College in the Latin Quarter, renamed the Irish Cultural Center in 2002.

A small island battered by ocean winds and known for its traditional Celtic storytelling, Ireland has always enjoyed the reputation of having the greatest density of writers per square mile. Yet, because of this turbulent history of censorship and continued warfare with Great Britain, its authors had written many of their great works in exile or self-exile abroad, particularly in France.

The illustrious figures of the twentieth century, James Joyce and Samuel Beckett, once considered unabashedly avant-garde, are now viewed as the mainstay of contemporary world literature. Our bookshop largely reveled in their success by organizing several events around their plays, poetry, and novels.

TRIBUTES TO JAMES JOYCE AND SAMUEL BECKETT

James Joyce in Pula

The name of James Joyce is inseparable from Paris, where he published his monumental opus *Ulysses*. And so, connecting the young Joyce to a place as relatively unknown as Pula in Croatia may seem a bit far-fetched. But it will all make sense. Failing to get a promised teaching position at the Berlitz School of Paris and, accompanied by his future wife Nora, in 1904, Joyce agreed to take a comparable job in Pula on the Adriatic Coast.*

Strangely enough, one day in 1984 a young Slovenian film-maker, **Željko Ivanjek**, arrived at the Village Voice and suggested he show us his short documentary about the six months Joyce spent in this hidden seafront city.

Produced by Zagreb Television and titled *A Day of Dappled Seaborne Clouds* after a line from *A Portrait of the Artist as a Young Man*, the projection took place in our bookshop on November 28, 1984. Crucial to the young writer, Pula's exceptionally rich library offered a wide range of books written in its official languages—Croatian, German, and Italian. Joyce learned German, translated Italian literature and wrote a critical essay on the Italian poet and playwright Gabriele D'Annunzio, all the while working on his future novel *Stephen Hero*. He also completed several short stories, later incorporated in *Dubliners*. In a letter to his brother Stanislaus, he described himself as "a hell of an industrious chap."[1]

Ivanjek's camera followed its imagined recollections of Joyce and Nora in their comings and goings around the Coliseum, the center of the antique city where they lived, here and there catching a glimpse of their various lodgings. Among the people interviewed, a few older ones provided snippets of faded memories

---

* Part of the Austro-Hungarian Empire before World War I. Very little is known about Joyce's brief stay there.

of the place at that time. The camera went along, imagining the couple's journey to the Brioni islands where, at the Miramar Café, the two celebrated the writer's twenty-third birthday, peppered with their passing erotic notes under the table. In their intimate language, Pula became synonymous with such hidden pleasures.

Unexpectedly, six months into their stay, a spy scandal forced the foreign community, including the Joyces, to pack up their bags, leaving behind this "Naval Siberia," as Joyce nicknamed the city. The couple set off for Trieste, farther north on the coast.

A big crowd attended this screening, attracted by such an unusual topic. There were officials from the Irish and British embassies, the writer Hélène Cixous who had written her PhD on Joyce, the filmmaker Agnès Varda who had produced a short documentary entitled *Ulysse* (having no relation to the novel), and the legendary photographer Gisèle Freund who, in 1938 and 1939, had photographed Joyce in his Parisian apartment.

Yet the true star of the evening was Stephen Joyce, the writer's grandson, who drew as much attention from the curious audience as the film itself. After the showing was over, the crowd pressed around him, but he quickly slipped out of sight. I never knew what he thought of the documentary, this modest but sensitive and informative attempt to resurrect a chapter of Joyce's life left in the dark for so many years.

SAMUEL BECKETT: TWO CONTRASTING PORTRAITS

Samuel Beckett, the other giant of twentieth-century Irish literature, lived in Paris his whole adult life. On different occasions he was honored in our bookstore by two of his lifetime friends: John Calder, his British publisher, and the American poet Anne Atik, the author of *How It Was*, her memories of Beckett that recounted thirty years of their friendship only interrupted by his death in December 1989.

John Calder

Britain's Scottish independent publisher with a prestigious literary catalog boasting eighteen Nobel Prizes, Calder gave four talks at the Village Voice about Beckett's novels and plays. On March 29, 2012, he presented his most recent essay *The Theology of Samuel Beckett*[2] that focused on Beckett's vision of a world without God. It highlighted the writings of the nihilist/existentialist writer, inspired by Arnold Geulincx, a seventeenth-century Flemish philosopher Beckett had discovered in his student years at Trinity College in Dublin. According to this theologian, "God was so far away that he couldn't hear us or care about us, leaving us human beings in a quandary."

Not wanting to offend his religious mother, Beckett never openly admitted to being an atheist, even though his writings clearly reflect the conviction that "man's future was nothingness and his tragedy was to have been born." He was a writer of philosophical thought, but Calder stressed that, above all, he was a writer who "out of the blackness of this world, has created an unparalleled literature, suffused with dry, gallows humor." "This underlying humor," he went on, "emphasizes Man's awareness of his tragedy. Humor is part of life, one of its traits, and Beckett could laugh, but tragedy is also the reality and intrinsic part of human nature."[3]

Samuel Beckett lived until the very end of the year 1989. For a number of years, we would have loved to organize a reading or book signing with him. However, Calder told us that he was too frail and would never be able to endure a signing session. The only contact we had with the author was, on his publisher's suggestion, sending him a complete Oxford English-French dictionary mailed to his retirement home. It meant a lot to us, knowing that Beckett was still fascinated by the world of words, wanting to probe their secrets and invent language games in English and French.

Anne Atik

A Parisian since 1959, the American poet Anne Atik launched *How It Was: A Memoir of Samuel Beckett*,[4] her own memoir of lifetime friend Samuel Beckett, at the Village Voice on December 4, 2003. Her portrait of him was very different from that of the dark, pessimistic philosopher Calder had cited. She remembered a warm, convivial person who spent a lot of time with his friends, showing a genuine interest in their children and even real affection for them.

Anne had met Beckett in the early sixties through her husband, Avigdor Arikha, the distinguished painter and art historian who was a very close friend of his. In her talk at our bookstore, she recounted the frequent dinners the three of them shared at the couple's home—Beckett, Avigdor, and herself, discussing literature, playing and listening to music and, most of all, reading poetry aloud. As they were all multilingual, they recited Yeats in English, Goethe in German, Dante in Italian, and contemporary French poetry in French, delivering their lines the way Beckett directed his actors. He would ask them to "keep the voice flat, leave off acting, and transmit the structure of the sentence as well as the pace and the music of the words themselves."[5] After dinner and their readings, Anne noted down details about their evening while her husband accompanied Beckett to his nearby home on boulevard Saint-Jacques.

Throughout her talk, she emphasized Beckett's revolutionary style. To him, words were like musical notes, each one with its own weight and resonance. Anne recalled a brief encounter between him and Stravinsky, the latter wanting to know how Beckett, "the maestro of language," had written his silences in *Waiting for Godot*.

In another vein, she told us that Arikha, convinced that "integrity in art was the artist's golden rule," admired his friend Beckett for "giving the ethics of aesthetics . . . For him, every dot, every word had to be justified. It was a question of truth." In all, she said, Beckett was the perfect example of the artist's "life and work meshing together so perfectly," both requiring "integrity."

LIVING IN WORDS TO TELL THE WORLD

In November 1989, the French Ministry of Culture organized Les Belles Étrangères, a festival of contemporary Irish literature, to enhance its visibility in France.[6] The Irish Cultural Center, an extension of the Irish College, was still several years away. One of the venues chosen for this important encounter was our bookshop, where novelists Jennifer Johnston and John McGahern, alongside poets John Montague and Derek Mahon, gave a joint reading on November 27, 1989.

Born into the interwar generation, these authors had started to publish in the sixties, when censorship in Ireland was still in effect. As a result, and like their predecessors, they had spent part of their writing lives abroad. For example, Johnston had lived for twenty years in London prior to returning home in 1980. Her novel *Fool's Sanctuary* (1987), presented that night, portrayed the tragedy of an Irish family torn in their allegiance between the Irish War of Independence and answering the call of the British military draft at the start of World War I. She was followed by John McGahern, one of the great Irish voices of the second half of the twentieth century, who had also lived many years abroad after his novel *The Dark* was banned for obscenity in 1965.

As for the poets, John Montague split his time among Ireland, Paris, and the South of France while Derek Mahon moved back and forth between Belfast, London, and Paris, always looking for "an elsewhere with beauty."[7]

By an extraordinary coincidence, this first Irish literary festival took place within a month of Beckett's death on December 22, closing one era and marking the beginning of a new one.

In the coming decades, along with the revival of Irish folklore, music, and literature, writers the likes of John Banville and Colm Tóibín who gave readings at our bookstore were being acclaimed by an international readership. An Irish artistic renaissance was in the air, and here we turn our attention to two young writers who lived in Paris for a full decade, from 1994 to 2004.

Harry Clifton and Deirdre Madden

A poet and a novelist respectively, Harry Clifton and Deirdre Madden arrived in the city from Italy, where they had spent a year in the rugged mountains of the Abruzzi. Seeking a quiet area to write, they settled down on the southern border of Montparnasse, and, within a decade, had completed and published seven books between the two of them, confirming their talents and rightful place in contemporary Irish letters.

Their first reading at the Village Voice took place on April 11, 1995, as a joint presentation of their works. Harry read from two of his poetry collections, *The Desert Route* and *Night Train Through the Brenner*,[8] and Deirdre discussed *Nothing Is Black*,[9] her fourth novel. In his preface to the poetry collection, Mahon had written that Clifton was a poet who "had taken the world as his province"[10] while it was clear that Madden was immersed in the private and intimate realm of women who were mothers, sisters, friends, and artists. Yet for each, their roots were inseparable from the landscapes and history of Ireland.

Lured to "other wheres" since youth, Harry had lived twenty years abroad, traveling through Europe, the Americas, Africa, and Asia, teaching and working with aid agencies. "The seventies were a time when we were getting out of university and felt there was little for us in Ireland," he told us, "but there was also a personal element in my continual wanderings . . . I come from a mixed background, an Irish father and a South American mother . . . representing an unknown country to me . . . My life has been polarized between Ireland and the world at large for twenty years. The ideal place for me is to exist between two places, between two polarities."[11]

On June 21, 2001, at his launch of *On the Spine of Italy: A Year in the Abruzzi*,[12] he was asked why as a renowned poet he had not written it in verse. He explained that "poetry was a way of looking inward while the year in the Abruzzi had been one of looking outward. . . . It was not a book about us, but about the people in the village. The place was unwritten, and I felt that there was something invaluable here to write about."[13] However, in her introduction, the American poet Ellen Hinsey praised his book as "pure poetry," comparing Clifton's lyrical language to the egg tempera technique used by the painters of the Italian Renaissance, "one suited to capture essential details and arresting images, such as a stitch in the sewing line of a garment, or the reflection on the face of a tear globe. Such a technique allowed a skilled rendering of the roughness of the place, filled with extraordinary descriptions and emotions."[14] Indeed, in his poem "Abruzzo" he expressed the physical, sensuous contact with this stony place and its villages: "All that was tangible, tasted, felt / Restored us to our senses / Like freezing mountain water / From the spigots . . ."[15]

Deirdre had shared that year in the Abruzzi with her husband, experiencing firsthand the harshness of the place: rain coming through the roof, freezing nights, and heavy snowfalls causing power cuts. In *Remembering Light and Stone*, her own memoir of their mountainous village, she recalls "the pleasure and fascination of other countries . . . yet," she confessed, "I do not belong here," but "I found out more about my own country, simply by not being in it."[16]

This country that she calls "my own" is Northern Ireland, a land of wild, sensuous beauty described with great affection and subtlety in all her works of fiction. It is also a country that has suffered from its colonial history, including the violence and senseless killings of the Ulster Troubles, depicted in her novel *One by One in the Darkness*, which she presented at the Village Voice on June 14, 1996.[17]

Introducing her work, Deirdre warned her audience: "It is not a book on the terrorists or the actions going on between the two camps. There are many accounts of those, thrillers essentially, but," she insisted, "what is most important for me is to talk about the ordinary lives of people, how they lived and died through the Troubles. I have a responsibility to it. I have a very strong connection with Northern Ireland, and I wouldn't want to lose it."[18]

In this story about a family tragedy caused by the random killing of the father, the narrator portrays his widow and their three daughters in their home setting. The love among them is the source of their resilience in the face of an uncertain future that, for one of them, includes the difficult path of an artistic calling.

Asked why she, a writer paying particular attention to language, often wrote about art and not the writing process, Deirdre replied that it would be "too self-referential. Also, I love painting, for example, a landscape in paintings and how to do the narrative of it." For her, painting means a physical, even intimate contact with the natural world of Northern Ireland and its elemental forces that include the debris of pebbles and shells cast on the sea coast and going back millions of years.[19]

Julia, the protagonist of her novel *Authenticity*, is a conceptual artist, building an art installation around the word "peat" or "turf," that clod of earth reminiscent of Ireland and commonly used until recent times as its domestic fuel. Engaged in her project, she is curious about what such a word means to people nowadays. Did it evoke the particular smell of its smoke or anything else? The responses varied widely but none of them bore a direct relation to the object itself: it could be "an odor of clean linen," "the memory of a betrayal," or "a day at sea with a father." For the author, one saw a landscape "as one remembered it or through something remembered."[20]

During their ten years in Paris, this couple never mentioned writing about the city, but in 2007, three years after going home, they were back in Paris to visit friends. On this occasion, Harry presented me with his new collection of poetry, *Secular Eden: Paris Notebooks 1994-2004*, actually written in his earlier Paris days. He opened it, pointing to a poem, "To the Fourteenth District": "a place to live and die, and go mad in."

Although dedicated to me as it was my neighborhood, more specifically it was a tribute to the writers and artists who, like Beckett, had lived in this part of the city. Likewise, this neighborhood had a particular resonance for Harry: it meant the memory of the three of us getting together at Le Bouquet d'Alésia for a drink, a bite to eat and a chat, enjoying an early evening where "the everydayness [was] raised to holy rite / at café tables."[21]

Harry Clifton, Odile Hellier, Deirdre Madden, editors Maggie Doyle and Cynthia Liebow. Village Voice Bookshop, April 11, 1995. © C. Deudon

7

Varieties of Exile[1]

TWO CANADIAN PARISIANS

Nancy Huston and Mavis Gallant

Born in bilingual Canada, Nancy Huston and Mavis Gallant are both native English-speaking authors who chose to live in Paris, Mavis from 1951 and Nancy, 1973. Unlike many North American expatriates who returned home after a few years, they remained in our city, making a life in writing.

When the Village Voice closed in 2012, Mavis had lived here for sixty years and Nancy almost forty. In fact, they were essentially viewed in their home country as Paris writers. Yet many differences separate these two women and their generations thirty years apart—their backgrounds, lives, works, and choice of language—Nancy writes almost exclusively in French while Mavis never departs from English. And, of course, their chosen city is a distinctive place for each of them. Mavis Gallant's stories resurrect the postwar Paris of the '50s, "a jumble of unsung lives and war survivors," including artists and intellectuals exiled from Central and Eastern Europe. On the other hand, Nancy Huston depicts Paris as a city of the mind at the vanguard of the various modes of thought and literary currents that stimulate ways of seeing and writing about the world.

Nancy Huston

"I went to Paris to find myself,
and I was not there either."[2]
—HUSTON,
    Village Voice reading, March 4, 2002.

"There was a stunning picture of Nancy Huston in *Le Monde*," Mavis Gallant wrote in a letter to me, "I've often heard her name, but I don't think that anyone told me that she was young and beautiful." This was in April of 1989, and I was surprised to learn that the paths of these two authors had never crossed in the sixteen years they had lived in the same city. Strange as it may seem, praised in the Anglophone world as a regular *New Yorker* contributor and a unique voice from Paris, Mavis was unknown in France, while Nancy was already much present on the French literary scene at the time.

Born in Calgary in "the least bilingual state of all Canada," Nancy Huston was raised in an English-speaking household and learned basic French at school. Later on, at Sarah Lawrence College in New York, her interest in contemporary French literature took her to Paris. During her junior year abroad, she wrote her thesis on the French language under the guidance of the eminent linguist and philosopher Roland Barthes. This remarkable achievement was to be the start of a long and rich writing career in France and in French.

Nancy gave a number of readings at the Village Voice and participated in many different literary events, introducing authors and organizing roundtables. I have selected her talk of March 14, 2002, when she ushered in her essay *Nord perdu*.[3] This work is an original, perceptive, and witty series of reflections she later translated herself as *Losing North: Musings on Land, Tongue and Self*. For her, transnational life or life in translation means a constant tug of war between two languages, cultures, and countries. If she airs grievances in this gem of a book, the author also comes to value the deep texturing of such an experience: a foreign accent immediately catches one's attention as this person might have a story to tell, that of another life in a distant country with its own compelling history and culture.

This topic was of particular interest to the Village Voice audience of writers, readers, and general public, often puzzled by

Nancy Huston, reading at Village Voice Bookshop, March 14, 2002. © Flavio Toma

French mores and cultural oddities. However, even more intriguing to us was Nancy's exceptional linguistic ability. It appeared that she had become a renowned French writer in no time, even compared to "a female Beckett" by Mavis Gallant.

At her presentation of Nord perdu, Nancy shed light on the bilingual writer's shift of language. It was not always evident, but she saw it as being individual and, in her case, grounded in her own life circumstances. Had Nancy and Mavis met to debate this question, they would have agreed that, in the end, the choice of language for a bilingual writer is deeply personal.

Q: "How did you come to be writing your fiction in French?"

Nancy Huston: "The basic reason for that strangeness is my mother: she left the family when I was six years old and my brother eight, and the way to deal with that blow was to abandon our mother tongue. Yet, there is another connection with my mother, and it is music. She played the piano, and usually young people leave playing at adolescence, but I continued to play, at least for a while, out of my desire for a connection with my mother. Both English and piano were abandoned and replaced by the French language and by the harpsichord that I associate with French. There are fewer emotions in the harpsichord, and the French language is very monochord. From the start, English was my mother's tongue, which, symbolically, also meant the piano fortissimo."

Q: "Do you feel French? And do your French readers see you as a French writer or a foreign author writing in French?"

Huston: "No, I don't feel French, and I'm not even Francophile. There is a Canadian adage that says: 'I went to Paris to find myself, and I was not there either.' I don't have a particular admiration for the French language, though, for a while, I was a Francophile, but for a very short time. For me, French was more like a territory full of musical possibilities."

Q: "You write your novels in French, but you also use English here and there, and translate some of your writings into English, such as this essay. Aren't you tempted to go back to your native language?"

Huston: "A few months ago, I could have answered such a question by saying that I write in the language of my characters, English or French, depending on their origins. However, now it's a little bit more complex; the process is more chaotic: I can't choose in which language to write, coming and going between French and English. I look at it negatively, as if I were handicapped, as if I didn't speak any language fluently. I talked about this with André Brink, the only author I know to be in my situation, going linguistically through the same thing as I do. Irrespective of the subject, he writes in English or Afrikaans and then translates himself in both directions. 'Go ahead,' he said, 'don't worry about it. We live twice; it's a privilege.' And so, I try to look at it this way."

Q: "Does your choice of language change the story you have in mind? After all, there are certain things one can express more easily in one language than in another."

Huston: "Going through my journals, I tried to find out whether I privileged one language over the other for certain topics, and I couldn't discern such a pattern. However, I'm much more at ease in French in theoretical discussions because it was the kind of French required for my studies in France, and it's easier for me to 'délirer et déconner' in English though I can still pretty well do it in French. [laughter] For me, the best moment in my writing is when I feel that I hear the same music in French and in English."

Mavis Gallant

"Paris is so different, so special,
so inexplicably home."
—GALLANT, letter to me, dated August 2001.

Born in French-speaking Montreal, Mavis fiercely clung to English, her mother tongue: "I owed it to children's books that I absorbed once and for all the rhythm of English prose. By eight, it was irremovably entrenched as the language of my imagination."[4]

When I first met Mavis Gallant in the mid-eighties, she had been a Parisian for more than thirty years, and most of her one hundred and sixteen stories—all written in English—had already appeared in *The New Yorker*, as well as been reprinted in various Canadian and US editions. A reference for regular readers of the US weekly, Mavis was often compared to Chekhov, the Russian master of the short story. However, in spite of her long stay in Paris, she remained virtually unheard of in France.

To me, this was a paradox. How could she be overlooked by French publishers when her Parisian social circle included French and European intellectuals and artists, as well as American literary figures, such as the famous novelist Mary McCarthy or Janet Flanner, the flamboyant Paris correspondent for *The New Yorker* until 1975? Furthermore, Gallant lived in the heart of Montparnasse, within walking distance of Saint-Germain-des-Prés, well known for its publishing houses and bookstores. Strangely enough, not one of them seems to have been aware of their distinguished and prolific neighbor.

Mavis gave a dozen readings in our bookstore, introduced a couple of times by Marta Dvorak.[5] Our author also put forward a number of Canadian writers such as Mordecai Richler and Margaret Atwood. Her own first book launch at the Village Voice took place in 1985 for her collection *Overhead in a Balloon: Stories of*

Paris,[6] published in Canada (Ontario). The reading was arranged by Simone Suchet of the Canadian Cultural Center, in charge of promoting English Canadian literature in France.

Mavis continued to be ignored by the French in her adopted city until 1988. It was the year when a new Parisian publishing house brought out her journal of May '68 to coincide with the twentieth anniversary of the student uprising.[7]

On May 17, 1988, she presented the work at the Village Voice, summoning up the scenes she had observed as she walked through garbage-strewn streets. Adventurous, she had immersed herself in the demonstrations, and now, reading to us from her journal, she conjured up the violent and confused mood of the time, depicting students standing on barricades and hurling heavy cobblestones at the police. With nowhere to go and not knowing what might happen, other astonished Parisians wandered aimlessly about.

De Gaulle had disappeared, leaving behind a shadow government and a population fearful of civil war. Still, Mavis Gallant was out there, braving the disorder to catch bits and pieces of various people's reactions. At one point, during the later May counter-demonstration, she heard people shouting "Cohn Bendit Dachau."* Only familiar with the German pronunciation of the death camp's name, she did not get the true meaning of the hideous slogan yelled out in a French accent. "I didn't include it in my account," she informed us, "as I had not heard it firsthand."[8]

Her book *Chroniques de mai 68* was widely reviewed, and its author, congenially nicknamed "Miss Barricades,"[9] was invited to talk about it on Bernard Pivot's *Apostrophes*, the most popular literary program on television in those years. As a result of this national exposure, her Paris stories in *Overhead in a Balloon* soon appeared under the French title *Rue de Lille*.[10] They were received with mixed reviews: Gallant's style was praised, but most readers

---

* The German sound of "ch" is pronounced "sh" in French, i.e., "Da-sh-o."

shunned the work. Her publisher argued that short stories did not sell well in France and dryly assumed that French people expected a Canadian writer to set her works not in Paris but amid Canada's wild landscapes.

Known as a *New Yorker* author, Gallant broadened her overall readership through the years, essentially through the US imprint of the *New York Review of Books* that published three volumes of her stories, reflecting the range of her imagination, style, and talent. In 2002, the first of the three featured her *Paris Stories*,[11] selected with an introduction by Michael Ondaatje, the Ontario author of *The English Patient*.

Soon enough, a Canadian TV crew was dispatched to Paris to interview her in the context of the city where she had chosen to be her true self, that is, a writer. Well intentioned, they took the author on a whirlwind tour, asking her to comment directly on the sights as they passed by them. In a letter to me, Mavis described this venture with some irritation, but also with her typical wit: "I let myself be trundled around like a passive spaniel (poodle might be more exact) to no real purpose clear to me, from the Bois de Boulogne to that little square at the bottom of rue Mouffetard. Everything seemed haphazard and random, I've no particular fondness or attachment for or to either—they are not part of my personal map of Paris."[12]

Actually, her "personal map of Paris" was the Paris of her heart, evoked in "The Other Paris"[13] through her character, Felix, a young Eastern European war orphan exiled in Paris, far afield from the cliché of the romantic "gay Paree" to be found in popular American songs and movies. Her Paris was a place with "people uprooted and in permanent transit, the ones I cared to write about throughout my life," she told us at a reading.[14]

These were the same people who had captured her imagination back in wartime Montreal. In the story "Varieties of Exile,"[15] Linnet Muir, the young journalist, aka Mavis Gallant, reports on the crowds of European refugees streaming into the country. "I was attracted to Europe and always knew that I would fit there."[16]

In Spain, our young, intrepid author wrote stories on a hungry stomach, desperately waiting for the payment of her first *New Yorker* stories. Later, in Florence, she had "a distinct 'déjà vu' experience, as if I knew every street and doorway," she wrote. "Even in cities that were postwar poor or still partially in ruins, I felt the continuity of art and literature."[17]

Traveling on to Germany, Mavis went from city to city—Berlin, Bayreuth, and Munich, asking people how they had experienced the war, and how they could have gone along with Hitler's policies. She was trying to get to the bottom of what had really occurred during their years under Nazi rule, but she admitted "I now know there is no such thing as 'what really happened' anywhere; yet I still scramble after the facts of the matter."[18] She also wanted to understand how Germans went about reconstructing their shattered lives in a country in complete disarray, just like that train stopped at the Pegnitz Junction in the middle of nowhere, its passengers stranded in transit, as depicted in her novella *The Pegnitz Junction*, her favorite among all of her stories.[19] In an afterword to her *Paris Stories*, Mavis confided that "no city in the world drew me as strongly as Paris."[20] It was **Michael Ondaatje**, the uprooted Sri Lankan Canadian, who understood that her Paris reflected the "underground map of Europe in the twentieth century with wanderers caught in a permanent in-between"[21] that resonated with his own fictional characters.

Inspired by the success of these *Paris Stories* in the NYRB edition, two other writers, great admirers of her work, published their respective selections of her anthology in that same US imprint. Russell Banks chose her Canadian characters for whom he felt "an abiding affection" under the title *Varieties of Exile*, while Pulitzer Prize winner Jhumpa Lahiri selected Gallant's *Early and Uncollected Stories*, published as *The Cost of Living*.[22]

Known for her affinities with Gallant's writing, Jhumpa Lahiri was commissioned by *Granta* to interview the author in Paris. The two women spent three days talking about their respective lives and works, concluding their stimulating and friendly exchanges with a joint reading at the Village Voice.[23]

On February 19, 2009, before a packed audience, Jhumpa revealed with some emotion that "to be here with Mavis is something I would never have dreamed until it happened this moment.... For years, Mavis has been a source of inspiration; she taught me the art of linking stories with the same character migrating from one story to another, and my work owes a lot to her." As a final tribute, she read a short excerpt from *The Unaccustomed Earth*, her recent collection of interrelated short stories.

Wearing the turquoise silk scarf Jhumpa had brought her as a gift, Mavis, in turn, enacted a passage from her only play, *What Is to Be Done?*[24] a satirical wartime comedy based on the nonsensical correspondence of two lovers across the Atlantic Ocean. In her letters, the young woman extols the war effort and their bright future while her fiancé primarily indulges in fantasies about their lovemaking.

Mavis's performance was a huge success, triggering uninterrupted fits of laughter from the audience. Duly applauded, she was beaming with a joy as I had never seen her express at any of her other readings. Several days later, I received a note from her, telling me how much she had enjoyed this evening of "complicité et amitié with Jhumpa Lahiri, such as I'd felt at that other reading with Michael Ondaatje—her kin-spirit."[25]

Mavis's last talk at the Village Voice took place on December 3, 2009, attended by the large circle of her Parisian friends and acquaintances. She chose to read "The Picnic," one of her earlier stories (1952) reprinted in Lahiri's *The Cost of Living*.

Mavis Gallant, Village Voice reading, February 19, 2009. © Steve Murez

The work is set in postwar France, in a small town in the East where American troops are stationed. Billeted with a local family, an officer decides to organize a Sunday picnic as a "symbol of unity between the two nations" which, rather than the expected cordial entente, only reveals engrained cultural prejudices on both sides. Mavis spoke in a voice that was intimate and let the irony come through, subtly expressing the complex, frustrating relationship between the French people and their American "saviors."

Several people in the audience then asked her to talk about her writing. It was the first time at a reading that she agreed to do it. She referred to "the presence of preexisting figures in the genesis of a new story," specifying that "these figures did not talk, but waited to be developed into full-blown characters. They are there, even their names are there, and I know what they are thinking . . . I also know how the story ends, but it requires from me that I write down pages and pages of dialogue that will not go into the story. I have to have them talk; I have to hear their voices and hear what they are thinking."[26]

Mavis lived her entire adult life in France, but she never became French, perhaps her way of holding onto her Canadian roots and the Montreal of her childhood, at once an enchantment and a place of inconsolable grief, brought upon by the loss of her father at an early age. Yet Canada had not left her and, more than once, I happened to find in the folds of her letters a dried maple leaf, inviting me "to imagine the beige tracings as brilliant yellow and the reddish tone as scarlet, and then imagine the whole tree."[27]

8

Dark Times

AN ANGLO-AMERICAN FOCUS ON THE VICHY REGIME
Raymond Federman, Carmen Callil, Alan Riding, Alice Kaplan on Louis Guilloux

Throughout the years, one particular issue that captured the attention of our public was the collaboration of the Vichy government with the Nazi occupancy during the Second World War. However, once the fighting was over, the image of an active Resistance movement had increasingly prevailed in the national narrative, obscuring the somber role this regime had played for the sake of the country's unity. In fact, one of the first artistic attempts in France to bear witness to the truth was Marcel Ophuls's documentary film *Le chagrin et la pitié* (*The Sorrow and the Pity*) that came out in 1969. Deemed too controversial, it was immediately censored and retracted.*

Meanwhile, American scholars were conducting research on Vichy and in 1972 the renowned historian Robert O. Paxton published *Vichy France: Old Guard and New Order, 1940-1944*, an in-depth account of this government's active collaboration with Nazi authorities in the deportation of foreign and French Jews to extermination camps.

Its revelations, based on documents found in a number of German archives collected by the US Army, were incriminating

---

* Two years later, in 1971, the film was discreetly released in movie theaters, shown on public television only in 1981.

evidence. Yet, if the truth could no longer be ignored, it was not always well received. At first rejected by Éditions Gallimard as inexact, Paxton's *Vichy France* was published by Le Seuil, causing an outcry that more or less amounted to "What right does this American have to come to France and unearth skeletons in our closets?"[1] While this incensed question didn't necessarily reflect the attitude of the entire population, it still revealed the private stirrings of a large number of French people. We will look at the works of four Anglophone writers who, each in their own way, take us to the very heart of the Vichy scandal, as well as the testimony of a French author who recounts his understanding of dubious US military wartime practices.

Raymond Federman

On July 16 and 17, 1942, the Vichy government stepped up its collaboration with the Gestapo by ordering its own Parisian police to arrest over thirteen thousand foreign-born Jews, including children, in the capital and Greater Paris area. They were to be held in a bicycle racing stadium in the fifteenth district before being deported to French internment camps and, ultimately, to Auschwitz.

One of the rare survivors of this tragedy, known as Rafle du Vélodrome d'Hiver (the Vel d'Hiv' Roundup) was the French-born American writer Raymond Federman who told his story at the Village Voice on March 25, 1986, as a prelude to the presentation of his recent novel *Smiles on Washington Square*.[2] In fact, he was thirteen at the time when he became an unseen witness to the arrest of his parents and sister at their home in Montrouge, just south of the Montparnasse district.

It was five thirty in the morning. His parents woke up to the voices of the police in the courtyard and that of the concierge indicating "the Federmans on the third floor." In a hurry, his mother got him out of bed, pushing him into a stairway closet where he would sit hidden and cramped for more than thirteen hours: "His tomb and his cradle, his death and his renaissance." These were the words going around in the boy's head in Yiddish, the language spoken by his parents in private. Sadly, they rang true, for no one in the family ever returned home to him. At the age of eighteen, Federman immigrated to the US, and much later, wrote *The Voice in the Closet*, the sober memoir of this secret hideout.[3]

Smiles on Washington Square did not, however, focus on the Vichy collaboration, but was a New York love story that, he specified, "was not about love, but rather about loneliness, the loneliness of two separate individuals who, instead of getting together, will only have an exchange of glances, a reconnaissance of one another through the eyes, on a rainy day in New York on Washington Square."[4]

This novel is one of missed opportunity, absence, and longing that pays particular attention to language and its multiple possibilities. Being bilingual, Federman experimented with the words and sonorities of the French and English languages. He likewise addressed his mostly bilingual public that evening as "the happy few and the happy fous,"[5] a play on words in line with the puns of Beckett whom he personally knew and highly admired, as seen in the two essays he wrote about him.

Yet if Beckett was the writer of silence, Federman wrote from silence. In the course of his reading with us, he jokingly announced that "my favorite key on my typewriter is 'delete.'" This definitive kind of erasure was also a feature of the work of Georges Perec, the French writer who shared with him the fate of a child orphaned by parents who had been expedited to the death camps.

An experimental writer himself, Perec was the author of *La disparition*, the unique example in world literature of a lengthy three-hundred-page novel in which the letter *e* has been entirely deleted. The work was later translated into English as *A Void*. All of these stark terms bring to mind the gaping hole left by the quasi-inexpressible blank space of Jewish lives that had been snuffed out so drastically in Vichy France.

Carmen Callil

This regime was much later laid bare by the Australian-born British writer Carmen Callil, the founder of Virago Press, which specialized in women's world classics in literature. Living in London, she had no particular ties to France and no apparent reason to write about Vichy until the unexpected 1970 suicide of her lifetime friend, Anne Darquier, which left her with unanswered questions.

A year later, as Callil was watching *The Sorrow and the Pity* on the BBC, through the subtitles she was able to identify the Frenchman shaking hands with the Nazi officer at the Ritz Hotel as none other than Anne's father. She told us that "there had never been a conversation in all those years I'd known Anne that could have indicated to me that she was aware that her father was a war criminal. Bewildered, I set out to reconstitute the puzzle by searching for, hunting and collecting all its pieces, which I patiently assembled into *Bad Faith: A Forgotten History of Family and Fatherland*."[6]

A strong-willed woman, Carmen Callil was at the Village Voice on April 18, 2006, to launch this personal investigative journey. Her editor, Marc Parent,[7] opened the evening by alerting the audience to the fact that *Bad Faith* had been rejected by seven French publishing houses before it reached him.[8] "The reason put forward was its length," he explained, "but the truth is that the Vichy collaboration is still a sensitive issue in today's France and now, barely out, *Bad Faith* in French is already the target of harsh critics so as to deflect the attention of the reader from the core of the issue at hand. A revisionist history is at work in this country," he offered, "and Petain's spirit is not dead, far from it."

Callil agreed with him, pointing to "the British obsession" with the French for not facing their war past. "The first villain of my book," she said, "is Vichy, a story of evil and a reflection about how a civilized country can find itself collaborating with the most horrible, horrifying system. Yet," she went on, "as in all tragedies, this one has its own lining of burlesque and black humor as it reveals the grotesque villain, Louis Darquier de Pellepoix, commissioner for Jewish Affairs in the Vichy government." As the executor of all policies against Jews, he organized the Vel d'Hiv roundup.*

She had heard of a book about the Vichy Commissariat aux Affaires Juives, the commissariat-general for Jewish affairs, written by a young French scholar, and wanted to find out if anyone in the audience knew anything about it. Someone in the audience quickly pointed out the presence of the author in question, and, in acknowledgment, a man raised his hand and stood up. Though he basically agreed with Callil, he stressed that "Darquier was incompetent and an immense opportunist." While going through the archives, he had come upon a letter written to Darquier by an admirer. It was a find, "a rarity," he added, "because, at the time, nobody paid attention to the man. He was just a puppet." Callil snapped back: ". . . and a dream for the Nazi occupant . . . someone greedy like him was a blessing for the Nazis whose strategy was to have the French to do the dirty jobs, and they found plenty of them to do it. [pause] And it took a foreigner to tell the story!" she angrily concluded.[9]

As a literary editor, Callil paid close attention to words, and especially those used in propaganda. They are "the same ones over and over again, and it is important to spell them out in order to uncover what goes on." She gave a probing and most chilling

---

* Darquier was under the command of René Bousquet, secretary general to the Vichy administration police. Brought to court after the war, Bousquet was acquitted in 1949. In 1991, he was finally charged with crimes against humanity. Two years later, he was assassinated, removing all possibility of a trial, and thus, any proceedings against the Vichy regime. In the late '80s and early '90s, the revelation of President Mitterrand's continued relationship with Bousquet caused a stir and even outrage.

example: "The Vel d'Hiv Roundup was referred to as 'vent prin-
tanier' or 'spring breeze' by Darquier & Company, disguising the
terrible reality as some sort of a spring-cleaning operation—a
renewal!"

Someone asked what had most surprised her in her enquiry.

Callil: "I would say the financing of the far-right movement and
anti-Semitic actions. The list of those sponsors is long, and I
will mention only a few: Coty—perfumes—Taittinger—cham-
pagne, admirer of Mussolini and Hitler—L'Oréal, the financier
of the most extreme and murderous fascist leagues that, after
the Liberation, provided hideouts for many war criminals.
It took me a full year to track that money and the payments
that went to intellectuals who used words to propagate the
venom of anti-Semitism through such newspapers as *Gringoire*
in which Colette wrote, and many others. Rosenberg, Himmler,
Goebbels, and the industrialist Krupp were a Nazi hotbed for
funding French intellectuals."[10]

The fact that Colette wrote for a French paper financed by the
Nazis is shocking, but she was not the only one. However, we
continue to wonder about the collaboration of influential artists
and intellectuals in a country so proud of its enlightened culture and literature. In his masterful and authoritative book about
artistic life in Paris under Vichy, Alan Riding, the *New York Times*
Paris bureau chief,[11] tries to answer this question that remains an
especially thorny one for the French.

Alan Riding

Frenzied Parisian cultural life under Nazi occupation was a paradox: artists continued to paint and exhibit their works in galleries,
musicians gave concerts, writers wrote, publishers published, and

films were made and shown. Who were the creators and intellectuals that joined the Nazis in this dance of death? The author's detailed and informative quest for facts sheds a new light on this dark episode of French culture.

The imposing Alan Riding introduced his work *And the Show Went On: Cultural Life in Nazi-Occupied Paris*[12] at the Village Voice on February 3, 2011, opening his reading with a friend's quip: "Sorry, dear friend, too many names, too many names." So, Riding assured us, "I'll stick to writers, not only because we are in a bookshop, but because they best illustrate the premise of my book which is, in my belief and somewhat supported by experience, that artists and especially writers have a special obligation." He also reminded the audience that "traditionally, writers in France enjoyed great prestige among the population—they spoke out on political issues and were listened to. For this reason, I set out to investigate to what extent French writers lived up to their moral duty under the Occupation."

He first traced the volatile political background of the Vichy years in a France torn between two extremist political currents: "There was no other choice in the thirties than being a communist or a fascist. No one wanted to be a 'democrat,'" Riding learned from French historians who had been students during that decade. He likewise quoted Beauvoir, who lamented the failure of European democracies: "Was there no place on earth where we could cling to hope?" Beauvoir wondered.[13]

With the Fall of France in June 1940, other writers were at a loss as to where to turn: to Vichy? Even the aforementioned Gide initially nodded to Pétain as a savior. This feeling of relief did not last long as the German occupant immediately implemented rigid forms of censorship in France. The number of banned books was soon staggering and, according to the Otto list alone, 2,242 tons of books were eventually burned.[14] However, the Nazi authorities decided to compromise with French publishers. Some publishers accepted money to keep their business going, but the majority of them went along with the ambiguous ruling of self-imposed censorship.[15]

As an example of the Nazi stranglehold on the French editorial profession, Riding brought up the case of Gallimard, the most prominent of all French publishers at the time (probably still today). Under some pressure, this company fired two of its most distinguished editors: Jacques Schiffrin, the founder and director of La Pléiade, because of his Jewish origins, and Jean Paulhan, the anti-collaborationist founder of the prestigious NRF (*Nouvelle Revue Française*). The latter was immediately replaced by Pierre Drieu La Rochelle, a rightist author and friend of Otto Abetz, the instigator of the outrageous list of banned books.

Even more puzzling was the attitude of the Jewish American writer Gertrude Stein during the Occupation. She enjoyed the protection of her friend, Bernard Faÿ, the director of the Bibliothèque Nationale under the thumb of the Otto List. Perhaps for this reason, the Gestapo left her in peace, even allowing her to hold on to her impressive collection of modern art. At the same time, this guarantee of safety came at a price: Faÿ asked her to translate a number of Pétain's speeches into English, and she complied with the request.[16]

The situation of other writers was even more complex: they could continue to write and publish books "as long as they didn't write for the collaborationist press."[17] With this rule in mind, most French authors resumed their work with their usual publishers under the pretext that, by doing so, they continued to defend French culture.

This being said, a few writers and publishers known as the Grands Résistants wrote and printed their books in clandestine reviews and presses, such as Les Éditions de Minuit, which published Le silence de la mer (1942) under the pseudonym of Vercors, the name of one of the largest Resistance networks in the country.

Fairly early on that year, British planes parachuted copies of the novel, along with weapons, over France, and the book became a lasting symbol of resistance against the enemy.

During the Liberation, business as usual replaced "the ideological maelstrom generated by the 'Purge'."[18] Among the intellectuals who had collaborated with the Nazis, only Robert Brasillach, the editor-in-chief of the collaborationist and anti-Semitic weekly Je suis partout was tried and executed (in his case, by firing squad). In response to a petition from intellectuals to pardon Brasillach, President de Gaulle declared that "people with more talent have more responsibility."[19]

On the other hand, Brasillach's expedited trial and death sentence left a number of questions unanswered; they were to be taken up by the American scholar Alice Kaplan in her outstanding biography The Collaborator: The Trial and Execution of Robert Brasillach.[20]

However, the book Alice discussed at the Village Voice was her more recent title, The Interpreter (2005). It dealt with another sensitive issue: the abuses and highly questionable practices within the US Armed Forces stationed in France.

Alice Kaplan

> "My role as interpreter made me feel important.
> But equally embarrassed, worried and distressed."
> —LOUIS GUILLOUX, epigraph of The Interpreter

The interpreter in question was Louis Guilloux, a French author known for his social realist novels and close friendships with

André Gide* and Albert Camus. He served as an interpreter at an American court martial in Brittany during the ongoing battle to liberate the region in November 1944. As the author of the book OK, Joe,[21] he was brought to Kaplan's attention by Roger Grenier, an eminent French writer and Gallimard editor who had earlier published her biography of Brasillach. Upon reading Guilloux's text, she was stunned by its revelations that unequivocally pointed to the biased racial discrimination in the 1944 war trials of the US military in France.

Alice launched The Interpreter at the Village Voice on October 6, 2005, and was introduced by Grenier himself, a life-long friend of Guilloux's whom he described as "a little man with a typical Breton face, his left hand always cradling a pipe." He then lauded Alice Kaplan for having undertaken a "formidable investigative journey for the writing of The Interpreter, going from local archives in France to the American Army Archives at College Park in Maryland where, in an archive kept secret by the army, she found the evidence that a number of American soldiers had been sentenced to death, hanged, and buried in an unmarked plot.

Gaining access to such sensitive files, whether those of Brasillach or those of the American Army, was a real obstacle course, but, Grenier added with a touch of humor, "Alice's most difficult challenge of all was getting permission from the local municipal library of Saint-Brieuc to have a look at Guilloux's manuscript of OK, Joe. [laughter] Each word," he stressed, "each sentence in Alice's book is true, but her book is not standard history."[22]

A gracious and vivacious woman with an expressive smile, Kaplan opened her reading with the inscription on the book's jacket that read: "The American Army executed seventy of its own

---

Guilloux participated in Le Congrès des écrivains anti-fascistes in 1935 (Palais Mutualité, Paris). In 1936, he traveled to the Soviet Union with his friends expres. and Gide. That same year, Gide published Retour d'U.R.S.S in which he 's disillusionment with the Soviet Union.

soldiers in Europe between 1943 and 1946. Almost all of them were Black, in an army that was overwhelmingly white. One Frenchman witnessed the injustice and never forgot." She followed with the description of the preparations for the execution by hanging of James E. Hendricks, a Black GI sentenced to death for the murder of a peasant in a small Breton village, specifying that this chosen form of capital punishment always took place in the community where the crime had occurred.*

She admitted she was startled at first by the title of Guilloux's book, as "*OK, Joe* was not a title a French intellectual, peer, and friend of Gide, Camus, and Malraux would use." However, it was the author's view of this war that had completely thrown her off, so radically different from any she had grown up with. "Like most Americans," she told us, "I was raised to think of World War II as the war which made a clear distinction between what was truly good from what was evil, a war where you knew who the enemy was." Kaplan went on to explain that Guilloux "was trying to make sense of a great democracy with a segregated army. As a witness of these trials, he had an insight into what was going on and detected racial biases in the decisions made at the highest levels."

Q: "Guilloux could have been influenced or tainted by a personal, distorted understanding of the situation at hand."

Kaplan: "The ethical universe I'm exploring in *The Interpreter* is murky and complex. When I read Guilloux's book, I did not know what was true and what was of the author's own making. He must have made up the case of the white American officer who had killed a French Resistance fighter, but was acquitted. 'Too dramatic to be true,' I thought, 'and probably not even referred to in local documents.' I was determined to go

---

* The GIs sentenced to death for war crimes were buried in a separate plot in the Oise-Aisne American Cemetery Memorial.

and find the historical records of what had happened, which took me to the next phase of my investigation. In addition to archives, obscure reports, and other resources, I interviewed descendants of the victims of the GIs and French people who remembered the American liberators. Most people mentioned by Guilloux were either alive or connected with the accounts in his book. In my acknowledgments, I thanked one hundred and forty people."

Q: "What were the attitudes or reactions of the French people you interviewed?"

Kaplan: "Some of them had witnessed a hanging, and they never forgot it. Others admitted that the hanging was justified, but I never felt any bitterness toward Americans, even among the people who had a crime in their family. People are still taking care of the graves of the GI's, very touching. Graveyards, by the way, were invaluable sources of information. In the Oise-Aisne American Cemetery, in the section reserved for executed soldiers, there were ninety-six graves, and among them, I found the grave of Louis Till, the father of Emmett Till."

Q: "Guilloux waited almost thirty years to publish his observations. Was it from fear of indelicacy toward the liberators?"

Kaplan: "He felt distressed; he felt 'like a cat who didn't dare to take a leap through the window,' he said. Myself, I wonder if he was not thinking of Richard Wright's Bigger Thomas, the man who doesn't speak."*

---

* Bigger Thomas, the protagonist of Richard Wright's *Native Son* (1940), who has killed a white woman, refuses to speak and so faces his destiny alone.

One Decade Ends, A New One Begins

At the close of the decade, in October 1989, the fall of the Berlin Wall sounded the knell of the Cold War, bringing on the collapse of the Soviet Union and the breakup of its satellite states.

Kept invisible behind the Iron Curtain and forced into silence for well over fifty years, these Eastern countries started to open up: in no time, Prague, Budapest, and Berlin became the emerging "happening capitals."[1]

The American novelist Arthur Phillips recounts this startling awakening in his novel *Prague*,[2] a reference to the emblematic port of call for these adventurers. As always, economic factors played an essential role in the shift: Paris had become too expensive for "these young bohemians and wannabe novelists"[3] while they could live well and cheaply in these new destinations. Likewise, Edmund White, the leading figure of the Third Wave, anticipates this culmination of an era in his literary memoir: "Mine was probably the last generation that took France seriously. We knew that we were ending a long glorious tradition of Americans in France."[4]

The exodus of American expatriates to more distant European horizons could have meant the closing of our bookstore, but by an extraordinary stroke of fortune, the 1980s brought about a literary renewal in the US. "A gale is blowing," Raymond Carver told us at the Village Voice in 1987. "American literature is going through a very healthy and productive period."

Characterized by its vitality and diversity, this effusion of writing would likewise become immensely popular in France and create a new interest in postwar American literature. In the late 1980s, and especially the 1990s, the display tables in Paris bookstores teemed with fiction rendered into French by a new generation of talented translators and published by dynamic, young publishers. These are the voices from the US explored in the following pages.

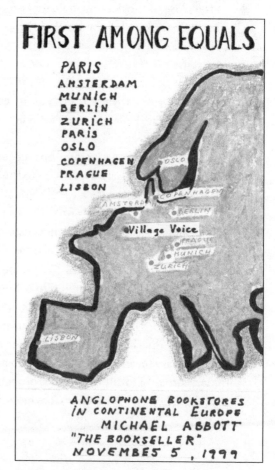

First Among Equals.
In the November
5, 1999, issue of the
British trade journal
The Bookseller.
Designed by
Katia Gerasimov.

PART TWO

A Literary Journey
across the United States

"The Village Voice Bookstore
is the scene of the city's love affair
with contemporary American fiction."
—EDMUND WHITE

"The listeners are upstairs, downstairs, in the stairs,
an inch away from the reader,
and, on the street outside the door;
it begins to feel like a crowded pigeon coop . . ."
—MICHAEL ONDAATJE

"And the writer,
for one brief evening,
feels like a star."
—HAZEL ROWLEY

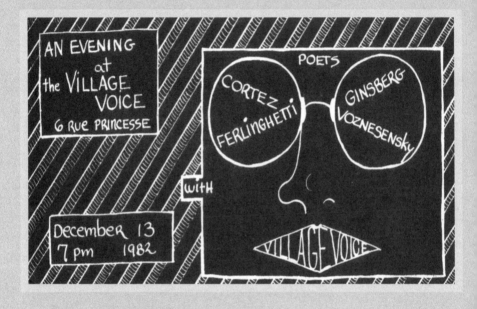

Invitation to a reading with Cortez, Ferlinghetti, Ginsberg, and Voznesensky
at the Village Voice Bookshop, December 13, 1982. © Rollin

An Era of Hope Leading to Disillusionment

Julian Beck, Judith Malina, Allen Ginsberg, Jayne Cortez, Andrei Voznesensky,
Lawrence Ferlinghetti, Kazuko Shiraishi, Hubert Selby Jr.,
William H. Gass, William Gaddis, Don DeLillo

"Literature has the function it always had:
it continues to reflect the realities of its time."
—ROBERT COOVER[1]

In spite of the lingering horrors of Hiroshima and the growing
threat of the nuclear race, the 1960s were a rich, innovative
time, when writers and other artists believed in "the regenerative power" of the ongoing protests and creative avant-gardes.
Yet, within the next few decades, the hope for freedom and justice
generated in their works did not last, giving way to a return to
ambivalence and searing doubt when it came to basic political and
societal promises taking root.

Starting in 1982, we had the opportunity to welcome a number
of pioneering authors from the US who experimented with the
complexities of language in drama, fiction, and poetry to render
the reality of these unsettling and changing times.

Julian Beck and Judith Malina

On October 2, 1982, three weeks after the official opening of our
bookshop, we were thrilled to host Julian Beck and Judith Malina,

two iconic personalities of the sixties. Jim Haynes,[2] their good friend from the days of his experimental Traverse Theatre in Edinburgh, had invited them to read with us. With some emotion, I remembered their staging of Sophocles's *Antigone* at the Festival of Avignon in the summer of 1968. It was a high-powered performance, an explosive happening of protest. In fact, the vision of Beck's sharp, eagle-like profile and Malina's eyes devouring the world had stayed with me.

However, as they appeared at the door, the two of them looked rather subdued, not at all like the actors who had once electrified crowds in Avignon. In a quiet voice, Beck started to read an excerpt from his memoir *The Life of the Theatre*,[3] a book that explored his dramatic techniques, principles, and politics. Then Malina chose to recite "Conversation with Julian" from a booklet of intimate poetry infused with melancholy: "You spoke in energetic time / I knew this was routed to despair / . . . If I could comprehend / the substance that is fire."[4]

Some acquaintances from their 1970s performance days travelling throughout France had come to hear them. Among those present were Henry Pillsbury, the director of the American Center in Paris, spearhead of American and French avant-garde creations,[5] as well as Robert Cordier, the director of the Paris drama school Acting International. Yet the joy of reuniting with friends did not dispel the palpable nostalgia for a spirited epoch seemingly long gone.

Allen Ginsberg

Several weeks later, on December 13, 1982, a crowd came to the Village Voice for a reading with Allen Ginsberg, organized by his French publisher, Christian Bourgois.[6] Ginsberg arrived accompanied by four of his friends: Lawrence Ferlinghetti, the San Francisco poet and founder of the City Lights bookstore; Jayne Cortez, the African American jazz poet; Andrei Voznesensky, one of the rare contemporary poets allowed by the Soviet authorities to travel abroad; and Kazuko Shiraishi, the Japanese Canadian Beat lyricist known as "the Ginsberg of Japan."[7] All five of them had been invited to participate in the International Poetry Festival War on War, organized in Paris under the aegis of UNESCO.

Sporting a bushy gray beard, Ginsberg stood on the stairs connecting the two-story, open-floor bookshop filled with people. Looking like a Celtic bard, he recited his internationally acclaimed *Howl*, his powerful voice filling up the whole space to the beat of a gong. His words exploded into visions of desolation, shadowy figures wandering through the ravaged world of drugs and despair in postwar America, the country he called "the Moloch."

Interpreted with passionate anger, *Howl* resonated with the audience, who hailed the end of his reading with thunderous applause. Off in his own corner, Ferlinghetti was lost in thought, perhaps reminiscing about Ginsberg's first public performance of this very poem in San Francisco in 1955. Thrilled, Ferlinghetti had immediately sent Ginsberg a telegram saying, "I was in the audience, when do we get the manuscript?" This moment marked the beginning of a long literary collaboration and friendship. And here they were, almost thirty years later—Ginsberg reading *Howl* and Ferlinghetti reliving the San Francisco scene, this time in Paris.

In sharp contrast to this flamboyant and rhythmic performance, **Ferlinghetti**'s own reading was flat, even somewhat dull. Attempting to sound ironic, he recited a few lines written in French, evocative of his youth in Paris. They started with "J'ai fait mon bac dans la rue du Bac," and then, suddenly, he blurted out "but I prefer train stations." It was a remark out of the blue, perhaps summoned up by the presence of his friend, Andrei, who may have reminded him of his eventful trans-Siberian journey in 1967.*

---

* Ferlinghetti had gotten "this romantic idea" of a trans-Siberian trip from the poet Blaise Cendrars. "Endless Siberia!" he wrote in his travel journal: "Lost land & Lost people . . . which bled & bled its white blood & its red blood . . ." of the millions of souls, including poets, who haunted those infinite "bare snowfields." Russian Winter Journal (February-March 1967) in *Writing Across the Landscape: Travel Journals 1960-2010* (New York: Liveright, 2019).

Born and brought up under Stalin's terror, **Andrei Voznesensky** was a young poet when he courageously defended Boris Pasternak, his mentor who was viciously attacked by the Kremlin and Soviet intelligentsia in the 1950s. With the advent of Khrushchev's Thaw, that brief period of cultural liberalization between 1954 and 1964, Voznesensky was one of the few writers authorized to travel abroad to give poetry recitals. This is how he, Ginsberg, and Ferlinghetti had become friends in San Francisco. Perhaps in deference to this Anglophone public at the Village Voice, the Russian poet read his poetry in English, sadly depriving the audience of his native musical language which, as I recall, used to transport his public at home and abroad in the mid-'60s.

Next, **Jayne Cortez** invigorated our spirits with her rich, low voice and powerful Beat rhythms as she recited her jazz poems with great heart, powerfully asserting her identity as a Black woman. She was followed by **Kazuko Shiraishi** who read "Odysseus,"[8] her poem about exile written in Japanese, which sounded like a meditative piece. When chanted by Ginsberg in his own English translation, it transformed into a Beat epic.

Ginsberg closed the event with a passage from "Kaddish for Naomi Ginsberg," a poem he had started in Paris in the fifties upon hearing of his mother's death. While *Howl* was a furious scream of anger at America, the embodiment of an evil society, these lines were a searing lament, the poet's cry of revolt and despair facing death and horror at his own physical dissolution to come. Standing once again on the staircase, a hieratic figure addressing the crowd upstairs and downstairs, he concluded his recital on a Buddhist note, chanting the mantra "OM . . . OM . . ."

In 2014, as I was browsing through William Gaddis's correspondence, I stumbled upon one of his letters to his daughter Sarah, describing a recent New York public performance of Ginsberg's as "avant-garde—which is suddenly old hat."* However, at that memorable reading at our bookshop, listening to Ginsberg and his friends, we were gladly carried back several years. Their stunning event had turned the spotlight on the Village Voice. We could not have imagined a better prelude to our soon-to-begin American Author Reading Series.

Hubert Selby Jr.

Another mythical figure of the sixties was Hubert Selby Jr., the author of *Last Exit to Brooklyn*,[9] a scandalous novel described by Ginsberg as "exploding like a rusty hellish bombshell over America, still to be eagerly read in a hundred years."[10] Written in 1957 and published in 1964 by Grove Press, it was banned for obscenity in Great Britain. After a trial made the work an instant underground success,[11] it was finally released in 1968. Two decades later, Selby's British publisher Marion Boyars arranged a reading of *Last Exit to Brooklyn* with the author at the Village Voice to mark the twentieth anniversary of its post-trial complete edition.

On October 25, 1988, the telephone rang all day with people wanting to make sure that they could be part of the evening. The crowd was overflowing into the street by the time Selby arrived, accompanied by Boyars and Philippe Manœuvre, a French jazz critic and editor of the magazine *Rock & Folk*, who was to introduce him. With some difficulty, the three of them managed to elbow their way through the excited throng at the door.

I had wrongly imagined Selby as a Bukowski type—a rough, macho guy from the fringes of L.A.—when, in fact, he was a small, thin, and frail-looking man who happened to write books about sex, drugs, and violence. How to explain such a large crowd? Some

---

* Gaddis refers to Ginsberg's reading and performance at "A Tribute to William Burroughs" at the Old Vic Theatre. Letter dated December 3, 1978, in *The Letters of William Gaddis* (Normal, IL: Dalkey Archive Press, 2013).

people in the audience may have expected a real low-lifer, but among them were also many fans of Manœuvre, a French TV celebrity.

The latter presented the author as a man following in "the great literary tradition of Melville, Poe, and Kerouac, all writers haunted by space. While Kerouac embarked on the road to discover the wide expanses of America," he continued, "Selby went deep into the netherworlds of misery, sex, and depravity and, even more forbiddingly, into his own tortured self."[12] Alluding to the author's epigraphs in his novel *The Demon*,[13] Manœuvre saw his protagonists "as men caught between two extremes—surrendering to evil and crying to God to be heard."

Selby then read the final pages of *Last Exit to Brooklyn*[14] with its violent domestic scene described as so crudely raw, and yet poignant. While the parents fought using foul language, the children withdrew into their own world of silence. Indeed, lack of family love and the loneliness of the child still haunted the author in the 1980s, as shown in the passage he delivered from his memoir in progress, *Seeds of Pain, Seeds of Love*.[15]

Here he recalled a boy torn between his longing for love and a seething desire for revenge to be acted out with the knife he had struggled to acquire. Selby cleared his throat and announced that "today . . . I am that boy I have chosen to remember, but that boy is not me, for that boy knows nothing of the person I have become and I am today." He read for a full hour at the request of his audience, clearly fascinated by the paradoxes of this humble man who could not conceal his inner torment. Later, sitting at the small table piled up with his books, he signed them with special attention to each one of his readers, appreciative of their warm welcome.

While these protest writers relied on expressive words and rhythms in order to be heard, the next three novelists—William H. Gass, William Gaddis, and Don DeLillo—were more concerned with inventing new forms of language that brought out the complexities and ambiguities of the disenchanted contemporary world.

William H. Gass

On February 6, 2007, William H. Gass was at the Village Voice to discuss *The Tunnel*,[16] a novel he had published in 1995, more than ten years prior. Claro, a French experimental novelist and outstanding translator, introduced him, admitting that it had taken him six years of hard work to translate this text, "though, much less than the twenty years it took the author to construe this six-hundred-fifty-page novel—a literary monster of scribbles, reflections, and meandering thoughts." He further stressed the point that "among his prolific production of fiction and nonfiction, *The Tunnel* stood out as Gass's most original and ambitious work, his literary testament, crowning a life of prize-winning fictions and essays."

Gass introduced the protagonist of his labyrinthine novel as a historian teaching in a small college. Having published a historical study called *Guilt and Innocence in Hitler's Germany*, the latter is now trying to write the introduction to his new book, "the best one," he thinks. However, overwhelmed by writer's block, he cannot continue. In a frenzy to move ahead, he starts covering his pages with "doodles and graffiti" which, Gass stressed, were "his own scribbles of a personal nature, and so personal that he wanted to hide them from his wife by sliding them inside the pages of his history book where, he knows, she will never look. In fact, he is mostly digging into his own past while digging a real tunnel of his own to hide his own dirt."[17]

Then, the author referred to his essays on language and writers in *The World Within the Word*[18] to show how he brought together the scattered pieces of his sprawling novel into a "musical structure, such as a fugue." To give us an idea of the range and diversity of styles in *The Tunnel*, Gass read three passages, each one stylistically different, each one an example of how "the sentence structure organizes the work." The first excerpt was an "effusive poem" he described as a "youth rhapsody," reminiscent of "Rilke's lyrical verses."[19] The next passage was a list of country wedding guests, mostly farmers and their families from the Dust Bowl at the time of the Great Depression.

Gass then switched to limericks, "those obscene and debasing short poems he himself enjoyed so much writing."[20] These three different pieces revealed not only the author's stylistic virtuosity, but also his remarkable taste for paradoxes.

Someone in the audience asked him: "Why such a split between ugly content and refined style?"

Gass: "This is the point: beauty is the aesthetic point from which to write about the disagreeable, whether hatred or criminal acts. World literature is all aesthetics of the form. At the beginning of the *Illiad*, there is nothing more powerful and beautiful or aesthetic than that massive massacre. There is a scene in one of the books of the novelist John Hawkes in which a man beats his wife to death with a wet newspaper. The reader is stunned: the beating is horrid, yet the scene is breathtakingly beautiful. This is what creates tension."

Q: "If we follow your reasoning, can there be aesthetics without some kind of vileness?"

Gass: "This is a question that is ever present: the discrepancy that exists in the human. The most erudite, sophisticated man will massacre thousands of people. These contradictions fascinate me: All Shakespeare is in this contradiction: 'smile and be a villain.' A view shared by Beckett: 'Tell me how horrific the world is, again and again.' And the way he told it makes me euphoric. I love it."

William Gaddis

On December 3, 1985, we welcomed William Gaddis to the Village Voice to talk about his new and third novel *Carpenter's Gothic*,[21] just out in the United States. He was on his way home from Moscow where he had been a member of a delegation of American writers that also included William H. Gass, Arthur Miller, and Allen Ginsberg, who had been invited to meet with Soviet writers and exchange ideas on their respective works. Now he was in the city for a brief visit with his daughter Sarah, an art student at the Parsons School of Design in Paris.

Gaddis was a name in America, but in the mid-eighties he was still little known to French readers. His first belatedly acclaimed novel *The Recognitions*, published in the US in 1955, had only come out in French translation in 1973, almost twenty years later.[22] However, he was studied in some French universities, and while our audience was mostly American, a number of local scholars attended the reading.

Gaddis was accompanied by his French publisher, Ivan Nabokov, his translator Marc Cholodenko, and Marc Chénetier,[23] the author of masterful papers on American postmodernism (including Gass and Gaddis) who was to introduce him. Compared to *The Recognitions* (almost a thousand pages) and *J R*[24] (seven hundred pages), the new novel was only two hundred fifty pages, but,

William Gaddis with French publisher Ivan Nabokov. September 2, 1988.
© Flavio Toma

as Chénetier pointed out, "like the earlier ones, *Carpenter's Gothic* is also a radioscopy of America at a given time."

In *The Recognitions*, a dense and sinuous novel, Gaddis first addressed the issue of authenticity among intellectuals and artists who, moved by greed, betray the very fundamentals of their calling. J R is the outlandish story of an eleven-year-old boy who builds his own financial empire—the ultimate American dream, reflecting its ruthless corporate world. *Carpenter's Gothic* portrayed the corrupting effects of the Vietnam War on nearly everyone—veterans, business-men, fundamentalists, and an heiress, all pushed into dodgy deals that work to their advantage. While poring over his epoch and his country with a magnifying glass, Gaddis proves to be a master of language that he considers to be the very substance of literature.

A discreet-looking man with a powerful, radiating presence, Gaddis opened his talk by referring to his brief stay in Moscow. It was 1985, a time when the collapse of the Soviet Union was still unimaginable, and our public was curious to hear the impressions of a writer reputed to be a keen observer of political and social realities.

"Back here in Paris, I'm in total disarray: in Moscow, we tried to explain our works, but realized that there was not much we could say, since the Soviet writers clung to their ideas of peace and happiness, but this is not what the plays of Arthur Miller or the writings of Gass are about, nor is my work. *The Recognitions*, published thirty years ago, is more about human shambles than happiness. Only Allen Ginsberg, playing the harmonica, tried to convey a kind of happiness that our works didn't."[25]

Gaddis went on to share an anecdote that pointed to the blind-ness or bad faith of the Soviet intelligentsia. At one of their meet-ings with the Union of Soviet Writers, Arthur Miller had asked about the authors who were in prisons or camps. One writer from the Union replied that "they were not writers, but ordinary para-sites who had broken the law." Miller insisted, handing them a list of writers he had compiled, which concerned some one hundred of them currently locked up. Gaddis acknowledged that in the end "Miller's persistence didn't get him anywhere."

Chénetier took over, asking Gaddis to read a short excerpt from his latest novel before going deeper into any discussion, but the author refused. He retorted that he didn't see any reason for doing so, explaining that "*Carpenter's Gothic* is not like a poem by Dylan Thomas that you can read in one breath. This novel is all dialogues and requires changing voices."

"To me," Gaddis went on, "the act of reading is a contract between the reader and what's written on the page, and it is up to the reader to make out of it whatever he can. The reader has to be left alone and do his part, that is, supplement the reading through his own experience. And this, I can say, often works to the disadvantage of the writer."

"What do you mean exactly by 'the disadvantage of the writer'?" someone in the audience asked.

Gaddis: "When J R was awarded the National Book Award, I was confident that it was going to stimulate sales. But the reality is there on paper: my latest royalty statement for J R, a book in print since its publication and which continues to be read, so I'm told, but when I see such a figure . . . I say . . . well, the millions of American readers must be passing around one single copy! [laughter] . . . and when I mentioned this to my publisher, he said: 'Oh, this is an elitist book, and the American Book Award is an elitist prize.' So, here we go: Danielle Steel has five million copies in print. All the boxes are ticked, nothing left up in the air, and no place is left either for the reader's imagination. In America, we definitely have two distinct things: books and literature . . . leading to my next point, why write?"

Q: "A crazy scenario like J R's story seems to contradict the 'facts,' an essential element in your own work. How do you reconcile the two?"

Gaddis: "In Gogol's *Dead Souls*, one of the greatest works of literature, here goes Chichikov buying the souls of the dead serfs not officially registered. This crazy, unimaginable scenario is also the most realistic panorama of Russian society at the time. In order to buy those souls, Chichikov has to penetrate every strata of the society, and, through the people he meets, he demonstrates the extraordinary foolishness of the human being. This is a con man of the first order, a hatter, and yet what can be more realistic than this novel? To me, the key phrase is 'the willing suspension of disbelief,'[26] when the reader suspends his judgment to accept the implausibility of the narrative, like in *Carpenter's Gothic*, when on the steps appears a stranger . . ."

Q: "Fundamentalism is central in your new novel. What is your relationship to religion?"

Gaddis: "My relationship to religion has become much colder than it was. In my youth I had a certain attraction to the Catholic religion. At the time, we didn't have anything like Buddhism. Today, religion is everywhere and is yielding to fundamentalism. . . . What about real religion? I do not see where it is. Anyhow, the number of priests is diminishing drastically, but religious cults are on the rise, and it would seem that the more outlandish, the better for business. To me, religion is the last refuge ignorance has from intelligence. You can't even argue with fundamentalists, and this is truly frightening. Reagan, for one, is convinced that America has been chosen by God . . . but it's not the only thing he is convinced of."

Three years later, on September 2, 1988, the French translation of *Carpenter's Gothic*, *Gothique charpentier*,[27] was launched at the Village Voice. At his previous talk, Gaddis had insisted that his novel, if read aloud, had to be done with "changing voices." His remark did not fall on deaf ears this time. His editor Ivan Nabokov invited two prominent French actors, Dominique Sanda, the mythic actress in Bertolucci's *The Conformist*, and Philippe Laudenbach, to be the distinct voices of the wife and her husband, the two main characters of the novel. The photos taken that evening convey the festive mood of this literary social gathering, with Sarah, the author's daughter, radiant with joy as she went around chatting with guests and friends.

During her own Parisian years, **Sarah Gaddis** was very much a part of the American community evolving around the Village Voice, and while pursuing her art studies, she also wrote her first book, *Swallow Hard*, a fictionalized memoir of her childhood. In it, Rollin, the protagonist, is born "a perfect combination of Southern mentality and Yankee cynicism."[28] In time, this obvious incompatibility leads her parents to go their separate ways.

Written with great sensitivity and an artist's eye for detail, the novel follows the divided life of Rollin growing up in two different worlds, torn between the American South of her mother and her father's exciting New York circle of writers and artists. The young painter also conjures up the magical summers she spent on Fire Island with her father's bohemian set of friends. She imbues this memory with much beauty, but just as disturbingly, draws a stark portrait of her father as inaccessible to her, absorbed as he is in his writing.

The sorrow she feels as a young girl desperately vying for his attention is captured in the illustration on the book cover: father and daughter sit apart on the steps of their summer house, the former deep in thought, probably mulling over the next sentence of his work in progress, while Rollin anxiously "watched him, waiting for some signal, some glance, but he didn't see her and turned back towards his work without a word."[29]

Sarah celebrated the publication of *Swallow Hard* at the Village Voice on April 23, 1991. That morning, most unexpectedly, her father appeared at the door of our bookstore with an armful of magnificent lilac blossoms to honor her reading some hours later.

William Gaddis had just landed in Paris to be by the side of his daughter on that special day.

Don DeLillo

At his reading, Gaddis had remarked that "religious cults are on the rise and the more outlandish, the better for business." This could be the epigraph of Don DeLillo's tenth novel, *Mao II*,[30] presented at the Village Voice on April 2, 1992.

DeLillo was the youngest of this group of American authors who tirelessly investigated the political, societal, and cultural issues of their time and country. In a congratulatory letter to DeLillo, Gaddis praised the way he married "style & content . . . embracing the American writer's historic obsession with getting the facts down clear," as earlier specified by Jack London: "Give me the fact, man, the irrefragable fact!"[31]

The two writers give detailed evidence that a fact is not just inscribed in the present, but acts as a codified warning sign of the future. To the twenty-first-century reader, these two writers appear as visionaries of a changing world, challenging our imagination and calling for reflection and concern.

DeLillo was introduced by his French publisher Hubert Nyssen, the founder and director of Actes Sud, then a young but fast-growing publishing house with, at the time, two prominent contemporary American novelists in its catalog: Russell Banks and Paul Auster, both of whom had recommended DeLillo. "This is how DeLillo became our third 'musketeer,'" Nyssen quipped, glancing over at the author.

He went on, observing that "while subjects in contemporary French novels are often ludicrous, American fiction shows us true heroes, deeply rooted in the territory where they evolve, thereby bringing out the realities specific to their own milieu. DeLillo has no fear of the issues he explores in his novels, speaking of obsessions, catastrophes, and fears haunting us, whether personally or collectively. Yet his stories have a highly symbolic significance that connects them to the great myths."[32]

Modest and/or seemingly impassive, DeLillo stood up and started to read the opening chapter of *Mao II*, called "At Yankee Stadium." In a low, matter-of-fact voice, he carefully detailed an actual and terrifying scene of a compact crowd of 6,500 couples, all followers of the Moon sect, standing in line and waiting their turn to be married by its Guru leader.

This depiction introduces the core issue of the novel—the disappearance of the individual into faceless and brainwashed crowds and, along with this phenomenon, the disappearance of literature. Its central protagonist, Bill Gray, a journalist and secluded writer, refuses to publish at a time when it is no longer possible "for a novelist to alter the inner life of the culture," and when "news of disaster is the only narrative people need."[33] An author condemned to silence, Gray reminded us of Salman Rushdie, publicly sentenced to death two years earlier for his own banned book *The Satanic Verses*, with copies of it being burned around the world.[34]

During the discussion that followed, Nyssen stressed that literature is not solely about facts: literature is also about language, and in DeLillo's narrative, "the wide gap that exists between the character's interior language and what he actually says is what creates the dramaturgy of the novel."

At the close of the evening, a young man in the audience thanked the author for writing novels that were not the soundbites of so many contemporary books, comparing him to "the Kabbalist who shows the way to the inner sanctum of language that bears a redemptive and humanizing meaning."

(above) Odile and Don DeLillo, Village Voice Bookshop, April 2, 1992.
© C. Deudon

(below) Jay McInerney, November 3, 1993. © C. Deudon

Bright Lights and Twilights[1]
Jay McInerney, Jerome Charyn, Richard Price, James Ellroy

I n 1984, reelected president Ronald Reagan continued his
supply-side economic policies, helping to propel Wall Street
to new heights, and thus making New York City the ideal
playground for quick money-making, ruthless ambition, and
undisguised cupidity. Disheartened and looking for more pro-
pitious cultural horizons, some young people went abroad, as
we have seen, while others, dazzled by the "Bright Lights" of
the "Big City," embraced its fast pace and frenzied rhythms. This
wondrous experience of the city as a dizzying whirlwind of late-
night bars, drug paradises, and outlandish fashion trends was the
subject of several novels of the 1980s.

The young writer Jay McInerney led the dance with his bestseller *Bright Lights, Big City* (1984), followed by Bret Easton Ellis's
Less Than Zero (1985) and Tama Janowitz's *Slaves of New York* (1986).
However, the celebrated city of this "Brat Pack" generation slowly
began to fade like an elusive dream. McInerney chronicled its
dramatic demise in *Brightness Falls*,[2] the third volume of his New
York trilogy,[3] presented at the Village Voice on November 9, 1993.

Jay McInerney

"The eighties were bad for Americans, but certainly
good for me."[4]

—MCINERNEY, Village Voice reading, November 3, 1993

A dashing Jay McInerney in a dark suit and pale blue turtleneck came into our bookshop, accompanied by his French publisher, Olivier Cohen, to discuss his novel *Brightness Falls*, just out under the French title *Trente ans et des poussières*.[5]

His translator Jean-Pierre Carasso introduced him, pointing out the radical departure of the author's most recent fiction from his previous novels: "McInerney has outgrown the 'slick and hip' label attached to the young writer of contemporary New York. The horrific eighties were behind, and the nineties were going through a time of increased consciousness and commitment to social justice."

The author opened his reading with an excerpt from the second volume of his trilogy, *Story of My Life* (1988), in which Alison, the twenty-year-old protagonist, a model and aspiring starlet, is caught up in "a coterie of club-hopping and coke-addicted friends," and racing toward a nervous breakdown.

This work is a prelude to *Brightness Falls* that depicts the stark reality of a new decade that awaited this generation whose "youth was gone, and fun and games were over."[6] Corinne Calloway[7] and her husband Russell are the dream New York couple, she a financial trader and he a publishing editor, doing two quintessential jobs of their time and class. However, "their bliss is also their curse," McInerney reminded us: "They are middle-aged, their marriage is going downhill, and they have become conscious of the fragility of life, afraid of losing jobs, spouse, or lover, making them more attentive and sensitive to the social realties around them."

"As I was walking down Fifth Avenue," the author went on, "my eye caught a typical New York scene: a celebrity, a billionaire, the known owner of multiple industries was standing on the pavement with his two bodyguards next to a man lying there at their feet, a pathetic-looking homeless guy. This is the kind of novel I would love to write, I thought, with those people in it."

And he did, with Corinne, a high-powered business woman who volunteers in a soup kitchen for the homeless, embodying the awakening spirit of her epoch with the emerging social consciousness Carasso referred to in his introduction. McInerney acknowledged that the voice of this complex female protagonist was "the one I enjoyed writing." As a broad social panorama of the New York of the early 1990s, this story of a contemporary New York couple spurred the audience to ask questions about the city's present and pressing societal issues.

Q: "Have you counted up the amount of cocaine consumed in your novel and the cost of it?" [giggles]

McInerney: "For me, the 'marching powder' (cocaine) defines this period of addiction and consumerism. Despite what you read in *Time* or other magazines, there is still lots of cocaine around, but on the decline, while heroin is on the rise. In the novel, one of the characters switches from cocaine to heroin to take the edge off his cocaine addiction." [more giggles]

Q: "Are you aware that your books may encourage the use of drugs?"

McInerney: "Drugs have been part of my social landscape since I was a teenager. How could I not write about this when they are part of the world I speak about? Not that I promote drugs, but they exist, and they are also a kind of metaphor for the treadmill consumption we have in the novel for consumerism. But it seems to me that's less fashionable than in the '80s."

Q: "What is the fashionable addiction in the '90s?"

McInerney: "Spirituality." [bursts of laughter]

Another woman asked what he thought about the politically correct movement that was raging in academic circles, on campuses and in all walks of life.

McInerney: "There is a frightening wind blowing in the US and Canada, which is this notion of political correctness: Blacks should talk about Blacks, whites about whites, men about men and women about women. There is a Black character in my novel, someone I like very much, and I was questioned by a critic about my right to write about a Black man. As a writer, you project yourself into all kinds of persons and experiences and, as a reader, you put yourself in someone else's shoes . . ."To me, political correctness is a creation of the left; it's a lack of humor or the sign of a defective humor gland. [laughter] In my opinion, artists and writers would do best to ignore it. It's a big debate on campuses: what authorizes the deconstruction of the old academic canon? Huge subject, big debate, vital issues are at stake. Sometimes, we trip over ridiculous things. In France you've had that debate over Céline for a long time. This debate is not over."

His answer sparked much dissent throughout the audience, with heated exchanges of pros and the cons. The sound of chairs scraping the floor signaled that a number of people were walking out.

"A book is not just a personal relation between the reader and the page. Texts have to be analyzed, and how could we remain silent about, say, Shakespeare's anti-Semitic prejudices?" a woman asked in an angry voice.

McInerney: "I was rather glib in my characterization of this. This is a quagmire, and it's chilling when authors start censoring themselves. On the other hand, it's constructive when they examine their own prejudices and if they have stereotypes and racial, sexual, or ethnic biases. I'd love to split here in the middle of the issue." [laughter]

A man stood up. He did not want to ask a question but rather share with the public something he had read not long ago: "In a publication on the recent Los Angeles riots (1992), the looters were described as 'alternative shoppers.'" [more laughter]

Jay McInerney concluded the evening by recalling the way critics punished him for the success of his first novel, the bestseller that brought him fame: "They did not like it. My fame, though, was limited to bookstores and bars where I was recognized." He was alluding to his renown as a connoisseur of fine wines who enjoyed tasting as much as writing books about their vintage years.

Jerome Charyn

The wild city nightlife of the eighties coexisted with another fast and furious New York: Manhattan's Lower East Side, the battlefield of gang violence, as seen in *War Cries over Avenue C*, the title of a novel by the prolific author Jerome Charyn. A native of the Bronx, familiar with the local mafias ready to defend their turf, he was at the Village Voice on May 7, 1997, to launch his latest novel, *El Bronx*.[8]

A tall, lanky man, somewhat aloof, with an ironic smile, Charyn divided his time between New York City and Paris where he taught film studies at the American University. At an earlier reading, he admitted to us that he didn't feel much like an American: "I don't go for America's set of values, materialism and all that, but I don't want either to be only an alien."[9]

Indeed, he had kept a certain distance from the American literary community in Paris, and remained firmly attached to his Big Apple city, New York, the preferred setting of many of his books. Yet he acknowledged that his novels were better understood in

France and Europe than in America, stressing that his artistic sensitivity was closer to that of Russian writers such as Dostoevsky or
Isaac Babel, the latter the subject of one of his literary biographies.

The author of an enormous output of fiction, short stories,
and nonfiction, Charyn was best known for his novels in which
"mafias—Cuban, Jewish, Latinos—fight against one another, their
only code of conduct being that 'murder is business and business
is murder.'"[10] There are lots of cops and robbers in his books, but
he disagreed that they were crime novels: "For one thing," he
stressed, "there is no plot; they are novels in which chaos and
energy are crossing."[11]

At his presentation of El Bronx, he was introduced by Daniel
Gunn, a Beckett scholar who pinpointed the tension in Charyn's
style: "It's the music of your language, its energy that carries the
novel," he noted, addressing the author. "Yours is not a literary
language; there is so much slang in it, but language exists by itself."

To illustrate this remark, the author read an excerpt from this
work, giving us a taste of his style that captures the swift movement of a confrontation between two gangs: "[They] are ready
to fight. The fight happens; they look like marionettes from the
distance, and then an extraordinary ballet of fists and legs; gone in
thirty seconds. But the police are arriving: a hundred guys with riot
control robots which, of course, precipitate another war. But now
there are guns on the roofs of the cars, fights and guys arrested."
It's a visual dance performance with the high energy of a *West Side
Story* ballet.

The Bronx, this place where he grew up, was a Russian town in the
1940s with its "Jewish gangster culture . . . people coming and going, a
population on the road. It was a place of poverty and poor education,"
he explained, "but there was something interesting here: being poor
was an education—you had to return to where you came from and
give back what you had received. This is how many Russian Jews
became teachers, doctors, lawyers serving the community."

Richard Price

While Jerome Charyn enjoys describing the aesthetics of a gang in movement, in his bestseller *Clockers*,[12] presented at the Village Voice on October 22, 1993, Richard Price takes his reader to the very heart of a city evocative of "the Bronx,"[13] and even into the thick of the harsh and violent realities of a population adrift. Price told us that he had just spent three years living in a particularly tough neighborhood in Jersey City, New Jersey (called "Dempsey" in his novel), getting to know young men who used to hang out day and night selling drugs on the sly (mostly cocaine) and, thus, getting connected with their families and local police officers.

He read an excerpt detailing the arrest of one such young man suspected of trafficking drugs and, possibly, committing a murder. We can visualize the thorough body search, the invectives of the police, and the crowd around encouraging the would-be offender: "'Fight the power, fight the power.' The mother of the kid arrives, all tears, screaming, defending her boy. The kid is embarked to the precinct to be placed under lock. The cops write their stuff."[14] In this dramatic scene, everyone takes part in what the author describes as "disrespect": "the cop disrespects the kid, the kid disrespects the cop, the family and friends disrespect the police, the police disrespect them, everything is 'dis' and you've got to play your part. And the cop concludes, 'We all did what we had to do'... and life goes on."

Price's decision to live three years in a rough and dangerous part of New Jersey intrigued the audience. The first few questions innocently, but perhaps justifiably, focused on him, his own fears, and even threats to his life.

Q: "Did you feel that you were taking risks?"
Price: "I'm too cowardly for that, but sometimes ambition is greater than cowardice. In going out with drug dealers and with cops, I had a good strategy: whether I was walking in the

Valley of Death, I was doing it with the guy who was the scariest of them all and, by the way, I was introduced to him by the cop himself. He was out of jail after he bought his release by giving out the name of the person he was getting the drugs from."

Q: "Nobody feared that you might be spying on them?"

Price: "I didn't want anybody to be paranoid or to hustle. From the start, people knew what I was doing. I told everybody—drug dealers, police, whomever—that I was writing a book. I was not a journalist and didn't look for information. I simply wanted to know how they lived day by day, made it through the day and how they survived. I just wanted to hang out."

Q: "How come this explosive mix of population agreed to be so closely observed and followed?"

Price: "'I'll pay you,' I said. 'I'm a writer. I'll make money from this book. To the kids, I would add, 'You're my research assistant' and to the cops, "You're my research associate.' Some people wouldn't take the money. They mainly wanted to talk, to blow their whistle, wanted some credit for participating in my project. For each favor, I tried to return it: I got a job for a kid; two other kids spent a summer with my family."

Q: "You never got caught in the crossfire between opposite camps or in a brush with death?"

Price: "Everyone is in it, and everyone needs each other. It's not when the guy is in jail that he'll give information. It's not a black and white picture, but more like in-between gray."

James Ellroy

The East Coast's New York City has its metropolis twin on the West Coast: Los Angeles, the "Movie Land, Hollywood and the Great American Dream Culture"[15] that has inspired many a writer.

Yet for James Ellroy, the celebrated author of political thrillers and suspense novels, this city of angels is not a dream, but rather a nightmare, and not just a setting, but a character—the ghost of his mother who had been raped and savagely murdered when he was a ten-year-old boy. He was to remain haunted by her story for the rest of his life.

On the chilly afternoon of April 19, 1995, Ellroy entered the Village Voice in a flowery Hawaiian shirt to talk about *American Tabloid*,[16] his eleventh novel and first volume of his *Underworld USA* trilogy, set in the arcane world of politics and crime during the Kennedy years. Tall, slender, and slightly stooped, sitting on the corner of a small table covered with piles of his books, he stared at his audience with piercing eyes behind thick glasses, and with a half-amused, half-cynical grin, called us: "the best-looking room . . . of degenerates,"—pause—"the last Clinton cabinet meeting."—giggling. How many of you here speak English?" he asked. Everyone raised a hand. Then he quipped, "You're fucked. I speak only my own LA patois and beatnik."

The tone was set for the reading, yet he kept his public in good spirits. Ellroy seemed to be raving. However, it was still a lot of fun listening to this elusive star talk nonsense. He started with "*American Tabloid* is my new masterpiece structure between my previous masterpieces and my masterpieces to come . . . a fucking novel: the truth of history is in fiction . . . I don't read, I think, I browse, I spin all this stuff, shift it in my head." "It's Barko," he went on, pointing to his bull terrier sitting at his feet (conspicuously absent), "who has written every one of my novels, channeled them in me. Barko, the heterosexual, the lover of most auspicious women," he added, providing a list of celebrity names. We soon realized that the author was not going to change his tune and, offended by his foul language, a few women started to walk out. Listening to the recording later on, I realized there was little I could salvage and nothing about the novel itself. There was only his absurdist sketch rendered as a live tabloid, a burlesque comedy of the political crimes and intrigues at the highest levels of state power, as portrayed in his novel.

In the end, enthralled by the author's disruptive yet highly entertaining talk, customers pressed around him to have their copies signed. Later on, expressing the ambivalent mood that prevailed throughout this odd reading, a friend confided to me: "I remember seeing my smiling face on a photo taken when he was signing my copy of his book, but I was devastated inside."

James Ellroy, Village Voice Bookshop reading, April 19, 1995. © C. Deudon

II

Highways and Byways

Barry Gifford, David Payne, John Biguenet, Terry Tempest Williams

We dreamed of Kerouac's journeys.
For us Americans, the idea that true life is
in the heart of the wild lands and not in the cities
goes back so much further in time, to Whitman."
—RUSSELL BANKS[1]

The increasing degradation of the large American metropolises in the 1980s and 1990s prompted some of their dwellers to escape to the countryside in an effort to get closer to nature. In *The Solace of Open Spaces* (1985), the Californian Gretel Ehrlich describes her harsh life on a ranch in the hostile but breathtakingly regenerative beauty of the wild landscapes of Wyoming. Her book was an immediate success. Renewing the tradition of Whitman, Emerson, and Thoreau, it inspired a new generation of writers to reconnect with nature in order to live a more authentic life and gain a modicum of self-knowledge.

With the development of highways, riding across the vast spaces of America generated feelings of infinite freedom, first extolled by Jack Kerouac's much earlier novel *On the Road*.[2] Embarking on such a journey across grandiose scenery, more writers awakened a new consciousness of the natural world. At the turn of the twenty-first century they continued to view the open road as a metaphor for freedom, "showing us a new destination . . . and a way of self-discovery."[3] But as we will see in this chapter, they also ventured onto byways to get a closer look at the mostly ignored or forgotten inner country and thus observe this invisible and mysterious natural world in its secret, ebullient, but fragile existence.

Speaking of "fragile existence," starting from Day One and throughout the next decade, the 9/11 attacks on the World Trade Center would regularly come up at our readings. In this section, two out of four authors address this pivotal moment which has now become an irreversible part of the country's history.

Barry Gifford

In his 1978 Jack's Book: An Oral Biography of Jack Kerouac,[4] Barry Gifford reinvents Kerouac's inspirational On the Road, weaving together interviews of the latter's friends, acquaintances, and the many people he and his companion, poet Neal Cassady, met during their cross-country ride. Gifford is able to portray in some detail this countercultural generation in their pursuit of wider horizons and a more intense spiritual life.

In 1990, in Wild at Heart,[5] Gifford updates the theme of the American highway in his neo-noir novel of two teenagers, Sailor and Lula, who, embarking on a ride across the South, leave behind families and any and all societal rules. Soon they get into trouble and are on the run. Their adventure becomes a nightmare of chases and escapes, reminiscent of both Kerouac's cross-country odyssey and Bonnie and Clyde, the popular gangster couple of the 1930s, also hot-footing it from the police.

Adapted to the screen by David Lynch (and awarded the Palme d'Or of the 1990 Cannes Festival), Wild at Heart became an instant bestseller with Sailor and Lula, the popular antiheroes of their time, bringing the author to write no fewer than seven sequels that follow his over-the-top characters between 1990 and 2015.

Easygoing and friendly, with a good sense of humor and a fecund imagination that produced enormous quantities of fiction, poetry, nonfiction, and screenplays, Gifford was a great supporter of our bookstore, writing pieces about it and giving several readings that revealed the wide range of his interests and themes, all the while showing his particular empathy for fictional characters on the fringes of society. He was also a sensitive poet in the Beat style, offering meditations on life in *Landscape with Traveler: The Pillow Book of Francis Reeves*[6] (1980). And there is his vivid depiction of a stifling, ominous atmosphere in the novel *Port Tropique*,[7] bearing a Conradian imprint and published by Black Lizard Press, a press he started himself to reprint the great, forgotten neo-noir classics of the 1930s and '40s.

His last reading at our bookstore took place on April 15, 2009, with the launching of *The Imagination of the Heart*[8] closing the lifelong saga of *Sailor and Lula*. It is a short, poetic, diary-form memoir of Lula's reminiscences of her life with the now-dead Sailor, her restrained emotions as she senses her own end coming, and her syncopated and visually expressive sentences tinged with Southern softness.

"About two years ago," Gifford said, introducing his novel, "I was between projects and getting older, like the rest of you."—[laughter]—"I started to think about Lula, my favorite among all my characters and who was now eighty years old. What was she doing and thinking now? I wondered. I started to imagine a new life for her, now alone, by giving her a new adventure, her final one as it were."

The epigraph of the book, "At the end of what is necessary, I have come to a place where there is no road" (Iris Murdoch), gives Lula's journey a special depth and poignancy. "I love my characters so much that I always have a hard time getting out of that sort of emotional state," Gifford confessed. "Now I think of Lula and she's gone, and I feel a kind of sadness."

Q: "Does this mean that fiction characters are real to you? If so, what makes them real?"

Gifford: "You indulge in your characters; you embark with them on their adventures. You play with them. You have to be them. I don't do research. It's all around, all the time. I just write how the people talk, and one of my intents in my books is to preserve that language. Even the language of Sailor and Lula is going away these days."

Barry Gifford, Village Voice Bookshop reading of *The Sinaloa Story*, June 11, 1998.
© C. Deudon

Q: "Your language is very colloquial. Your books have been translated into some thirty languages. How do you know that they are true to your writer's voice or voices?"

Gifford: "To tell the truth, there are some passages I don't know how translators can reproduce, especially some of my dialogues. My French translator, Jean-Paul Gratias, who's here tonight, has translated a dozen books of mine. It's astounding the way he renders them, and I still don't understand how he does it, all the more since he's never been to the South nor to Chicago where the voices are so different. I've nothing but praise for such translators. You're only as good as your translator, whatever country you're in. You don't have control over them."[9]

Q: "There's a lot of violence in your novels: corpses cut into pieces, cannibalism, kidnapping."

Gifford: "Violence? There's a lot of tragedy and death around. If things get a little bit overboard, it's to make a point, and if you don't have a sense of humor, it's not worth living. These people in my novels—I did not invent them. They do exist, but they have no protection and no voice. This is probably why I write about them."

Q: "What was your reaction to Lynch's adaptation of *Wild at Heart* for the screen?"

Gifford: "Lynch showed in the film things that were hardly mentioned in the text. He made certain decisions to make the story more visual, more graphic. I had no control. I always prefer now to be involved in the composition of the screenplay. It's a language that's very different from writing novels. The only thing I'd say: novels or screenplays, both necessitate the use of words."

David Payne

The author of the much-praised novel *Confessions of a Taoist on Wall Street* was in Paris to launch the French translation of his new novel, *Gravesend Light*.[10] We scheduled his reading at the Village

Voice for September 13, 2001, which, unfortunately, turned out
to be two days after the attack on the World Trade Center in New
York. The American community in Paris was in shock and fear
was in the air, but neither the author nor his publisher cancelled
his evening and we kept the date. As I had done on a number of
previous occasions, whenever there was tension in the city caused
by fears of terrorism, I asked our neighborhood police to keep a
discreet watch over the bookshop during our public event.

Payne opened his presentation by admitting that he was at a
loss for words: "I wish I had something profound to offer, but,
despite the horror and the sadness of the occasion, the only
response to such shock is continuity, going forward."

Gravesend Light is set in North Carolina, the native state of the
author and of his protagonist, Joey Madden, an anthropologist
who wants to study an isolated fishing community and observe
its traditions going back to Elizabethan times, that is, Sir Walter
Raleigh's first colony of settlers on Roanoke Island. Madden's
growing admiration for the island's fishermen, for their simple ways of life and their deep-rooted family and moral values,
instilled by the local Pentecostal Christian Church, increasingly
clashes with the critical attitude of his partner, a female obstetri-
cian who has opened a small medical office to provide birth and
abortion services to the neighboring population.

Payne read the passage about a terrifying storm at sea that calls
for exceptional skills on behalf of the fishermen to keep their
boat afloat. Answering a question from the audience about his
surprising technical knowledge in his description of the on-board
operations, he explained that he had worked as a fisherman for a
year after leaving college.

Payne: "I was in storms, but never like this one in my book, truly
frightening. This narrow passage that the fishermen have to
get through to go to sea is probably the most dangerous one in
the whole country. Many people die, and about fifty boats run

aground every year. These fishermen have lived a long time in the hope that the government would build jetties to stabilize the gully, but they have waited for twenty, thirty years, and it will probably never happen."

Q: "You seem to have a strong interest in this community. Why?"

Payne: "I grew up in North Carolina, and the fishermen's plight is somewhat alike to the tobacco farmers'. Even though tobacco is quite unpopular in the US these days, the tobacco farmers practice an old, honorable trade going back twelve generations. It's a highly skilled profession, now threatened like that of the fishermen facing the disappearance of fish species. Oceans are being depleted while the idea of jetties to stop the course of nature is probably futile. Nevertheless, these fishermen have to go out day after day and face death. In an increasingly globalized world, these professions become more and more marginalized. I got interested in those two because they are vanishing and they won't be around fifteen, twenty years from now."

Q: "Did you get along with those fishermen when you were working with them?"

Payne: "Those fishermen are tough. They have been there on that island on the Outer Banks—that line of islands, thirty miles of open sea between them and the mainland, for a very long time, and it won't be easy to cast them aside. They have been broken by life, but they're so tough that when they enter a bar, people discreetly leave. Yet, that hard life has also given them a breadth of perspective and a level of self-awareness that no one else in the novel has."

Q: "The second excerpt you read is the virulent ranting of a fundamentalist pastor against the new mores appearing in his community. Can this kind of sermon disappear with the older generation?"

Payne: "The public dialogue has been broken down in a shouting match between contradictory systems of beliefs. This Christian fundamentalism I describe is not so far from Islamic fundamentalism. Each one turns back to a time when the world was simpler and things were more identifiable. That's why doctors who per-form abortions are getting shot and clinics close down."

John Biguenet

The New Orleans playwright and author of the celebrated *Rising Water* trilogy plays set in the city after the passage of Hurricane Katrina, John Biguenet was teaching at the Paris American Academy in the summer of 2008. We took advantage of his presence to invite him to talk about his novel *Oyster*, just out in French translation.[11] Similar to David Payne's North Carolina fishermen, Biguenet explores the lives and hardships of Louisiana's traditional oyster farmers, desperately struggling with the daily realities of their dying trade.

The novel takes place in 1957. "I chose this date," Biguenet stressed, "for it was a time of transition in the Deep South. That year, Eisenhower sent his troops to the South to enforce inte-gration. . . . The small communities lost their power to federal power,* and, with the oil contamination of the brackish waters, oysters were becoming increasingly scarce, giving rise to rivalries, often between blood-related families vying for survival. These two elements put together—pollution and increasing loss of power—created a feeling of uneasiness pervading this community at the edge of omnipresent water and on the eve of a transition from their known world to one unknown."

Q: "What incited you to write on such an unusual topic?"
Biguenet: "The drama of this novel revolves around Therese, a
    young woman with a strong character who refuses to marry a
    man to cancel a debt. 'I don't get bought by no damn boat,' she
    declares. I was inspired by Zola's novel *Thérèse Raquin* and was

---

* Reference to *Brown vs. Board of Education*, the 1954 Supreme Court decision that established racial segregation in public schools as unconstitutional in all states; a seminal victory for the civil rights movement.

drawn to his observations of manual labor, and particularly his attention to the work of human beings, especially of women. I tried to be very careful about depicting exactly how the job of raising oysters was being done by men and also by women, as such labor involved the entire family."

A woman from New Orleans wondered about the future of the place with the increasing oil drilling. "We live in an area far removed from the oil spills," she told us, "yet the oil is there now, and the whole ecosystem is gone."

Biguenet: "An oyster takes seven years to mature. The last secured investment has been lost, so the next one will take another seven years for the oyster beds to produce, and the families will have long left to live somewhere else. Now it is family against family, and that culture is dead. I doubt that my wife and I will ever again eat oysters from the South."[12]

Terry Tempest Williams

"My medium has been earth" was Terry's opening remark at her Village Voice reading of March 17, 2009—a thread that runs throughout her writings.

A conservationist and "citizen writer," she gave four readings in our bookshop, including her landmark narrative *Refuge: An Unnatural History of Family and Place*,[13] the story of tragic events brought on by human violations against nature. Every single one of her books, whether a memoir, personal narrative, or essay is concerned with nature and the author's struggle to protect it from the pillaging of its resources.

We will focus on her talk on *Finding Beauty in a Broken World*,[14] her last reading at the Village Voice, when she shared at length her reflections on the necessity of recovering and creating beauty in a world torn apart by wars and the destruction of nature. "I'm desperate to find beauty," she declared. "When this book began some eight years ago, I was in a state of brokenness, distressed over the political condition in the US."

Indeed, when the 2001 attack on New York City occurred, she was in the Corcoran Gallery of Art, next to the White House, for a press conference on a photography exhibit of the natural world. "We had just begun when a guard stormed into the room announcing, 'the Twin Towers have just been hit, the Pentagon struck and there is no reason not to believe that the White House is next.' There was nothing that could have prepared us for what we had just been told, and we continued our conversation. A few minutes later, the guard came back with 'You did not understand. Run.' I remember grabbing a bunch of photographs and rushing into the street. Fumes were rising above the Pentagon."

Not being able to fly back to Utah for five or six days, Williams wandered around D.C., realizing how quickly the country had changed. "The only word defining that moment was 'terror,'" she recalled, "everyone pointing to the alleged enemy." Yet, as a conservationist, she had likewise learned that terror could take on many different forms, once affirming that "when oil companies spoke about oil drilling and exploitation of the Arctic Ocean, their terms were not 'if,' but 'when.'"

Terry lived in Southern Utah, which she described as having the most beautiful scenery with five National Parks,[15] red rocks, canyons rising up, and yet "there were forty thousand trucks crossing that fragile desert. So much had already been broken, including laws, to expedite this oil that finding beauty was difficult at such a time . . . nevertheless, finding beauty was creating beauty."

Inspired by the word "mosaic," which came to her in a meditative moment, she went to Ravenna, Italy, to learn its craft. While engaging in this artwork, she discovered that it was "an art of integration." On her way home, as she was driving, she saw the horizon as a long horizontal line with a small vertical one reminding her of mosaic art: on the horizontal line you place the tesserae, that small piece of cut stone, vertically. That vertical line on the horizontal line was a prairie dog, and she realized that her practice of mosaic art had changed her vision. "Suddenly," she said, "the landscape of my home appeared to me as an ecological mosaic—broken and beautiful."

The public began asking questions with humorist David Sedaris wondering out loud, "What is a prairie dog?"

Williams: "You're not the only one who does not know them. Recently, while talking with a journalist about my current work, he also asked me what a prairie dog was. 'Something like a wolf?' he inquired. [laughter] Wanting to be polite and not humiliate him, I mentioned that Lewis and Clark, those two great explorers, thought they were small dogs, but nowadays, they are considered to be vermin, and if my father were here with us, he would have told you that he had shot thousands of them in his lifetime."

She went back to the fact that Lewis and Clark estimated that, at the time, around 1803-1806, there were about five billion of them living in communities in the Grasslands (mostly on the Great Plains of the Midwest, the prairie of eastern Washington, and lands to the Southwest). Today, according to a *New York Times* article, they are part of an endangered species, fated to extinction.

"Yet nobody cares. We have forgotten how useful they are. Following the stampede hooves of the buffaloes, the prairie dogs stir the soil so as to let the rain soak through, maintaining it fertile. They also have their own language," Williams said with excitement in her voice, explaining how a biologist devoted to the study of their language had taken sound slices and identified up to a hundred words for communication among prairie dogs. "A prairie dog is called a keystone species, on which other species depend for their subsistence," Williams informed us. "Destroy prairie dogs, you destroy a varied world."

Finding Beauty in a Broken World is, in fact, a mosaic of different narratives. As well as this one on the mysterious world of prairie dogs, there is a chapter on her experience as a "barefoot artist" engaged in the Rwanda Healing Project to reconstruct villages destroyed during the Rwandan Civil War (1990-1994). She was taken to task by some American critics for putting prairie dogs in a book about the Rwanda genocide. "You can't do that," they protested. In reply to them, she strongly affirmed that "the extermination of a species and the extermination of the people are calculated on the same input which is: prejudice, cruelty, arrogance, and ignorance. If we cannot begin to see the world as a whole, we'll continue to see a world fragmented, fractured—the seedbed of wars."[16]

Terry Tempest Williams. March 17, 2009. © Village Voice video

Spectacular Sceneries, Ordinary Lives

AMERICAN WRITERS REEL
IN THE FRENCH IMAGINATION

Jim Harrison, Raymond Carver, Richard Ford, Russell Banks

"The novel is one that combines thoughts, meditations, insights, yet is deeply grounded in the daily reality of the hero . . . "

—RICHARD FORD

In the 1980s and '90s, American literature held a prominent place within France's literary panorama. Its readers were drawn to this new crop of fiction that appeared in bookstore window displays and talked about "the things that count, the things that move us," in the words of Raymond Carver,[1] the author who, alongside Jim Harrison, Richard Ford, and Russell Banks, was among the four most popular American writers of the time. Yet they couldn't have been more different from one another, in subject matter or style. So what exactly made their work so attractive to the French public?

Long accustomed to scenes of tamed nature and marked-off farmlands, these readers were now being exposed to America's wilderness and grandiose landscapes. They came to associate three authors—Harrison, Carver, and Ford—with the Great American West and, in fact, identified them as "Montana writers."

It is true that, fleeing the rush and demands of big cities, a number of authors had moved to the largest and least populated of the Western states, seeking silence and spiritual renewal through the breathtaking mountains, glaciers, deep forests, rivers, and immense ranchlands. They hailed from elsewhere, but had managed to turn Montana into a grandiose symbol for their fans abroad.

There was another element that captured the interest of the French. As large-scale, mechanized agriculture was reorganizing their own farmlands, and their cities were growing into sprawling metropolises, in these novels they discovered a close contact with real people, be they laborers, woodcutters, ranchers, or blue-collar workers, who were grappling with the realities of survival. Grown weary of a literature focused on the self and experimental stylistics, the French embraced these American fictions peopled with ordinary men and women determined to forge their own destinies.

Jim Harrison

An admired writer of the American West, as well as poet and essayist, Jim Harrison divided his time between Michigan, his birthplace, Montana, his home, and the American Indian plains of Arizona. In Paris for the launch of the French translation of Julip,[2] a collection of three novellas—Julip, The Seven-Ounce Man, and The Beige Dolorosa, his French publisher Christian Bourgois invited him to present at the Village Voice.

On May 16, 1995, a sturdy, jovial man in a floral-print shirt came into the bookshop accompanied by his longstanding friend and translator Brice Matthieussent. As we shook hands, Harrison alluded to the wild night just spent with some French pals, touring the famous bars of the capital, already whetting our appetite for his countless vivid anecdotes.

In his introduction, Matthieussent mentioned that Jim was often compared to Hemingway. "Both are natives of Michigan," he told us, "and, confronted with perilous situations, both are ready to show their manhood." Interrupting him, our author declared that he did not like Hemingway as "he had built up an image of himself as a macho hunter and fisherman prone to violence and never got out of this characterization. As for his style, a style that is perfect is one that says you're dead."[3]

Matthieussent then focused on the pivotal role of Edward Curtis in Harrison's life. This American ethno-photographer of Native Americans was a nomad who had documented tribes and their specific cultures. He was the tutelary figure for Harrison, who was deeply interested in Native American cultures and their folklore, particularly in myths of metamorphosis of man into animal and vice versa. Traveling from one reservation to another, his mentor had collected legends and anecdotes of such radical changes.[4]

One of Harrison's favorite characters, if not his alter ego, is Brown Dog, a vagabond half-man, half-dog, who becomes a bear in his dreams. At night, his life depends on his bearskin, and when it is stolen from him while he sleeps, he goes searching for it everywhere in an effort to recover his bear identity. It seems that the line between animals and humans is very thin, even diffuse in Harrison's fiction.

In his novel *Dalva*, a coyote's smile resembles that of a human being, and Julip, a trainer of hunting dogs, is said to handle men the way she handles her dogs.[5] All in all, the writer's animals are often even seen in a better light than men, as with Brown Dog, a man with an animal "soul" who, banished to the fringes of society, becomes the only character who is totally free in his physical movements and unrestrained thoughts.

Most dominant in all of Harrison's works of fiction and poetry is the presence of bears. "I have four bears I regularly check on in North Michigan," Harrison announced with fatherly pride. "There was that bear who lived in a cabin close by. He was enormous, some three hundred pounds. When I would come back at night from a bar, he would push his face on the side of the window as if to lift it. If there were too many bugs in the summer, he would roll about in the dirt, get into the river, and come back and roll again, all covered with mud, and look over at me. 'Ah, ah! how wonderful!' he seemed to gush."[6]

In the poem "My Friend the Bear" he recalls with emotion "her huge head on my shoulder / her breathing like a god's." Yet this sacred animal is also the prey of hunters. With a heavy heart, Julip recalls the anonymous shooting of a bear cub that had ventured close to her house. She rushed out and saw the cub was in its last throes of suffering. In an analogous poem "Bear," "[he] died standing up / paws on log / howling. Shot / right through the heart." After visualizing these two scenes for us, Harrison spoke at length of the violence in America in all its forms, an issue of great concern to him.[7]

In his final novella, *The Beige Dolorosa*, a retired professor is a bird-lover who has undertaken an eccentric project "à la Apollinaire"[8] to rename all the birds of America. "Their names are so boring," the author quipped, "so trivial, like that bird called 'Brown Thatcher.' [laughter] I renamed it 'Beige Dolorosa'; it's a much nicer name, don't you think? Yet I got a letter from the Audubon Bird Watch Society saying that you must not change the names of birds, such as Booby. Suddenly, I was a threat to the birds. I told them that there was one name I wouldn't change, and it was 'Hot Sunny and Get Wet.'"[9] [more laughter]

He next confided that every night in his hotel overlooking the elegant Matignon Gardens[10] he heard an owl hooting, and asked his audience, "Would someone know what kind of owl it might be?" . . . long silence. His attention to the bird's cries above the city's roaring traffic once again highlights this poet's acute sensitivity to all kinds of animal life, even in an urban setting.

Nevertheless, this author of some eighteen collections of verse is not a romantic. When someone asked him if nature was comforting, a sort of refuge or redemption, he replied, "None of those. Nature is not a palliative. One man enters the forest caring for animals, another comes and kills them . . . Watch a bear and you'll realize he is your cousin."

Poster for a reading by Raymond Carver, Richard Ford, and Jonathan Raban, introduced by Edmund White at the Village Voice Bookshop, June 26, 1987.

Raymond Carver

Reading the short stories of Raymond Carver, the writer from the scenic states of Oregon and Washington, one looks in vain for the spectacular landscapes of his homelands. Although nature is ever present in his poetry (river fly-fishing is his favorite outdoor activity), Carver's prose is about people, ordinary men and women in a quandary who tend to reveal themselves in their confusion, fragility, and anguish. The writer conveys these states with empathy, using spare words, even silences.

With some emotion, I remember the first time the author appeared at the Village Voice on April 7, 1987. He was to read from his collection of short stories *Will You Please Be Quiet, Please*[11] in the context of its French publication. Bundled up in a beige trench coat and looking almost "bearish," as his good friend Richard Ford once described him, Carver had a gentle look on his face that emanated kindness and vulnerability.

Edmund White, who was to introduce him, first acknowledged the writer Peter Taylor in the room. Taylor's novel, *A Summons to Memphis*,[12] had just been awarded the Ritz Hemingway Prize that afternoon during a reception at the Ritz hotel itself.* Then Carver reminded the audience of Taylor's role in giving the short story its rightful place in American literature.

Our author had already emerged as the advocate of a pared-down style that was being taught in writing workshops all over the States. Often called the "American Chekhov," Carver saw himself as a poet whose "poetry is a song, and often the song of the essential," as the writer Denis Hirson[13] defined him many years later.

This word "essential" pinpoints his art as one whose objective is to dive deeply into his characters, revealing their thoughts, concerns, and feelings, by suggesting rather than describing. That

---

* This prize was established in honor of Ernest Hemingway who, in his own words, had "liberated" the Ritz Bar from Nazi occupation in August 1944.

evening, Carver read "Collectors," "the one I still prefer of all my stories,"[14] he told us. It was the same story he had read in 1976 at the Southern Methodist University of Dallas when Richard Ford was in the audience. "Carver's reading," Ford wrote in his 1998 *New Yorker* article "Good Raymond," was "a startling experience, wondrous in all ways."[15] Meeting that night for the first time, the two writers became friends for life.

As in all his short fiction, nothing much happens in "Collectors," at least on the surface: a man is alone at home, "waiting for news from the North." His pacing back and forth and his regular glances at the window and at the mail slot in the door betray acute anxiety. Suddenly, a man shows up at the door, a salesman forcing his way through to demonstrate his wares, in this case, a vacuum cleaner. What follows is an absurd sequence as if from a silent movie, with each character obstinately locked into his own obsession. Unsuccessful in his sales pitch, the salesman finally packs up his things and rushes outside, inadvertently collecting, in his haste, a letter just dropped on the floor.

Referring to this story, Carver had already said in another interview that "many people do find it hard to communicate, and there's always a mystery in every story. Something else is going on under the surface. But things get said, do get done. Sometimes, the meanings are a little askew, but things do transpire."[16]

Carver is often seen as the writer of the ordinary man boxed into his specific social category, but, in fact, his attention is focused on the inner thoughts and hidden emotions of his characters and their difficulties: "My stories are never about the social, but the personal,"[17] he insisted to us that evening. Years later, in a conversation with Robert Altman, the director of the film *Short Cuts* based on a number of Carver's stories, the latter's widow, poet Tess Gallagher, likewise confessed to him that she "had missed the interiority of Carver's characters in the film." Altman's movie was "more societal than Ray was in his work."[18]

After their tour in Europe, Carver and Tess were back at the Village Voice on June 26, 1987, this time for a joint reading with his friend, the rising young American novelist Richard Ford, and the British travel writer Jonathan Raban, all three recently published by Christopher MacLehose (Collins Harvill), who had arranged the evening. Edmund White introduced these three authors to a packed house.

A strikingly handsome man, Ford was expected to present a passage from *Rock Springs*, his collection of stories recently published in New York. Instead, he read from his first novel, *A Piece of My Heart*, published in the US in 1976 and just out in Great Britain.[19] Beforehand, White had compared Ford's style and technique to Hemingway's "naked dialogue in action." "But there is a difference," he went on, stressing the fact that Ford's characters, "seemingly tough and resilient, are also fragile: a false step, one false response in a dialogue, or a lack of emotional intelligence and everything can derail."[20]

Next, **Jonathan Raban's** *Coasting*[21] took us on a sailing journey around the British Isles in search of memories of the places and people of his youth. Dropping anchor in local harbors along its western coast, he met and gave voice to fishermen and the populations of small towns, all hard-hit by Thatcher's economic policies and her distant and costly war in the Falklands.

Carver closed the evening with his poem "In a Marine Light near Sequim, Washington" from his collection *In a Marine Light*.[22] His reading called up the ubiquitous miracle of words that allows the poet to be driving along the Pacific Ocean with his wife next to him, and, at the same time, be in Paris: "The beauty of driving / that country road. Talking of Paris, our Paris . . . / And then you finding that place in the book/and reading to me about Anna Akhmatova's stay there with / Modigliani . . . / Them sitting on a bench in the Luxembourg Gardens."

This poem evokes two places close to his heart—his home, Port Angeles, Washington, on the Pacific Ocean, and Paris, "our Paris," weaving together the here and there and the now and then, the Luxembourg Gardens two steps away from the bookshop where he was presently reciting these lines.

After the event, we all went to La Cafetière, a restaurant on the rue Dauphine, close to the Village Voice, where Bruce Chatwin, a young British author renowned for his art and travel writings, joined us. His book *Songlines*, retracing his steps along the trails of the Australian Aboriginals, had recently come out in England to critical acclaim. An art expert turned globetrotter, there was something of a Rimbaud in him. Shod in wooden clogs that night, he was wearing the traditional black overalls of Norman peasants, once adopted by the Impressionist painters.

It was a warm and friendly gathering of publishers and authors. They all knew one another, and we could feel lightness in the air, sitting together around the table, happily chatting, drinking, eating, and exchanging anecdotes and memories of other get-togethers. British publisher Christopher MacLehose and his wife Koukla hosted this celebratory dinner, bringing together their authors—Ray Carver and his wife Tess Gallagher, Richard Ford and Jonathan Raban, Carver's French publisher Olivier Cohen, and author Edmund White accompanied by his close friend Marie-Claude de Brunhoff, the literary agent who presided over a Parisian salon at Saint-Germain-des-Prés. Edmund entertained us all with "beau monde" anecdotes, told with his usual wit. Everyone looked happy, untouched by the future. A year later, Ray Carver and Bruce Chatwin would be gone.

In the weeks following Carver's passing, Tess sent me a framed picture of his last port of call, a shrub of multicolored flowers in a field overlooking the Pacific Ocean that blended into the hazy sky of Port Angeles. And a few years later, she returned to Paris with her latest collection of poems, *Moon Crossing Bridge*. She read some of them that alluded to her life with Carver and, more particularly, her moving "Embers": "To speak aloud at a grave / breaks silence so another heat / shows through. Not speaking, but the glow / of what we spoke."[23]

Richard Ford

After his first appearance at our bookstore with Carver in the summer of 1987, Richard Ford returned to the Village Voice on March 29, 1989, this time to present his collection of short stories *Rock Springs*.[24] In a sense, this reading was a tribute to his friend "Good Raymond" who had died a few months earlier. He had previously written that it was Carver's "infectious sentences . . . so easy to write, it seemed, so natural, with their concision and strong feeling" that had reconciled him with the short story genre: "Stories had failed me and reading Ray's suddenly made the prospect of short stories appealing again."[25]

Yet he specified that Carver did not have any real influence on his work. As Ford understood Carver's experience, it was "simply to be moved by what you like, to understand you can never replicate it, to feel encouraged, and then to move on alone."[26]

Edmund White introduced our guest, calling Ford a key participant in the renewal of contemporary American literature: "In these stories, like in his novels," he pointed out, "the author fulfills with extraordinary energy and remarkable depth and range of feelings the writer's mission which, according to Gérard de Nerval,[27] is 'to analyze sincerely what his characters feel under serious conditions.'"[28]

Cool but with a commanding presence, Ford read "Optimists," a story of shattered dreams, in which nothing has prepared its protagonists to face the tragedy that has suddenly befallen them. A man has accidentally killed his neighbor, and his family members, who had always tried to be "decent people," are crushed by the randomness of this act: the man disappears into the night, his son enrolls in the army, and his wife's life is turned upside down. "What's going to happen to these three characters?" Ford asked, "How will they keep on going? What will it take to find the strength to live their new lives as best as possible?" These are the questions that come from a writer profoundly interested in thwarted human destinies.

Someone in the audience saw these characters as victims. "No," Ford retorted, adamantly rejecting this interpretation. "These

Richard Ford, Village Voice reading, March 29, 1989. © C. Deudon

characters are men in the dark, but they are left with the possibility to grope their way out of the situation and reinvent a new life
for themselves." In this sense, there is a major difference between
Carver's characters, often stuck in a dead end, and Ford's protagonists who "are given a chance, even if the prospect is far from
being inviting."[29] When facing a pivotal moment in life with a
crucial decision to be made, a direction to be taken—falling by
the wayside or keeping on—how is one to make the right choice?

These are Ford's existential interrogations in his fiction that
traces the inner journey of his characters in seemingly no-win
situations. For him, the only way out is through the process of
thinking, searching, interrogating, or meditating in an effort to
know oneself, so as to make the right choice. "The novel," he said,
"is one that combines thought, meditation, insights, yet is deeply
grounded in the daily realities of the hero." In fact, he would much
later insist that "these are never intellectual discursions, but always
arising from the lived experience."[30]

In the novels *The Sportswriter*, *Independence Day*, and *The Lay of the
Land* that form his *Bascombe* trilogy,[31] Ford follows his central character Frank Bascombe through the three decisive stages of his adult
life, bringing on a flux of thoughts and philosophical insights.

In *The Sportswriter*, Frank Bascombe has suffered consid-
erable setbacks: the loss of his regular job as a sportswriter for
a newspaper, a divorce, and the shattering death of a child.
In *Independence Day*, through his new job as a realtor, he wills himself out of his slump by reaching out to others, and especially his
elder son, estranged since the divorce of his parents and the fate
of his small brother. Finally, in *The Lay of the Land*, Bascombe has
entered the autumn of his life, and, on one Thanksgiving weekend,
his mind is preoccupied by the political uncertainty and social
disarray of his country—Bill Clinton's impeachment, George W.
Bush's election, and 9/11, but just as equally, the real intimations
of his own mortality.

Ford's fiction of introspective exploration is also a literature of displacement, a central motif of much contemporary fiction. "Changing places" comes to mean looking for a new house and, in fact, a better life. As a realtor, Bascombe explores the nooks and crannies of his country, helping people from all strata of society find the house of their dreams. This new home will allow them "to go up" to a better, more secure rung of life. In addition, he also becomes the fomenter of the unrealistic dreams of these house-hunters who, more often than not, end up bitterly disappointed with their choices.

This gap between dreams and realities reveals the author's rather dark sense of humor, and his deft irony often slipped into an anecdote about himself: "I probably looked at six hundred houses," Ford confessed, "driving hours and days looking for the one I had in mind—on a hilltop . . . only to put there a disfiguring house! Hilarious! You need a dose of self-irony here not to go to despair, but you're safe if you can say to yourself, 'This is ridiculous.'"[32]

As Ford had alluded to his nomadic past, having lived in Mississippi, Vermont, New Jersey, and now in Montana, someone in the audience wondered what had compelled him to move to so many different places.[33]

Ford: "I'm from Mississippi, and Mississippians have a lot to explain to themselves. When you think of all the stresses in Faulkner and Eudora Welty . . . Coming from Mississippi caused me to be the kind of a guy I am and the writer I am."

Q: "Is constant movement compatible with reflection and writing?"

Ford: "Movement through space can reflect inner movement, change inside. The American dream is about conquest which is movement."

Q: "Is Frank Bascombe your alter ego?"

Ford: "My character Frank Bascombe is not me in all kinds of ways. Making up a character represents my sense of will: this is what I want to do. This is what 'author' means, the one who authorizes. Bascombe is entirely made up out of language, out of dialogues, of phrases I've heard. The excitement that comes from reading a novel is not what's going on in someone's head, walking, shopping, etc. . . . The excitement comes from the language we have on the page in front of us. For me, language is one kind of action. This is what I do in my novels. Much of my time is spent getting bad words out and right words in the right places."

Richard Ford concluded his stimulating discussion with this reflection on the relationship between the novel and the reader: "I think that novels are supposed to bring you, the reader, back to your own life, with a great sense of its importance, and this is accomplished by having the characters pay attention to life and their thinking, brought to you through language."

Russell Banks

The author of more than a dozen novels and six collections of short stories, Russell Banks gave three readings at the Village Voice. The first one was on January 27, 1987, for the launch of the French publication of *Continental Drift*,[34] a novel with powerful resonance years after it had come out. In it, a blue-collar worker at the end of his rope quits his job and leaves his family for Florida, hoping for a better life. What awaits him is a nightmare that involves the smuggling of Haitian migrants into the country. According to Banks, "the novel's title points to the explosive social and political collisions created by displacements of populations inside and between countries: a contemporary and ongoing issue the world over."[35]

Some twenty years later, on November 17, 2006, he returned to the Village Voice, this time to present his eleventh novel, *The Darling*,[36] the story of the American Hannah Musgrave, a former member of the 1970s radical Weather Underground, who fled to West Africa, fleeing a US court of justice. Banks read the first pages of his work, projecting us into the past life of his protagonist. She had just woken up from a dream about Africa with a vague premonition that she is to return where she once was a wife and mother of three boys.

Since coming back to her native New England, she has been running a commercial farm, trying to submerge the "terrible years" in Liberia in the "dark waters of her memory." Nevertheless, she continues to be haunted by the memory of her lost family and the rescued chimpanzees she had to abandon to the civil war raging there.

Russell Banks, Village Voice Bookshop reading, March 4, 2008. © Flavio Toma

"What incited the male Banks to explore this figure of Hannah, this inspiring female character from our generation?" a woman asked.

Banks: "The Darling was generated remembering my twenties, a time of activism with the civil rights movement and the anti-war protests. There were lots of women in them and yet we, as young men, did not pay much attention to those women who, in fact, put themselves at risk, really sacrificing much more of their lives than men did. I started to think how wonderful they had been then, and wondered who they were now at sixty."

Q: "Why this choice of Africa where Hannah fled from America? Why Liberia and not another country?"

Banks: "I was interested in the history of the relation between Liberia and the United States. I wanted to get a feel of where the ferocity of Liberia's civil war came from, one of unspeakable violence. I had to research this special link with America, especially when I became involved in the project of my novel Cloudsplitter[37] about John Brown and the early abolitionist movement. The history of Liberia is a complex, complicated relationship with the United States since its founding and up to the Liberian Civil War, which erupted in 1991. That history is like an umbilical cord that stretched from Liberia to the US, spreading poison. Having investigated this link, I wanted to write that particular chapter of the race history of the US."

It is true that Hannah is an exceptional person who has undertaken each one of her projects with passion and compassion: from youthful protests for justice within the civil rights movement, to the sanctuary for chimpanzees she set up in Liberia while braving death all around her, to starting, later in life, a farm, a commercial operation she runs in the middle of the Adirondacks.

At the request of the audience, Banks read the excerpt in which Hannah is back in Liberia in order to find out what has happened to her chimpanzees. Their shadows and the echoes of their plaintive cries now haunt the small island of burnt dry grass in the middle of the river where she had once brought them to safety. This passage aroused so much emotion in the audience that people were curious about where such interest in chimpanzees came from.

Banks: "This is difficult to explain, but the element that brought everything together is exactly the chimpanzees. I came upon a sanctuary near my home, in Quebec of all places, just across the Canadian border, with chimpanzees rescued after being abused in medical and pharmaceutical experimentation. Visiting other sanctuaries in Atlanta and Sierra Leone, West Africa, I began to notice that the people who devoted their lives to protecting chimpanzees and high primates were generally women, very much like the ones I had known in the '60s and '70s in the civil rights and anti-war movements. They were from privileged backgrounds, white, well-educated women, almost an archetype. They had strong opinions, strong political principles, very much like my character Hannah Musgrave, and it all brought the material together for me."

Hannah is not the only unusual woman in Russell Banks's fiction. In his novel *The Reserve*,[38] launched at the Village Voice on March 4, 2008, he brings to life Vanessa Cole, a New England heiress and mysterious woman, a Baudelairian female figure, "beautiful as a dream of stone," a sort of antithesis to Hannah.[39] Her character as a femme fatale is most unexpected from the author of novels concerned with social issues. She is involved in a romance with Jordan Grove, a local artist of international fame. Their love affair unfolds against the fairy-tale backdrop of the "vast enclosed space between lake and forest, and mountain and sky . . . at the exact center of wilderness" in the Adirondack Mountains, the author's home and beloved retreat.*

Nonetheless, this romantic pairing that takes place in this exclusive estate is "doomed not only by their mutual narcissistic involvement," but also by larger events. As the story takes place in the very narrow framework of a summer, between July 14 and September 1, 1936, threatening clouds of history are gathering on the horizon.

Like other contemporary American writers, the author alludes to historical circumstances to contextualize his novels, but for Banks, "a major event ought to be written with clarity and with coherence if it is to be recorded as a historical document, whereas in fiction it goes differently. As we are sitting here, wars in Iraq and Afghanistan are going on and, however boring and pressing our lives may be, these wars are the italicized part of our lives right now. Four months away, 1937 was not just any year. It was the year Jordan[40] engaged in the Abraham Lincoln Brigade that fought in Spain, and the Hindenburg Zeppelin exploded into flames over the northern shore of the New Jersey coast."

Both events were "the rising ashes foreboding the forthcoming disaster, and such major events," Banks insisted, "I could only apprehend them in a metaphorical way. What I was trying to do in my novel was to give the shadows, as it were, of the historical context of the lives of my characters as they engage in betrayal, adultery, and complicated kinds of domestic events."[41]

Returning to the here and now, he saw the explosion of the Hindenburg as an echo of what happened on 9/11. "It is the only approach I can have for historical events of that scope," he concluded.

---

* "The Adirondacks is a familiar place, where every single detail is of significance, the beauty, the smell, the noise of the wind, the birds, the traffic, whatever it is, it has the resonance of it all, like a dream . . ." Banks said at Village Voice reading, March 4, 2008.

13

Four Remarkable Women

BREAKING FROM CONVENTION

Hazel Rowley, Grace Paley, Adrienne Rich, Susan Sontag

"[The] success of women writers has been empower-
ing women, has given them a sense of possibility."
—GRACE PALEY, Village Voice reading

"**K**ate Millett is the true groundbreaker and not Simone
de Beauvoir. Perhaps this is so for subjective reasons,
but Millett wrote things I had been thinking for a long
time, and when her first writings appeared, I remember feeling a
great sense of relief! Enfin!"*

This note from Mavis Gallant, received on the morning of a
Millett reading at the Village Voice,** brings together two significant feminist theorists of the twentieth century who sought
to revolutionize the lives of women in both public and private
spheres. In The Second Sex (1949) Beauvoir had demonstrated their
subordinate condition as a second-class gender; twenty years later,
in Sexual Politics (1970), Millett decried the enduring male culture

---

* On her way to Montreal, Mavis Gallant couldn't attend Millett's reading and sent
me these few words, dated October 24, 1991.
** Kate Millett, Village Voice reading, October 24, 1991, a presentation of her new,
full-length essay The "Loony Bin Trip that denounces the clinical treatment of
depression at the time, leading to her losing control of her life.

inherited from centuries of patriarchal societies that perpetuated the image of women as sexual objects.

These seminal works called for the emergence of a new consciousness that appeared in the 1970s with the creation of departments of women's studies and the huge success of writing workshops and book clubs—all of them circles of reflection that helped female authors diversify and broaden the scope of their writing. In the next two decades, their literature experienced an unprecedented boom, addressing as it did a more varied and larger readership. If their life stories were still a source of inspiration, their literary expression gained in vision and universal significance, now starting to capture the imagination of people of both genders.

Among the great number of unparalleled women authors who read at the Village Voice, we will highlight the voices of four whose critical biography, fiction, poetry, and essays have left an indelible mark on American and other literatures.

Hazel Rowley

> "I write to discover: I wanted to understand how this relationship worked."
> —ROWLEY, Village Voice reading, January 12, 2006.

British-born Australian and naturalized American writer Hazel Rowley is the author of four notable biographies, three of them about singular women and one the edifying life story of the African American writer Richard Wright,[1] whose 1946 exile to Paris was made possible by Sartre and Beauvoir. As a feminist early on in her life, the subject of Hazel Rowley's third biography, *Tête-à-Tête: Simone de Beauvoir and Jean-Paul Sartre*, was Beauvoir herself, known worldwide as the author of *The Second Sex* and taken on as a role model by so many women, now revealed in a unique and unexpected light.[2]

Our author had been a reader of Beauvoir's works since her youth and an admirer of this independent female figure. Intrigued by Beauvoir's unconditional dedication to Sartre, never eclipsed by any of her various other love affairs, not even her longest and most passionate one with Nelson Algren, Rowley made up her mind to choose this feminist icon as the subject of her doctorate dissertation, even managing with some difficulty to secure a private appointment with Beauvoir in Paris.

The interview took place in 1976 in the latter's studio, but Rowley's high expectations quickly dissipated as she told us that "Beauvoir was evasive in her replies about the 'pact' binding her for life to Sartre, and her very automatic pistol-like answers betrayed her irritation." She sensed that Beauvoir was a woman who was "attached to her own myth . . . polishing up her image, not really telling much and even holding onto certain truths."[3]

Seventeen years later, in 1993, after the death of both Sartre and Beauvoir, out of the blue, a scandal broke out with the publication of *Mémoires d'une jeune fille dérangée*[4] (a satirical pun on Beauvoir's title of her youthful memoir) by Bianca Bienenfeld-Lamblin, a former philosophy student of Beauvoir's. According to her, this teacher had abused her professorial authority by seducing her students and then passing them on to Sartre. It is perhaps not too far-fetched to say that Rowley's intuition of malaise during her studio visit had not been a simple impression.

Beauvoir's unfailing attachment to her lifelong partner was far more complex than she had made it appear in her journals and autobiographical fiction. Hazel Rowley was now finding it nearly impossible to consider her life and publications as separate from Sartre's role in them. In fact, she was the first feminist biographer to try to really understand how this unique couple "worked." She

presented her insightful portrait of their relationship at the Village
Voice on January 12, 2006.

Tall, slender, and elegant in a dark gray tailored suit, Hazel,
"Azelle la Gazelle" for her French friends, opened her talk with the
word "passion" which, she felt, "best expressed the driving force
of Beauvoir and Sartre's lives. It was not the kind of passion that
bonded Abelard and Héloïse, but an intellectual passion, a passion
for a life lived in ideas. Indeed, the title *Tête-à-Tête* conveyed the
idea of a relationship that had more to do with their heads than
with their bodies." She stressed the complexity of Beauvoir herself
who, in 1947, two years before the publication of *The Second Sex*,
had written an essay on "The Ethics of Ambiguity,"[5] which she
dedicated to Bianca, the lover she had given to Sartre, himself
the author of the following epigraph to the second volume of *The
Second Sex*: "Half victim, half accomplice, like everyone."[6]

Rowley reminded us that "truly, they were clear about their
ambivalence and claimed it as part of their philosophy, yet certain
mores that were easily accepted in France in the 1950s were no
longer in the 1990s." When Lamblin's revelations came out "it was
not as much the crude details that caused scandal as the duplicity and the deception of the couple, much greater than anyone
had imagined. Everyone had been conned, the women for whom
Beauvoir had been an inspiration and Sartre's former girlfriends,
who could now read in the archived letters the unpleasant things
that Sartre and Beauvoir had said behind their backs."

The biography was received in the United States to critical
acclaim, and Hazel was eager to see it published in France where,
she was convinced, it belonged more than anywhere else. At the
time of our bookstore launch, its French translation was being
finalized, but publication was postponed to October 2006 when
it immediately faced widespread outrage.

The saga of this short-lived translation provides some insight
into the Parisian intelligentsia of the time, all-powerful but

not without its own prejudices. Attacked from all sides, Hazel explained that "one priority of the biographer is to understand their characters with their complexities, their history, psychic particularities, and emotions."[7] She was an adventurous biographer,[8] as she described herself, the kind of biographer who will "press her nose on the windowpane to see inside,"[9] ever curious and eager to probe her characters' interiorities.

Yet her explanations did not appease the outcry, and she was disconcerted by the review in *Le Monde* that dismissed "la Britannique installée à New York,"[10] implying that as a foreigner she had no business meddling in uniquely French matters. Even more unsettling was the attitude of Claude Lanzmann, the internationally known

Hazel Rowley at the Village Voice, summer 2005, Village Voice archive.

author of the documentary film *Shoah*, Beauvoir's former lover, and Sartre's close collaborator at the review *Les Temps Modernes*, who had granted Hazel several interviews.[11] He was furious about her reference to an affair that had turned sour between his sister, the actress Évelyne Rey, and Sartre, a seventy-year-old story that had already been cited in one memoir and written about in the press.[12] Lanzmann threatened Rowley's French publisher with a lawsuit if the book was not immediately withdrawn.

Under pressure, Rowley's publisher spelled out to her the French laws on privacy and the public domain: "No matter if the material has already appeared in seventeen different books, the notion of 'public domain' doesn't exist in France." So, after a short life on bookstore tables, all copies of *Tête-à-Tête* were recalled and pulped. No one raised a voice of protest in France, not even a single female writer. In 2008, an expurgated second edition was reprinted, but booksellers did not reorder it, and so the French translation vanished completely.

Even more scandalous to Rowley was her "right of reply" denied by the two major French dailies, *Le Monde* and *Le Figaro*. She expressed her indignation in an article, "Censorship in France,"[13] reminding her detractors that Sartre and Beauvoir had made it clear that "they would like the public to know the truth about their personal lives." To further strengthen her position, she pointed out that "neither of them destroyed any of their private correspondence and journals even when it did not make them look good." Had not Sartre himself written, "So much the better if this means I will be . . . transparent to posterity?"[14]

If she showed the flaws of her characters, Hazel also stressed their dedication to work, to worthy causes, and enduring friendships. Answering a woman in the audience who wondered if the couple's "pact of love" had profited both partners equally, she paused for a while, then affirmed that she "sincerely believed that Beauvoir had gained more from the relationship than Sartre." Her answer caused a stir, given the revelations heard that evening, but after a pause, she went on, "it was Sartre who had stimulated Beauvoir, pushed her to go into the world, have lovers, and adventures. . . . 'Dare to put yourself in your writing; screw up your courage and take risks,' he had told her."

Hazel's conclusion was taken as encouragement by author Ayaan Hirsi Ali, who was sitting in the first row that evening. Born in Somalia, Hirsi Ali is an international political activist who has dedicated her life to supporting the rights of Muslim women throughout the world and, as a result, has become the target of death threats.[15] Accompanied by six bodyguards who, the day before, had checked out the nooks and crannies of our bookshop, she was in the process of writing her autobiography and had looked forward to hearing Hazel speak about Beauvoir.

Likewise, Constance Borde and Sheila Malovany-Chevallier attended the reading. Socially and politically active women in the circle of Democrats Abroad, they had recently taken on the daunting task of a new and complete English translation of Le deuxième sexe.[16] Four years later, they would launch their work at the Village Voice on January 14, 2010, extending the influence of Beauvoir's feminist ideas in the US, as well as the English-speaking world.

I might add that while she was engaged in her research work in Paris, Hazel had become a personal friend and constant supporter of our Village Voice bookstore, which she described in an elaborate and wonderful article published in Australia and in the US.[17]

On March 1, 2011, the eve of her Australian book tour to promote her new and highly praised biography on the exceptional marriage of Franklin and Eleanor Roosevelt,[18] the news of her sudden death came as an enormous shock, plunging us all, her friends in Paris and many other places in the world, into grief and dismay.

Two months later, a number of us gathered for a tribute to Hazel at the Village Voice, her "home away from home" during her Paris years. Still stunned and sorrowed, we decided to share our fond memories of her. Coming first, Jake Lamar's moving anecdote was a reminder of the ups and downs of her career as a biographer.[19] He reminisced about the first time he met Hazel by chance after one of our bookstore readings, everyone mingling and chatting with a glass of wine in their hands. Jake told us he suddenly realized that the person he was talking with was none other than the author of Richard Wright's biography that he had favorably reviewed for the *Washington Post*. With the usual bio elements and photo missing in his review copy, he had always assumed that "this person was a male Jamaican, and this male Jamaican turned out to be white, a woman, and an Australian." Enjoying this confusion of genres, Hazel had then concluded, "It's the best compliment I've ever got."

Another of her Paris friends, Virginia Larner, closed the evening by describing our friend as a woman of the world: "Hazel had lived in London, Australia, Cambridge (Mass), Paris, and New York. . . . At times it made me wonder where home was and what it was for her." Reflecting on the remark of Adam Gopnik's wife that their family "had had a beautiful existence in Paris but one missing a full life," Virginia insisted that "Hazel had fought to the end to keep both registers alive and vibrantly so . . . always happiest living with others."

The following year, on the first anniversary of Hazel's passing, her sister Della flew all the way from Australia to New York with close friends of hers to attend a tribute to Hazel at the Roosevelt House/Hunter College on February 9, 2012. The day before, in the biting cold, a few of us had gathered at the Eleanor Roosevelt Memorial in Riverside Park, not far from where Hazel had lived and where I had spent a few days with her in June 2010.

Sitting on the wooden bench with the memorial plaque Della had dedicated to her, we looked at the pensive figure of Eleanor while revisiting in our minds the warm and vivid portrait Hazel had drawn of this revered figure in her recent biography. Then, in loving memory of her sister, Della scattered a handful of her ashes at the foot of the statue in the park where Hazel had loved to walk.

Two days later, Sarah Gaddis, a friend since her Paris stay in the 1980s, welcomed me at her home in the Lower Hudson Valley. She had discreetly left on my bed a box of letters her father, William Gaddis, had sent his mother from abroad when he was a young writer already working on his monumental novel *The Recognitions*. Back in 1999, Sarah had invited me to attend the memorial tribute to her father at the American Academy of Arts and Letters in New York City. Sharing this intimate correspondence with me before the letters were to be published beautifully reflected our mutual trust and friendship. Sarah had given me the room at the top of the house where she usually worked, a cozy place infused with the concentration of her own writing.

It was nightfall. I stood at the window watching the snow dancing in the light of the street lamps, reminiscing about Hazel but also about Sarah's father, with the last words of James Joyce's "The Dead" filling my thoughts: "His soul swooned slowly, as he heard the snow falling faintly through the universe and faintly falling, like the descent of their last end, upon all the living and the dead."[20]

Grace Paley

> "She will listen. It's her work.
> She will be the listener in the story of the stories."
> —GRACE PALEY[21]

Grace Paley gave three readings at the Village Voice, the last one on March 28, 1999, for the launch of *Just as I Thought*,[22] a semi-autobiographical collection of essays, reports, and talks. She was introduced by Noëlle Batt, professor of contemporary American literature and author of an essay on Paley.[23] In the photo taken that day, Grace Paley looks like the French writer Colette with her mane of tousled, curly white hair framing an open, jovial face. A mother, a friend, and an anti-nuclear and anti-war activist, she had made her opinions heard in public stands and in writings that defended civil and women's rights. Famous for her sharp wit and humor, hers was truly a unique voice among us.

Paley opened the reading with "The Man in the Sky Is the Killer," her account of her 1972 visit to Vietnam as a member of the Peace Movement on a mission to escort three liberated POWs back home. The title of this piece was the name given by the North Vietnamese to the US jet fliers bombing their country where, Paley quipped, "they had no business to be." Asked about his war experience, one of the three soldiers ingenuously replied: "Gosh! Grace, I have to admit it, I really loved bombing." Whereas at home the POWs were hailed by politicians and newsmen "as though they had been kidnapped from a farm in Iowa or out of a canoe paddling in the waters of Minnesota." [laughter] As for their wives, they waited for their husbands, refusing to acknowledge the reality of the deadly havoc they had caused with "Oh, Mrs. Paley, villages and people! My husband wouldn't do that."

Paley followed with a seventeen-minute memoir, "Six Days: Some Rememberings"—her unforgettable six days in prison that she revived with much humor and tenderness for her inmate sisters. Arrested for sitting down in the middle of the street to slow down a military parade, Paley was taken to the Women's Detention Center in the middle of Greenwich Village, her own neighborhood. Tears running down her face, she caught the attention of the other women already inside.

"Hey, you, white girl," a Black woman called out, "you've never been arrested before?"

Putting her arms around Paley's shoulder, she said, "It ain't so hard . . . I've got thirty years. What's your time, sugar?"

"I've got six days."

"You've got six days? What the fuck for? You've got six days for sitting in front of a horse? Those cops are getting crazier, meaner and stupider. We'll get you out of here." [laughter]

A woman in the audience asked her if she considered this piece to be fiction or nonfiction. Paley: "The border is thin between the two, and I don't particularly like borders." [laughter]

Grace Paley, March 28, 1999. © Noëlle Batt

Q: "What is your take on America these days?"

Paley: "It's a hard question. We're all very anxious.[24] Many of us, like me, hope for less war, less racism. Yet struggles that happened in the past are still there. Let's take the fight against racism that started with the civil rights movement. If things seem worse now, it's because racism has become a lot clearer: it is the great curse of the United States, like anti-Semitism is the great curse of Europe, but women-hating is the great curse of the whole world. [laughter] Really, all around the world, it has been how to keep women down.... It may look to many people that it is all about oil, but it's more like making and maintaining a patriarchal state."

Q: "You said in one of your interviews that writing for you came from life. Could you elaborate on this?"

Paley: "The sound of the story comes first. My lesson came from the poet Auden. I attended his class. I admired him a lot. I was shy, but I gave him some poems to read. He pointed to a couple of words and asked me, 'Grace, is it the way you talk?' I immediately realized that I had been writing Jewish all along, and I suddenly understood the richness of my background, a community of Jewish immigrants in the Bronx, with Yiddish talk all around. I really learned from poetry to write stories."

Q: "After a whole life in Greenwich Village, how does it feel to live in Vermont?"

Paley: "I don't feel a stranger, but I miss New York. I met Isaac Babel's wife who lived in France with their daughter. Babel would come to visit them in Paris, but always would return to Moscow. Why? I asked her, until 1935, the year of Stalin's Great Purges, he could have stayed in Paris. 'He used to tell me,' she said, 'that Paris was good for strolling, but Moscow was good for work.' The way I feel is that New York is good for strolling, and it's also good for work." [laughter]

Adrienne Rich

The author of a significant body of poetry and essays, both awarded prestigious prizes, Adrienne Rich graciously agreed to make a stopover in Paris on her way back home from England where she had been presented with a new award. She was to read from her latest collection *The School among the Ruins*[25] and the event, organized by our mutual friend Steven Barclay, had been set for July 18, 2006. It turned out to be the hottest day of that summer's heat wave. With people massing at the door, we left it open, rendering our antiquated air-conditioning system pretty useless. Suffering from the high temperatures, but also from a bout of arthritis, with some difficulty Adrienne made her way through the dense crowd gathered outside and inside the bookshop, helped by her partner, the writer Michelle Cliff. Though tired from the flight the day before, she displayed a big smile and even began to look somewhat sprightly.

Adrienne Rich, July 18, 2006. Village Voice archival video.

Sitting poised at the microphone with a sparkle in her eyes, Rich gazed around her, acknowledging friends in the room, among them the poet Marilyn Hacker who had written about her poetry. In the packed audience were American writers living in Paris, as well as her Norton publisher from London and her French, Italian, and Spanish translators. Likewise, there was also a number of women from the States who remembered Rich as the feminist advocate and activist whose writings, poetry performances, and clear public stances on gender issues had made a difference in their lives.

Ellen Hinsey,* a young and talented American poet living in Paris, introduced Adrienne Rich. Like Rich fifty years beforehand, Ellen had been awarded the Yale Younger Poets Prize in 1996 for *Cities of Memory*,[26] her first volume of poetry. She immediately began by stressing the impact of Rich's writings on several generations of women, including her own, describing her poems as "those seemingly simple things which had changed their lives." "I'm sure," Hinsey went on, "that everyone in this room has their own version of them. Adrienne's poems were read, passed on, discussed, carried in notebooks and wallets, returning even in dreams. . . . The driving force of her poetry and essays is her desire to reach the other, to be in dialogue with the other."[27]

Rich opened her reading with the poem "The Art of Translation,"[28] a dialogue between the author and the translator. In this way she greeted her three translators in the room,[29] insisting that "her life would be unthinkable without poetry translation." She too had put works from different languages and cultures into English and knew the difficulties, the obstacles, and the duplicity inherent in this demanding art.

In her poem "The Art of Translation," she intimates that such dangers betray the original language, its ideas, and its internal

---

* As a poet, Hinsey is featured in Part IV of this book, dedicated to American poets based in Paris.

rhythms. Here the translator is likened to a would-be smuggler at "passport control," unable to prove that the translated poem is not "contraband," or its words subversive messages. "If translation is a dangerous art," Rich ventured, "it's nonetheless an indispensable one with a crucial social responsibility." "However," she added, "translating a poem is also to create a new poem."[30]

Though a writer of numerous essays, Rich stands out as the poet who asserts that "what I know, I know through poetry."[31] Beyond knowledge, this literary genre is the path to the advent of "the dream of a common language" between men and women. For her, since the very existence of patriarchal societies, language had developed according to the male view of the world, fashioned by his will to dominate through power.

In her poem "Fox" she shows how male vision and language have deprived women of the "recognition" of their own "history" and with it, their own vision of the world and the language to represent it. Only through a radical change may the "dream of a common language" become reality. "Change" is another key word in Rich's poetry and essays and the very precondition for the birth of "the yet-to-be human child" and "the-yet-to-be woman," as shown in the final act of the vixen in "Fox." She is the one who, by giving life, incarnates hope for the new being to come.

Rich dated each one of her poetical works, placing them "in a historical continuity," she said, thus charting her personal involvement in their composition. She concluded the reading with the title poem from *The School among the Ruins*, depicting a classroom of children in a city which has just been bombed.

Dated 2001, the poem hints at crucial events in recent American history taking place within a crossfire of American foreign wars, both past and present. Still, beyond the larger scope of deadly world catastrophes, in this "school among the ruins," the teacher urges her children to pay attention to the stray cat that has taken refuge in their still standing classroom: "Don't let your faces turn to stone / Don't stop asking me why / Let's pay attention to our cat she needs us."[32]

A few weeks after the reelection of George W. Bush, Adrienne sent me a postcard dated November 29, 2004, conveying the atmosphere of the country at that particular moment and her own sadness: "It is a time when one would gladly think oneself outside the US, or the grotesque profile of what calls itself culture here & now. Yet there is something else, partly invisible, partly confused perhaps—the end of illusions, of adolescent egotism—but it is coming at a huge price for the vulnerable of the world. One writes, one reads, one speaks, one remembers dreams that were not illusions and tries to re-imagine them."[33]

Susan Sontag

> "What is a writer but a mental traveler?"
> —SONTAG, Village Voice reading, March 28, 2002.

Susan Sontag had lived in Paris in the 1960s and returned to the city regularly. During my Washington, DC, days in the seventies, I had discovered her essays on French and other European writers and artists, deepening my understanding of the earlier decade's protest culture within my own country. On the other hand, her essays on the United States—"Notes on Camp" (1964), "What's Happening in America" (1966), and "Trip to Hanoi" (1969)—gave me clues to decipher the country I was now living in, helping me discern the perpetually shifting contours of its political and cultural trends.

I can honestly say that this writer's intelligence, her vast culture, her overarching approach to the world, all expressed in a style that was unpretentious, direct, and yet elegant, simply carried me away.

In Paris, told by French booksellers close to the Village Voice that Sontag was a regular of their bookstores, I asked them to put in a word for us, but their reply was, "It's no use. Sontag does not come to Paris to buy American books; she can find them around her corner in New York."

Then, one day she pushed open the door of our shop. It was a late afternoon during the Christmas holidays. The writer was wearing dark, loose pants, a black flyer jacket, and walking boots. The following times, she never arrived alone, rather always with one friend or another, dashing straight away to our section on Central and Eastern European literatures in English. I learned that when she was just a teenager, Sontag's veneration for Thomas Mann's *The Magic Mountain* was so strong that it had led a friend of hers to set up a seemingly implausible meeting with the great writer exiled in Los Angeles. Never forgetting that enchanted moment, all her life she remained attentive to the literatures from that part of the world.

Her famous essays "On Photography,"[34] "Illness as Metaphor,"[35] "AIDS and Its Metaphors,"[36] and "Regarding the Pain of Others"[37] stand as crucial testimonies of our time by a major American voice whose observations and reflections have opened our eyes and minds and sharpened our discernment.

Then, in the 1990s, the preeminent essayist revealed she was an equally brilliant storyteller with two powerful novels, *The Volcano Lover*[38] and *In America*,[39] each featuring an inspiring and memorable female character: Emma in the first novel and Marina in the second.

One day, as she was browsing in the bookstore, Sontag approached me, saying: "Odile, I would love to give a reading at the bookshop." I was thrilled. I had been too shy to ask her and here we were, setting up the date—March 28, 2002—for the launch of her new book, *Where the Stress Falls*.[40] It was a collection of essays laying out her aesthetic credo in literature and reflection on what it takes "to be a great writer" who also acts as a kind of societal conscience.

On that March evening, Sontag arrived with her French publishers, Christian and Dominique Bourgois, followed by her sister, Judith Rosenblatt, and Chantal Thomas, a renowned French novelist and essayist who was to introduce her. Our author apologized for being a few minutes late as she had "recklessly" accepted a friend's invitation to go and visit the Vézelay Abbey in Burgundy, a site already familiar to her, but, she added with an apologetic smile, "I've only got three days in Paris and I had to do it."

Our bookstore was packed upstairs, downstairs, and there was a crowd standing on the stairs in between.[41] She opened her talk by confiding that "the fact of this evening was a confluence of affinities and affections: this bookshop an eccentric place, and the discovery of Chantal Thomas[42] who interviewed me for *France-Culture*. It was stupendous. I realized we had so many authors in common, starting with Thomas Bernhard and Roland Barthes."

Thomas: "In these essays collected in *Where the Stress Falls*, you explore a new space with writers and artists from many different horizons, and most of them are displaced: they are writers, travelers, and wanderers. This book communicates your ardor for travel, reading, and writing. How do you conciliate all three?"

Sontag: "The first travel book I read, and certainly one of the most important books of my young life, was *Book of Marvels* by Richard Halliburton[43] describing the wonders he visited all over the world, including the Great Wall of China, where my father and mother lived at the time. His adventures fired up my imagination. I was seven years old and, in my child's mind, to be a traveler, to be a writer, started off as the same thing. Both travel and writing meant to embrace the world."

Thomas: "'Travel is to embrace the world,' you say, but do you write when you travel? Elizabeth Bishop in your epigraph wonders, 'Should we have stayed home?'[44] What about you?"

Sontag: "I don't write when I travel, but I like very much to be a foreigner. I don't think that travel involves detachment; on the contrary, it is a higher, passionate form of intensified experience. In many ways, it is also simply living in a big city. I grew up in the Southwest of the US and went to New York when I was twenty-six. New York is foreign to me."

Thomas: "How does this experience of being a foreigner translate into your writing?"

Sontag: "Migrants, wanderers, travelers are themes of my fiction. Actually, as a fiction writer,[45] I wanted to encompass a great deal more reality, but did not know how to do it, did not have the inner freedom to do it. It was not that I did not have ideas, but there is a difference between what's going on in your head and what's going onto paper."

Thomas: "What about your essays?"

Sontag: "I drifted into writing essays, the seduction of certain kinds of debates that were going on, getting much attention from the beginning. But I went back to fiction: screenplays, plays, play directing. Fiction was what I wanted; essays are monophonic while fiction is polyphonic. I'm still trying to keep the muzzle on the essayist dog in the basement. But suddenly, in the 1980s, the gates swung open. I don't know why. I began taking in much more reality and liberating my gift as a storyteller."

Thomas: "Your two major novels, *The Volcano Lover* and *In America*, are works of a storyteller?"

Sontag: "Yes, in these two novels I discovered that I was a storyteller. I was proud of the act of making a story: how you invent a story, a character, names, relationships, future events. The writer is God, and, hence, the master of the destiny of his characters. It is in the process of writing fiction that I came to some kind of unified relationship with myself as a writer. I felt that I was taking care of the person who wrote this book."

Thomas: "Marina, the protagonist in your novel In America—is she your self-portrait? So many details seem to indicate it, like her origins, her ardor . . ."

Sontag: "No, not at all. Marina is not me. My family came a hundred and thirty years ago, too far back. I do not look in that direction. I have no family apart from David, my son, and my sister who is here tonight. As much Europeanized as I may be, I'm ready to let the past go. In 'Singleness,' one of the essays in this book, I address this question of the author and their double. My books are not me. They are not a portrait of me, but the work comes from me. It took almost thirty years to write a book I really liked, The Volcano Lover. There is an even deeper reason why my books are not me: my life. I've always felt it like a becoming. And still do. Once the books are finished, they liberate me to do, to be, to feel, and aspire to something else."

Thomas: "Sartre writes against someone or something; by contrast, each one of your essays is a tribute to a writer or to an artist, a form of love."

Sontag: "That's absolutely true. I once wrote an attack, and it was an accident. It was my piece on Leni Riefenstahl. Not because of her association with Hitler or fascism, but I discovered doing my research on her that she was even more infamous than I thought . . . all those lies. The question I ask myself when I am writing on something: 'Is this worth doing?' I have to go beyond my subject. I have to have a larger point. The larger point here was not to discuss the work of Riefenstahl per se, but to explore the idea of fascism as an aesthetic point of view. Benjamin speaks of 'le fascisme esthétisant' (the creation of a fascist aesthetics). In every one of my essays, I try to highlight a theme, a body of work, a style, and I do so out of enthusiasm and admiration. I don't know if I could have a main character I could not like or identify with. It's not that I am not able to deal in my fiction with the horrors of the world, but the main character could not be an executioner. I don't think that my creative process works that way. I write to share."

Someone in the audience asked, "What does it mean to you to be an intellectual today?"

Sontag: "When the word 'intellectual' is pronounced, I substitute it with 'writer' because that's what it is, and myself, I react not as a writer, but as a citizen, as any citizen reacts to public things. However, if I do not have firsthand access to the event in order for me to form my own opinion, I do not talk. I prefer silence."

"Silence? But you always spoke and took public stands on the major events of the past years, didn't you?" someone interjected.

Sontag: "I did not speak about what was happening in Yugoslavia until I had been there, and I did go to have information first-hand, be a witness and ask people how they felt.[46] 9/11 was a terrible crime, but after my piece in *The New Yorker*,[47] I was to be drawn and quartered, stripped of my citizenship. The *New Republic* went as far as putting me in the same bag as Hussein with 'What they have in common: they both wish the destruction of America.' The atmosphere of conformity is drastic. I've never been attacked so much in my whole life even during the anti-war movement of which I was one of the founders. As for Iraq, I'm appalled and horrified because I have from a sure source that all is imminent, decided. I have it from authority. Everything is in the works . . . only logistical details are being worked out."

Q: "What do you feel when you write?"

Sontag: "Good question. To write feels as if I were rowing my frail boat to the very big ocean, and that ocean is made up of words, language, fragments of words. It's a great adventure, a great challenge. Writing is a tremendous journey in which you get lost. Yes, lost. Sailing his frail Chinese junk, Halliburton had disappeared in the Pacific Ocean. Writing fiction was no different from a risky sea-faring journey; it was the great and challenging adventure of the mental traveler."

On November 3, 2008, David Rieff was at the Village Voice to read from *Swimming in a Sea of Death: A Son's Memoir*,[48] his sober recollections of the last months of his mother's life.

Three years earlier, on January 17, 2005, at her burial at the Montparnasse Cemetery in Paris, as one of her friends was quoting Emma in *The Volcano Lover*, it was the voice of Susan Sontag we heard: "I will not allow that I was moved by justice rather than love, for justice is also a form of love."

Native American Renaissance
STORYTELLING AS REPOSSESSION
James Welch, Louise Erdrich, Sherman Alexie, David Treuer

"In American literature there's a lot happening.
How wonderful it is to hear Native American writers,
African American writers and writers from other
countries. All those diverse voices make up the
country, make it whole."
—GRACE PALEY,
    Village Voice reading, March 28, 1999.

"To tell stories in order to keep alive,
and through stories, the history
 and all the ghosts are part of it."
—SHERMAN ALEXIE,
    Village Voice reading, January 9, 1997.

The first event centering Native American authors at the Village Voice took place in 1986 with the presentation of an anthology of contemporary Native American poetry, *The Clouds Threw This Light*,[1] brought together and edited by the polyglot Edouard Roditi.[2] Opening the reading, he expressed his regret that the collection was not multilingual, "an impossible task," he admitted, "since it included seventy-seven poets from as many different tribes and languages."

The poems he read in English highlighted "the importance given to the land in which Native Americans had lived for four thousand years without exhausting its bountiful resources." One of their aspirations was a return to their roots, as seen in William Jay Smith's iconic poem "The Tall Poets" with "Come down here to join me in my pirogue / and together we shall thread our way through the innumerable / Louisiana bayous / . . . / the land of my birth."[3] Roditi spotted Jill Scott Momaday in the audience, the daughter of N. Scott Momaday, the first Native American author to be awarded the prestigious Pulitzer Prize (1969) for his novel *House Made of Dawn*[4] and, unceremoniously, he began to recite her father's poem "The Wound": "The force lay there in the rupture of the flesh, there in the center of the wound." This wound of the land had become the source of a new Indigenous literature that started to flourish in the 1980s: the Native American Renaissance.

At the time, in France this writing genre was hardly visible, and, if published at all, was rarely identified as such. However, in 1992 a young editor, Francis Geffard,[5] with a passion for Native American cultures and arts, created the collection he called *Terre indienne*. Over the years, he would bring most of the great voices of the Native American Renaissance to the public eye here.

James Welch

> "Are you Indian? And, if you're not Indian,
> Who are you?"
> —WELCH, Village Voice reading, May 10, 1992.

Raised on two different Montana Indian reservations, James Welch was at the Village Voice on May 10, 1992, to launch the French translation of *Winter in the Blood*,[6] eighteen years after its American publication. Having left his reservation in central

Montana, the unnamed protagonist of the novel is without a future. After many years away and most distraught, he returns home seeking to reconnect with his roots from the past. He goes to meet the oldest man on the land, Yellow Calf, a blind yet wise hermit who, living alone in close contact with nature, embodies the memory of the place, its history, and even the lives of its successive generations.

A gentle man with sad eyes, but a big, illuminating smile, Welch read the poignant passage of his main character's visit to

Odile, James Welch, and his French translator Michel Lederer, May 10, 1992. © C. Deudon

this venerable old figure. Among other stories of the reservation, Yellow Calf describes the massacre of their tribe, the Blackfeet. In that terrible Montana winter of 1870,* Yellow Calf witnessed its horror, but set out to save the life of a woman who turns out to be the protagonist's once beloved but now dead grandmother.

"The process of cultural recovery has started," Welch told us. Slowly reconnecting with his origins, this wanderer recognizes the elder as his own grandfather. "Identity and knowledge of the tribal self are linked," the author concluded. We might add that, uprooted and exiled from their homeland over so many years, the Native American who longs to return to their origins will become a recurring motif in Welch's novels and Native American literature in general.

Q: "Do you have someone in your family who witnessed the massacre referred to by this old man?"

Welch: "My great-great-grandmother lived to be so old that I learned from her what she had seen in that time when reservations were not formed. They lived a nomadic life, and she told my father many stories about it, including the massacre of a village in which everyone was killed and the lodges burned down with bodies inside. It was these details that haunted me as I was writing my novel *Fools Crow*.[7] I tried to set a record of those events and of their consequences, and, among them, the worsening of the relations between Indians and whites, but also the strife they occasioned between tribes, tearing them apart. Writing *Fools Crow* from the point of view of an Indian was my attempt at an oral history of that time, even though I wrote it in the European form of a novel."

---

* The author refers to the Marias Massacre of the Piegan Blackfeet Native peoples that took place on January 23, 1870, in Montana Territory, when two hundred Blackfeet, mostly women, children, and older people, were killed by the US Army.

Q: "Writing your novels in English, do you lose something of the way you want to convey ancestral stories or describe Indian life?"

Welch: "Indians don't use oral traditions anymore. We write like Americans; we put the work into the form the American people can read. Do not forget that most Native American writers are not full-blooded Indians, but mixed blood from European descent, and therefore, are bicultural. However, every Native American writer is influenced by their own tribal language. The naming of each detail of the environment and of the reservation life, apprehended in the tribal language, gives a density to the English language which the English word alone cannot give, but words in English do not always translate the meaning and the rhythm the poet carries in his mind."

Q: "Is your novel autobiographical?"

Welch: "Most of my life, I lived away from my reservation and felt a lack of a close connection with the tribal community and even forgot my language which I used to speak growing up on the reservation in the 1940s and '50s. It was a time of forced assimilation: children were torn from their parents and sent to boarding schools, cut off from their roots, their families, their communities, and their languages. For many decades, Indians could not speak their own languages."

Reconnecting with the Native reservation was not easy, and Welch recalled his own experience: "Going home after a long absence, all my body ached, my throat, my bad knees, my head."[8]

Louise Erdrich

"These stories come out of the earth—where the
people are from."
—ERDRICH,
    Village Voice reading, October 1, 2008, quoting from
    The Plague of Doves

The Native American author (mixed German-Chippewa-Ojibwe
blood) of more than twenty novels, collections of poetry, nonfiction, and children's books, many of them awarded literary prizes,
Louise Erdrich stands out as one of the dominant voices of contemporary American literature. To enter her world of fiction is to get
tangled in the skein of her stories about ordinary and extraordinary
Indigenous American characters of varied tribal and multiracial
origins. Grounded in the complex realities of Native American life,
her tales are infused with memories of true historical events and
ancestral lore laced with magical realism and trickster wit.

I vividly recall that spring-like day of February 16, 1988, when
Louise and the Native American writer Michael Dorris, her husband at the time, appeared at the door of the bookshop. Michael
shook hands with me before introducing her, a tall, elegant figure
in a beige trench coat, shyly holding a bouquet of daffodils she
extended with a gracious smile.

Fame had preceded their performance and the place was
packed with people eager to meet this celebrity couple, particularly Louise, the author of *Love Medicine*,[9] her debut novel and a
bestseller in the States that was to set the literary trend of linked
stories in a long narrative.

In her preface to the reading, the scholar Joëlle Rostkowski,
author of *Le renouveau indien aux Etats Unis*,[10] identified the two
authors in light of recent developments in Native American literature. "These new writers," she explained, "are aware of the risk

of being confined to the category 'Indian American literature,' but they are ready to take it on in order to be part of the American literary scene and of the new generation of American novelists. Having attended universities, these young, talented artists are not living on reservations, but live and function in two different universes. Their works have the merit and interest of being a bridge between two different cultures."

"There is some confusion here," the scholar Marc Chénetier interjected, stressing that "American literature is one, *not* divided into different categories. These writers are not Indian writers or Indian American writers, or women writers or male writers; they are *good* writers. I do believe in the specificity of their works, obviously, but it seems that the great features of American literature are those we see in them, namely a prodigious sense of place, space, and voices."[11]

Reacting to Chénetier's reference to "confusion," quick-witted Louise bantered that she was adding even more of it with her fiction characters of Polish and French descent. She first read a short passage from *Love Medicine* in which Lipsha, "her beloved character" and the typical trickster of Native American folklore, tries to resurrect the lost love between his grandparents through the "love medicine" he has concocted. Alas! His potion turns out to be fatal to his Grandpa who, luckily, appears in a dream to his widow, declaring eternal love to her.

Erdrich then followed with an excerpt of magical realism from *The Beet Queen*,[12] depicting a scene in which a mother brings her two children to the fairgrounds where the Great Omar accomplishes stupendous airplane stunts to the amazement of the crowd. Invited to climb into his cockpit, their mother rises into the sky with the pilot, while, powerless and mesmerized, the two children watch the plane disappearing away . . . "soon only a white dot . . . and to vanish." Abandoned, the children now have to face an unknown life, one they could never have imagined before.

Stories of such forsaken youngsters are "a recurring reality of Indian life and theme of Native American literature," Michael Dorris said, introducing his first novel, *A Yellow Raft in Blue Water*.[13] The father of three adopted Native American children, he described his novel as yet another story of abandoned offspring.

On October 1, 2008, after too many years of absence, we were thrilled to welcome back Louise Erdrich for a joint reading with the American scholar and author Peter Nabokov.

In his introduction, their French publisher, Francis Geffard, hailed the growing popularity of Erdrich in France and identified Nabokov as an anthropologist renowned for his fieldwork among hundreds of different native tribes throughout North America.

Nabokov opened his talk by referencing his *Where the Lightning Strikes: The Lives of American Indian Sacred Places*[14] as a book about the ways Native Americans relate to nature: "Their relationship to their land is a dimensional space with which Indian peoples have to negotiate in multiple ways for subsistence. The sacred places are what Pierre Nora in France calls *Lieux de mémoire*, or sites of memory, sacred, because they evoke fear and even terror, feelings connected with a kind of power these places conceal and which has to be handled very carefully."

Asked by someone in the audience if these sacred lands were sites with a specific telluric energy, Nabokov did not go along with such an idea, preferring an approach based on cosmology or cosmic configurations of the landscape. He told us how for Native Americans, "Indian lands are inhabited by the invisible which they say they see, claiming that the white man lives in another land. Yet a sacred place was not necessarily the grandiose landscape we may imagine and could just be a spot of moisture, for moisture means beans, butterflies, tadpoles, rainbows, life, and subsistence."

A woman of decided charisma, Erdrich then introduced *The Plague of Doves*, her twelfth novel, "the one closer to my own life on the reservation where I grew up," she explained. Philip Roth called her recent narrative saga "a dazzling masterpiece," a remark that reminded me of a conversation with Louise years beforehand. She had told me that one of the authors she admired the most was Tolstoy and, once a year, she would reread *Anna Karenina*.

Louise Erdrich at her first Village Voice reading, February 16, 1988. © C. Deudon

The idea for this novel had come to her from a notice in an old newspaper recounting the lynching of three thirteen-year-old Native American boys, hung from a tree where swarms of doves congregated each year, "flying from afar, through woodlands to descend on the fields and destroy harvests." Due to a lack of suspects and witnesses, the boys had been blamed for the murder of an entire family. "I have long been haunted by this story," Erdrich told us.

Set in a fictitious town in North Dakota with the foreboding name of Pluto, it follows the tense relationships among several families whose silences and long-buried secrets have been kept through generations, leaving enduring scars. "This novel," she stressed, "is a series of stories about what happens when there is no justice and what it generates in the town through blood-related generations."[15]

Q: "Where do your [stories] come from?"

Erdrich: "As a child and growing up, I always loved being around the older generation, something common with the older child in the family. I grew up listening not to stories told around campfires, but from people at the power plant, at school laundry, at grandfather's butcher shop. I listened to all kinds of people and not only to Indians, but also to people of other origins.

I'm from the Turtle Mountains, not really mountains, rather hills in North Dakota, the land of Dakota and Lakota. In a very small part of that region, there is a reservation where my mother is from. My grandfather is a Chippewa, and my mother a Métis whose language is a mixture of Cree and French eighteenth-century language, similar to French Canadian. My father is of German origin. I wrote about both sides of my family. My mother and father are both teachers.

Q: "Would you say that the dominant trait of Native American cultures is storytelling?"

Erdrich: "People crave to tell stories. I don't know why, but they do . . . and telling those stories, they laugh a lot. This is why I'm learning Ojibwe, to understand why people laugh so much."

At the end of this session, Louise spoke about her bookshop in Minneapolis, Birchbark Books & Native Arts, an Indian community bookstore for the advancement of Native cultures and languages. At that time, the community was working on a large-sized map of the Indian lands of North Dakota, replacing all the American names with their original ones.

Sherman Alexie

"I think Indian writers write about the kind of
Indians we wish we were,
and I write about the kind of Indians we are,
with all our strengths and weaknesses."
—ALEXIE, Village Voice reading, January 9, 1997.

For his first appearance at the Village Voice on January 9, 1997, Sherman Alexie arrived late, greeting the audience with an explosive "Hello, I'm tired although they bumped me up to first class. Amazing! All night horizontal. Better than my house. I've been traveling around, and I'm 'the Indian du jour.'" [laughter]

The star of the day looked like the Native American of childhood imaginings with his long, jet black hair plaited in the back, a jocular, impressive, but also most endearing young man ready to conquer the world. Over the years, Alexie presented two of his books at our bookstore—his novel *Indian Killer* on January 9, 1997, and *Flight* on May 15, 2008. The following exchanges are taken from these two readings.

As a prologue to his first reading, he described the decor of the place he came from—the Spokane reservation, an isolated community "with many conservative, small-minded people who have their own strange ideas of what Indians are. On the other hand, when I started traveling, I met people who knew little about Indians."

Q: "Touring abroad, do you find a difference between reactions at home and those of European audiences?"

Alexie: "In my reading tours I have more questions about my hair than about my writings, and when I travel abroad and end up on a panel discussion, usually I'll be the only American with a bunch of international folks. Everyone is just hammering on the US which they hate, and they just go on and on. . . . One of the great ironies is that here I am the only American, and an Indian at that, suddenly feeling patriotic and who ends up defending the US. [laughter] I've never been more of a patriot than abroad. Then, I feel that it's time to go home. so that I can start hating my country again. [laughter] Oh Dreamland! The rage to return to it!"

Q: "How did oral tradition shape your own voice?"

Alexie: "I grew up in two different traditions in my house: one the Buffalo, the bully, all alcoholic liars, and the other one, Coeur d'Alene, the female side of my family, a sacred traditional environment far more involved in the daily culture, ceremonial tradition, powwows and the rest of it. Its emblem is the salmon . . . [looking around the audience] the sleek and persistent salmon. [laughter] It makes me feel so good to hear so much laughter. I grew up on the Rez, in federal government housing, and these stories of the people I grew up with end up in a bookstore in Paris! It feels like an epic journey! It also feels vaguely silly, like all human endeavors being vaguely silly."

Q: "What about the salmon?"

Alexie: "Yes, to come back to the reservation—a dam was built upstream on the river, precisely the part of the river that flows through the reservation, and the dam eliminated the salmon—the very focus of our cultural, religious, and economic life, and now there is no salmon. We fought the Washington Water Power and they had to pay the reservation millions of dollars in damages. But mostly we lose. There is also uranium mining on the reservation; employment rose dramatically, but cancer is also on the rise."

Q: "Are structural and mining projects imposed on reservations or negotiated?"

Alexie: "The situation of Indians comes down to treaties. Every Indian nation signed a peace treaty with the federal government. We agreed to quit fighting in return for certain rights: hunting rights, fishing rights, land rights, mining rights, the right to determine our economic future, the right to be a sovereign nation. According to those treaties, we are supposed to exist as nations within the nation of the US. We are supposed to be separate and equal."

Q: "And on the ground, how is it going?"

Alexie: "Well, you guessed it. The reality is something else. What happened is that the American government threw tribes on lands they thought totally useless, but, in their infinite wisdom, they put Indians on lands which were rich in minerals and oil. [laughter] Over fifty percent of oil deposits are on Indian lands: seventy percent of uranium deposits, twenty percent of ancient forests, all together representing a GNP superior to any country in the world. Well, the US government couldn't let us have rights over those; it would mean that we would have serious political power. As a result, no treaty has ever been honored, and our lives are a continued fight to win pieces, bits, of treaties."

Q: "You've written a number of books for young adults. Did you read much in your boyhood?"

Alexie: "I read a lot very early on, and I read everything from Steinbeck to Stephen King. People in my family knew that I loved books, and my grandma gave me books all the time. She spoke English, but did not write it or even read it well.

She bought books by the cover and bought all the ones with an Indian on the cover [laughter], most of them being Indian romances with warriors. When I got to college, I took a poetry writing class and my professor, a Chinese man, guided me through contemporary Native American poetry. I was twenty years old, and nobody had ever shown me anything written by an Indian. The book was four hundred pages long, and I read it through and through in one night. I was just amazed. I had no idea that any-body wrote about our lives this way. I read the poem 'Oh Uncle Adrian, I'm in the Reservation of My Mind' by Adrian Louis.

I read it and that was it. . . . [pensive pause] That was it! That night, I wrote five poems, and I've never stopped since. I still think I live in poems. I wrote seven drafts the past couple of days in France . . . but forgot them on the train!"

Q: "Is poetry your religion?"

Alexie: "I question everything, I don't believe in any God. I believe in stories. They are my gods."

David Treuer

> "People tend to read Indian American fiction as a
> work of anthropology. I want to unhinge my books
> from that kind of reading."
> —TREUER, Village Voice reading, May 15, 2008.

At the time of his reading at the Village Voice on May 17, 2002, David Treuer was the youngest of the Native American writers featured in this chapter and the author of two novels, *Little* (1995) and *The Hiawatha* (1999).[16] He was the son of an Ojibwe mother and a father whose family had fled Austria and Nazism to immigrate to the US in 1938. After a wandering life he met his future wife, a

Native American woman, and together they settled on her Leech Lake Reservation in Northern Minnesota.

In *Rez Life: An Indian's Journey Through Reservation Life* (2012), Treuer provides a close portrait of his father: "Here (on the Rez), [he] felt safe for the first time in his life. More than that, he felt he had found, with his new friends and new family, something that had eluded him all the years before. He devoted his life (and still devotes it) to the community he has come to call his own, and is

David Treuer, May 17, 2002. © C. Deudon

as passionate today about the rights and respect owed to Indians as he was when he moved to Indian country in the 1950s."[17]

In his introduction to the author, Francis Geffard highlighted the originality of his work, explaining that "only recently, a Native American writer such as David Treuer could tell Indian stories outside the Native American context and its myths."

A slender man with the look of an adolescent, his piercing dark eyes behind small round glasses, Treuer read the first chapter of his novel *The Hiawatha*. It opens with the unforgettable scene of a fawn gone astray in a parking lot where homeless people let it wander freely. But a gentle hand on its fur soon startles it. "In an instant, it is running. It jumps once, and then again. In two leaps it is over the fence. . . . The men watch the deer bound down the weedy and trash-strewn slope to the freeway and into the traffic. . . . The deer is dead."[18]

Simon, the novel's protagonist, witnesses this frightening scene on his way to a reunion with his mother he has not seen during the ten years he has been in prison. The fate of the deer seems to foreshadow the horrific revelation to come that he was the one who murdered his own brother.

Q: "In the scene you've just read, there is no lead indicating that the mother and the son are Indians. Could the deer stand symbolically for the destiny of Native Americans?"

Treuer: "People tend to read Indian American fiction as a work of anthropology; they think that Indian American novels show what it's like to be an Indian whether on a reservation or in the city. But nobody says, 'Ah, I've just finished Proust, and I know exactly what it was like in Paris in 1902 and what it's like to be French.' Nobody would say that because it's idiotic. I want to unhinge the book from that kind of reading. I want a book that you couldn't use to comment on what life is like. Stendhal compared the work of the writer to that of a mirror drawn along a path. But it's much more than that. It's not landscape portraiture. What we have here is something brand new."

Q: "What do you mean by 'brand new'?"

Treuer: "We think and see through very narrow channels. I say 'Indian' and, immediately, there are certain things that will occur in most people. When I moved to Minneapolis, I noticed the degree to which people did not want to see Indians and did not see them. Their eyes would skip the Indian over because he did not fit their fantasy."

Q: "You mean a denial of Indian existence?"

Treuer: "To people, the word 'Indian' summons up more a concept than a geographical reality. To us, it evokes reunions with family and friends on reservations amidst immensities, wondrous spaces, but it also evokes what someone recently told me: 'We have less of everything.' For my part, I consider that we have more of everything—more poverty, more skills to keep our heads above water, more laws, but also more resilience and resistance, more intensity in relationships, more desperate tragedies.

Something is happening today. Children claim their Indian past more than ever, but they tend to keep lower standards. I'll say to them: 'Strive for the best and get personal . . . don't go on repeating 'I'm Indian,' but say, 'This is my life, my personal life.'"

Q: "You put the accent on the personal, the individual, rather than on being 'Indian.' How can Native American literature reflect this without losing its specificity?"

Treuer: "For me, writing became an opportunity to get into the individual, allowing surprise and revelation, but this can only happen through the writer's freedom to show that his character's life is significant for him alone. If my character has made a mistake, like Simon in this novel, for instance, it's not because he's Indian, not because the family moved to the city, not because of this or that. There's no good reason for what he did. There's no compelling rationale for what he did: murder his brother. It is his deep personal tragedy. That's what it is."[19]

"Me and you . . . we need some kind of tomorrow."*

OPEN WOUNDS IN
AFRICAN AMERICAN LITERATURE

Jake Lamar, John Edgar Wideman, Paule Marshall,
Barbara Chase-Riboud, Jayne Cortez, Sapphire, Toni Morrison

"As writers, what we do is remember.
And to remember this world is to create it."
—TONI MORRISON

During an interview in Nanterre, on the outskirts of Paris in 2011, Toni Morrison traced the relatively recent existence of the African American novel back to the folklore of the West African storyteller, the griot.[1] For three centuries, African Americans had used music and coded songs to communicate among themselves and pass on traditions from one generation to another. "But," she explained, "when spirituals, gospels, blues, and jazz became world music, losing their specificity as guardians of the past, then the novel became an absolute necessity to keep their tradition threatened to be erased and made invisible, and revisit the history of slavery not from the point of view of the conqueror, but from the point of view of the conquered, told in an imaginative way."

---

* From Toni Morrison's Beloved. Full quote is: "Me and you, we got more yesterday than anybody. We need some kind of tomorrow." (New York: Picador USA, 1987).

This is what the African American postwar novelists Richard Wright and James Baldwin had done, showing in their novels and essays the social and mental ravages of racism born out of slavery. Among other factors, their writings sowed the seeds of the civil rights movement that was to bring on its culminating act of 1964, raising hopes of an equal, nondiscriminatory society.

Yet, by the 1990s, the picture of African American life, as depicted by an emerging generation of African American writers, bore little resemblance to the promises of this landmark law. The roots of racism lay deep, and if this could not be expressed overtly anymore, it nevertheless persisted, morphing into new forms and expressions that included "innuendoes," "power play," and "humiliations," as Jake Lamar reminded us at the Village Voice.[2]

Jake Lamar

> "Fiction allows one to go below the surface and explore the underlying consciousness of being Black and facing racism."
> — LAMAR, Village Voice reading, April 25, 1999.

We have already met the author of *Bourgeois Blues*,[3] a Harvard graduate and a journalist for *Time* magazine. He belonged to the generation who had grown up with promises of civil rights increasingly tinged with disillusionment.

A major voice of African American expatriates in Paris, Jake has continued to live in a multicultural northern Paris neighborhood, where he observes the racist remnants of France's colonial past while continuing to scrutinize his native land from a wider angle. Though his novels and thrillers are filled with resilient African American characters, they are often set in a country resoundingly beset with innate racism.

On April 25, 1999, Jake launched his second American novel *Close to the Bone*[4] at the Village Voice, introduced by Bob Swaim, an American film director living in France.[5] The two had met at a prior Village Voice reading, and it was clear that their shared passion for movies would keep them close. As well a writer of screenplays, Swaim praised the cinematic style of Lamar "who could spin a damned good yarn. His novels speak of racism, but they essentially speak to all of us, regardless of race, creed, color, or gender."

Jake Lamar opened his talk by telling us that he had added "a new confusion to the problem of racial identities" in his latest novel. Among three young couples, one of his main characters, Walker Dupree, is mixed-blood, born of a white father, a fact he conceals from his girlfriend Sadie Broom, a middle-class African American.

Learning that Walker is not only Black, Sadie blurts out that she will not have mixed-race children, arguing that "she would not feel close to them." Her admission shocks Walker, but another irritant soon comes into play with the O. J. Simpson affair that was exacerbating the American race debate at the time. Contrary to prevailing public opinion, Sadie defends Simpson, claiming that "if the victim were a Black woman, America wouldn't care."

A woman in the audience wondered why the author had wanted to show racism in the particular light of a mixed-race and middle-class character.

Lamar: "Racism has been underlying the past two hundred years of American history, but it varies with generations. African American literature has traditionally shown blatant, oppressive racism, especially in novels taking place in the past. Of course, with a new Black middle class, there is no doubt that the issue has become all the more complex and subversive, and this is what I'm trying to show."

Q: "How was this novel received in America?"

Lamar: "In America, all these nuances, ambivalences, complexities are immediately understood. But there are other elements now in America playing a part in the debate, such as the politically correct. In one case, the reading my publisher organized for me long in advance was cancelled at the last minute by a bookseller in Chicago for fear of offending her customers. Sometimes, readers do not know what to make of the situations I create in my works."

Q: "How would you describe those 'situations'?"

Lamar: "I deal with ambivalences in my Black characters who question their place in the world and what I call 'barriers of consciousness,' like Sadie's biased approach to the Simpson trial. The traditional divide between Black and white doesn't take into consideration the new Black middle class with the relatively new Black access to professional jobs. Such ambivalences require a more nuanced approach to racism which, I admit, knocks people off kilter."

Q: "Do you think that living abroad gives you the distance to treat the issue of American racism differently?"

Lamar: "Certainly, living in France gives me a more detached perspective on America, and following the blown-up O. J. Simpson affair, I saw the weirdness of America more acutely. The O. J. Simpson affair is a thread running through the book, and at the end of it, my characters are at one another's throats over him, reflecting the reality of the country. People were consumed by its every detail. Following the case from France, I had some distance, allowing me to be more interested in the effects such a trial was having on people. Perceptions of racism are varied and complex, and in fiction you can examine those perceptions from many different angles."

Q: "For a long time, the debate on racism was inseparable from the class issue, yet the title of your memoir *Bourgeois Blues* clearly implies that the access of African Americans to middle- and even upper-class jobs doesn't protect them from racist attacks. Has the traditional pairing of class-race become obsolete?"

Lamar: "True. For a long time, race has been assimilated to class. And there is a term that defines this pairing of race and class: it is the 'caste system.' The heritage of slavery, segregation, and lynching are in the many stereotypes and images that stick, that are glued to your skin. Caste consciousness is not just about color or class; it has to do with all those images brought to you from the past."

Q: "There are many African Americans working in the film industry today; they are film directors and actors. Do you think that their films have changed or are changing the way Americans look at African Americans?"

Lamar: "Right. There are many African Americans in American films, but generally those actors prefer to play neutral roles. The movie business, being what it is, wants to show stereotypes out of which two are common: the Black man as a macho thug out of the hood, or the nonthreatening type, a clown. Both are the defining stereotypes, and the business wants images that can be easily digested. . . . Complexity doesn't go well with Hollywood, but for me it's the reverse. The more complex, the better."

John Edgar Wideman

> "Listen to the music that young people create.
> Really listen."
> —J.E. WIDEMAN,
>   Village Voice reading, February 2, 1992.

In early February 1992, John Edgar Wideman read from his gripping memoir *Brothers and Keepers*,[6] just published in France under the title *Suis-je le gardien de mon frère?* The Biblical reference, more obvious in French, points to the responsibility, even guilt, the author, a university professor, feels toward his younger brother who has been given a life sentence in prison. They were both raised in the same family but their destinies stand at the two extremes of the social spectrum. How did this happen?

To begin with, Wideman explained that this portrait was an "attempt to free my brother from his prison and to help free myself from a metaphysical prison, which is part of growing up Black in America."[7] The passage he chose to recite was the long, passionate, and angry "epitaph" written by his brother, his recollections of his involvement in the 1968 protest events he had organized at school in a moment of exaltation, but only ended up with "locks and cops."

Q: "Did you yourself take part in that movement?"

Wideman: "I was naive politically then. I was starting an African American studies program at U. Penn that was important to me as I tried to bring more Black students into my university. I was working on it and writing my books at the same time. I had no idea of my brother's involvement in those militant activities at school. When I began to write this book, during my visits to him in prison, I learned about him, and I learned about myself. So, in the process I discovered that my brother had a certain kind of wisdom, a certain kind of understanding."

Q: "Writing this book did not resolve your brother's predicament; he is still in prison. But did it help you in any way?"

Wideman: "Discovering this side of my brother's life was an education for me because, had I been alert and conscious at the time, I would have seen the connections between what I was trying to do at the level of the university and what he was doing on the street, and we could have been allies. But the distance between us corresponded probably to the distance between the heads of the Black Power movement and the actual lumpen proletariat in the street, workers and poor people rebelling in different fashions . . ."

Q: "The picture you describe of the African American predicament today is very dark, especially in your latest novel, *Philadelphia Fire*.[8] How do you see the future?"

John Edgar Wideman, Village Voice reading, February 1992. © C. Deudon

Wideman: "The present is a nightmare, and it's very discouraging as we don't see many good signs. America is a big place, and there are Black families that are very strong, Black families that are middle-class and Blacks in the lower class that are confronting their problems in a communal way. There are new schools and other improvements. However, in the face of the tremendous deterioration of the actual conditions in which Black people live and of the general breakdown of the cities, America is tied up, becoming like South America: the middle class is fast disappearing, and between the Haves and the Have-Nots there is a wasteland, and Black people are in there. And if you want another witness to that, listen to the music that young people create. Really listen."

Q: "Do you have in mind rap music and such groups as the ones included in your recent novel *Philadelphia Fire?* The lyrics are very violent. What is your approach to this new expression of anger?"

Wideman: "Like I am towards most things, I'm ambivalent about it. I listen to that music and enjoy most of it. I hear in those groups traditions I do know about and watched them develop over time, and so I have a perspective, historical in that sense, and I'm very excited by this continued tradition. Whether I like them or not, they are performing a crucial function in the culture."

Q: "What kind of function? Could you elaborate?"

Wideman: "Such popular creations represent spaces cut out for ourselves to try to preserve something basic of the African American culture. They may not be all good, but it's a space we need to create to keep a distance from the immense pressure and immense danger we are exposed to. People did not go out and create music simply for fun. It came out of a sense of being in danger: 'I'm not listened to'; 'Nobody cares'; 'My face is not on the TV screen'; 'My voice is not in the music I

listen to'... [raising his voice in anger] 'Who am I?' [pause]
Yet opening the door and inviting them to marry my daughter?
NO. [laughter] You sense my ambivalence about this. But it's
a hope, and it's coming not only from the street but also from
younger people. And how many lifelines have we managed
to throw down to them? That's how they make that music
themselves."

For a long time, African American literature meant signature
works, such as those of the Harlem Renaissance poet Langston
Hughes or of the novelists Richard Wright and James Baldwin.
With the women's movement of the 1970s, feminist presses resurrected a prestigious tradition of eminent Black female writers more or less forgotten, including Zora Neale Hurston, the
Harlem Renaissance author of *Their Eyes Were Watching God* (1937);
Gwendolyn Brooks, the first African American poet to be awarded
the Pulitzer Prize for Poetry (1950); or Lorraine Hansberry, whose
play *A Raisin in the Sun* was produced on Broadway in 1959. Similar
to these prestigious female writers, Paule Marshall, the author
of *Brown Girl, Brownstones* (1959) was rediscovered by the Feminist
Press in 1981.[9]

Paule Marshall

In her novel, Marshall introduces this work as an intimate dialogue of a young African American woman of West Indian origin.
Selina is coming of age in the New York of the 1930s when jazz
was all the rage. We follow her through her search for a real
identity, her sexual awakening and her encounter with the brutality of racism as she strives to conciliate disparate selves and
become whole.

On April 22 of 1983, Marshall was invited to Paris by her French
publisher to launch the translation of her novel *Fille noire, pierre*

sombre[10] at the Village Voice. She introduced it as a "breakthrough" back in the 1950s. Then, it was rare to find a young, Black female character with a consciousness of her inner life and a determination to overcome seemingly impossible obstacles in order to grow into her own person.

Q: "What inspired you to write this book at that moment?"
Marshall: "It was my hunger for literature. I had been a voracious reader since my younger age. I could identify with heroes and heroines of all the books I read, but I could feel there was something missing. I was thirteen when I picked up an anthology of poetry in my neighborhood library and opened it to the photo of a Black poet. I read a couple of poems; they were talking directly to me. There was even a poem about passionate love between a Black man and a Black woman, a theme that was not present in literature before."

"Yet," she added, "I had likewise discovered the 'miracle of literature' through my mother's imaginative and colorful ways of speaking, especially when she was with her Barbadian friends talking in Bajan Creole, a mix of English and Creole."

Selina's decision to leave exhilarating New York for her parents' native island where she has never been is thus intimately connected with this maternal language which, Marshall stressed, was her mother's "homeland." From it, she wanted to capture something of the poetry that imbued her with power and spirit in an attempt to bring together her own broken identity.

Whereas in the 1960s it was vital for the African American women to join the ranks of their Black brothers to defend the cause of the civil rights movement, the feminist movement of the 1970s was also a turning point in literature by African American women. Female writers started to explore more personal issues, from the family and social milieus to the intimate self, encompassing original writing styles that extended from fiction to poetry.

In her novel *Sally Hemings*, the writer and sculptor **Barbara Chase-Riboud** resurrects the life of the female slave in the service of Thomas Jefferson.[11] He had made her his lover, the woman who bore him at least six children, but "What was her role in history? What was her personal life like, what were her feelings toward Jefferson?" and "How could she have freely loved the man who had the power to free her, but never did?" the author wonders out loud.

In her anthology of jazz poetry *Firespitter*[12] activist, poet, and performance artist **Jayne Cortez** cries out in anger on behalf of Black women experiencing both racial and sexual violence. In her well-known poem "If the Drum Is a Woman," she pleads in a jazz invocation: "don't abuse your drum, don't abuse your drum, don't abuse your drum . . ."

Then, on April 6, 2004, came **Sapphire**, a bold, young, and unconventional New Yorker to present her novel-poem *Push*[13] that recounts the life of Precious, an illiterate, unwed mother from Harlem, sexually abused since childhood by her father. Her schoolteacher gives her a chance to change her life by teaching her how to read and write. The story of Precious is bleak, but the girl's language—"oral speak," with its limited syntax and vocabulary—is transformed by her colorful imagery and darting rhythms. As she performed a passage from this stream-of-consciousness dialect, Sapphire conjured up Precious's language that metamorphizes a dismal fate into fireworks of images, sounds, and a liberating tempo.

All these voices continued a long tradition of eminent Black female writers, forgotten, resurrected, and now flourishing, with the Nobel Prize in Literature awarded to Toni Morrison in 1993, giving African American women literature worldwide exposure and long overdue recognition.

Toni Morrison

"It is language that seals and reclaims the singularity
of existence."

—TONI MORRISON

Toni Morrison was invited to France in September 1989 to launch
the translation of her novel *Beloved*,[14] winner of the Pulitzer Prize
the year beforehand.[15] Her publisher had planned such a full
schedule of events that we welcomed his offer to organize a signing in place of the reading we had been eagerly expecting.

Morrison's novel about the tragedy of Sethe, a slave woman
driven to kill her small daughter to save her from being sold back
into slavery, captured the hearts and imagination of French readers.
Morrison had become the stellar figure of American literature in
France.

However, well before becoming world famous for her prestigious literary awards, this New York editor and writer used to drop
by the Village Voice whenever she was in Paris visiting friends and
fellow editors. A distinguished, beautiful woman, Morrison was
an imposing yet highly accessible presence.

Back in the 1980s, Morrison was hardly known in France but
was a name among our American customers, and her first novel,
The Bluest Eye (1970), was taught in international schools in Paris
and the French university system. We carried all her published
titles in the bookstore, modest paperbacks, I confess, yet she had
always graciously signed them and never failed to buy copies of
her own books as gifts for her close friends here.

Among them were Michel and Geneviève Fabre, scholars in
African American studies.[16] One night they invited me over for
a dinner with Morrison. Their house was located in one of those
narrow cobblestoned lanes in Paris, bordered by small gardens
full of fragrant flowers and plants and illuminated by antique

street lamps. It was a cozy evening, the four of us sitting around an inviting dinner table. I didn't talk much, eager to listen to the conversation on their respective works and mutual acquaintances, often interspersed with vivid anecdotes about the scholars and writers they knew. The chatting was light and lively, spiced with

Barbara Hendricks and Toni Morrison, September 7, 1989. © Roberta Fineberg

in-jokes—not always clear to me, but setting off great bursts of laughter in Morrison.

The grand launch of *Beloved* in Paris, planned by her publisher Christian Bourgois, included our afternoon signing session that attracted a long line of readers happy to exchange a few words with the author, followed by a recital at the Théâtre des Champs-Elysées.

That night, accompanied by her friend Barbara Hendricks, the renowned operatic soprano, Toni Morrison read excerpts from *Beloved* in front of "le Tout-Paris" and an international audience of intellectuals and artists. In turn, Hendricks rendered the same passages in French that alternated with her singing of Black spirituals.

In her memoir *Lifting My Voice*, Hendricks meaningfully revives the duo's performance: "Toni Morrison read her own words with such passion . . . I tried to read mine with all the same involvement, as if I were singing."[17]

Shadow Lands

THE HERE AND THERE IN
AMERICAN STORIES OF EXILE

André Aciman, Amy Tan, Jamaica Kincaid,
Dinaw Mengestu, Junot Díaz, Azar Nafisi

There are as many literatures of exile as there are individual experiences of it, but all of them are infused with the memory of an elsewhere, glimpses of a former life that slip into focus in strangely kaleidoscopic ways. The nature and force of this memory always vary, while the significance of exile will often depend on whether writers are immigrants themselves or second- or third-generation children of their adopted country. How they transmute this raw material from the past into personal narratives or fictional stories is the essence of this chapter on the United States as a land of exile.

André Aciman

> "Exile is to inhabit a world of shadows.
> Shadows of memory, of thoughts,
> of cities, of selves."
> —ACIMAN, Village Voice reading, November 5, 2010.

Few authors have captured the dual aspect of exile as André Aciman has: a life experienced as a reality shifting between two worlds—the

here and there, the now and then—suddenly perturbed by fragments of memories that cling to you like slivered "shadows."

André Aciman, the New York–based writer, son of French-
speaking Sephardic Jews, was born in Alexandria, the Greek city
of ancient Egypt and a place of exile.* Its founder, Alexander the
Great of Macedon, a foreigner who had crossed several lands to
conquer this kingdom, had also envisioned his port of call, his
namesake Alexandria, as a city open to travelers, passersby, and
would-be settlers. During his reign, the memories of these wanderers were carefully consigned and thus kept alive in thousands
of papyrus scrolls amassed in its Great Library, the other visionary
dream of Alexander, eventually fully realized by his followers.

It is said that his city was burnt down but remained a symbol of
Hellenic knowledge and literary treasures in the ancient world, even
during its decline. Yet in the middle of the twentieth century, the
happy medley of civilizations, cultures, and religions was to vanish.

In 1966, along with his parents, the fifteen-year-old Aciman was
forced to leave his home there, the place to which "his mind would
always turn." In his essay "Alexandria: The Capital of Memory,"
Aciman revisits his native land thirty-five years later, but he remains
resolutely attached to the Alexandria of his youth, claiming "I'll
always end up there, even if I never come back," an echo of the great
Alexandrian poet C. P. Cavafy's poem on exile: "For you won't find
a new country, won't find a new shore, the city will always pursue
you, / and no ship will ever take you away from yourself."[1]

André Aciman was at the Village Voice on November 5, 2010,
to speak about his new novel *Eight White Nights*.[2] The French music
critic and producer Renaud Machart introduced him, referring to
his friend's complicated relationship with Paris, describing his
novel as a Proustian musical piece.

---

* After leaving Egypt, Aciman was raised in Italy and then France, where he felt
he belonged; denied a residency permit, he left for the United States where he has
lived since.

In fact, the two had met at a Proust evening in one of New York City's reputed concert halls. To Machart's surprise, the place was bursting at the seams. On the stage were several notable speakers, including the composer and diarist Ned Rorem who had invited him as the French translator of his memoir *The Paris Diary* (1966).

There was also a man who spoke French the way a native would. Intrigued, Machart rushed out to buy a book by this author, as yet unknown to him. Moved by Aciman's *False Papers: Essays on Exile and Memory*,[3] Machart immediately arranged an interview with him for the French daily *Le Monde*. They were to meet at Straus Park on the Upper West Side, a favorite place of the mysterious writer and often featured in various essays and even on the jacket of his recent novel.

Machart set the scene for us: "It was raining and cold, there was snow and homeless men were lying on benches, and, all around, drug dealers and police cars. It was miserable, and my first words to Aciman when he arrived was, 'I now know what literature is all about: it's about transfiguration.'"[4]

This word "transfiguration" captures the essence of the author's *Eight White Nights* and its surreal atmosphere. Aciman read a passage from it in which his two protagonists, the unnamed narrator and Clara, meet for the first time at a crowded Christmas party in a fashionable Upper West Side apartment. They have come out-side onto the terrace and, standing there in the cold, they look in silence at the enchanting view of snow-topped Manhattan with the "lights speckling the New Jersey shoreline . . . From (their) high perch, the silver-purple city looked aerial and distant and superterrestrial, a beguiling kingdom . . ."[5]

"It is a moment of transformation, the beginning of a romance," the writer commented. "Time is suspended and the narrator and Clara are in a magical sphere," leading to a mesmerizing vision:

"Bellagio," he said.

"What about Bellagio?" Clara asks.

"On special evenings, Bellagio is almost a fingertip away, an illuminated paradise. . . . On other nights, it seems . . . a lifetime away, unattainable. This right now is a Bellagio moment."

"What is a Bellagio moment?" Clara wonders. [. . .]

"Life on the other bank, life as it's meant to be, not as we end up living it. Bellagio, not New Jersey. Byzantium."[6]

Thousands of miles and just as many years separate Manhattan and Bellagio, but, in that brief interval of suspended time, the present and the past coexist together. Surely "a Proustian moment."

"How would you describe such a 'Proustian moment'? As a reverie?" someone in the audience asked.

Aciman: "The narrator is not daydreaming, nor fantasizing; he is more likely thinking in a temporal space which is not inhabited by the present, but which, as in Proust, constantly slips into the present. He is in an 'in-between' or better yet . . . everything is in transit towards *something*."

Q: "You were introduced by your friend as someone having a complicated relationship with Paris. Does it have to do with nostalgia?"

Aciman: "Just before the reading, I had a conversation with a friend who is sitting on the staircase tonight" (the bookstore was packed) "and I was telling him that coming to Paris is troubling to me because it's coming back to a place which should have been home and never was. Coming back is to revive the feeling of a 'rendez-vous manqué.' Every time I come to Paris, it's like being home and it's not home."

Q: "Is Paris one of the 'shadow cities' of your essays?"

Aciman: "There is not only the shadow city; there is the shadow person, the shadow memory, the shadow self. You inherit a life of shadows which is as concrete as the life you live in."

Q: "Does your title allude in any way to Dostoevsky's novella *White Nights*?"

Aciman: "The echo I wanted in my novel was James Joyce's 'The Dead,' probably the most beautiful prose piece of the twentieth century."

Amy Tan

"The language of my novel is typically
the language of my mother. "
—TAN, Village Voice reading, June 2, 2005.

Amy Tan is the author of the bestseller *The Joy Luck Club*,[7] a semi-fictional contemporary novel that plays with the many differences between two generations of Chinese women, those who have come

Odile and Amy Tan, Village Voice reading, June 2, 2005. © Flavio Toma

to America as immigrants, and their daughters, born in the States and Americans above all.

The writer was at the Village Voice on June 2, 2005, to talk about her memoir *The Opposite of Fate: Memories of a Writing Life*.[8] Dressed in a stylish silk outfit, with her two cute Yorkshires pressed against her, Tan introduced her work by objecting to being classified as an author of "ethnic literature": "Some critics have written that I wish to capture the immigrant experience and demystify Chinese culture; the truth is that I write for myself. I write because I enjoy stories and make-believe. . . . I write about secrets, lies, and contradictions. I write stories about life. . . . To be sure, it's a Chinese American life, and it's the only one I've got so far."

After entrusting her little darlings to her husband in the audience, she read an excerpt from the first chapter describing the process by which, as a child and adolescent, born and schooled in the States, she began to perceive everything her mother was not, and all that she herself was, i.e., an American.

"My linguistic style is from California where I was raised. It is my voice, especially in this memoir where there is so much of me growing up in America. Nevertheless, what I try to do here is to look at the language I grew up with. I call it my mother's tongue which is a different kind of English. Her language was full of imaginary, and, I should say, amazing imagery that created a profusion of pictures for me. The language of my characters is typically my mother's voice."

Q: "If your voice is Californian, how can it be that your language is your mother's voice?"

Tan: "My mother was inhabited by anxiety and fears. She believed in the invisible and fateful powers acting upon our lives: How does everything happen? Is it by faith, is it by a curse, is it by your own will or by the action of other people? How does the world happen? The voice is, in a way, the person being in the world."

Insisting on the importance of language in her work, Tan said that one of the reasons she had become a writer was her fascination for it and how it works in so many different ways. Acknowledging the richness of her mother's original, imaginative expressions, the Californian writer Amy Tan told us how she felt lucky to have been raised "in two different forms of language and imagery"—the very core of her writing style. "After my mother's death, as I was starting to work on my new novel, I heard her voice that reassured me with her comforting words: 'I can be your narrator. I do not have to be your mother anymore.'"

Jamaica Kincaid

> "It is writing that saved me."
> —KINCAID, Village Voice reading, January 14, 2000.

In 1966, Jamaica Kincaid, a young Antiguan woman, immigrated from the West Indies to New York. She was seventeen when she turned her back on her native island, abandoning her family and the Creole tongue she hastened to forget, even inventing a name that suited her new self. For twenty years she would not visit her island, that "small place,"[9] fraught with poverty, humiliation, and feelings of jealousy towards her three brothers, all favorites of her mother. As a young girl assigned to look after the youngest of them, she had ignored her task and, instead, immersed herself in a world of books. "In anger, my mother gathered all my books, poured spirits over them and then burned them."[10]

This dramatic turning point led her to choose exile, cutting off all connections with her past and the family that had literally reduced her dream of alternative lives imagined from her readings to ashes.

Nonetheless, "at once familiar and hostile," both island and family would relentlessly capture her imagination, haunting her in book after book as the irreplaceable source of literary inspiration.

A stately woman with an aura of mystery about her, Jamaica Kincaid was at the Village Voice on January 14, 2000, to present My Brother,[11] the companion book to her previous narrative The Autobiography of My Mother,[12] both nonfictional portrayals of her mother and her younger brother. In it she examines in depth the complex and tormented feelings she has towards each one of them.

She read the passage from My Brother that depicts her transit at a Miami airport after leaving Antigua where she has just had the heart-wrenching experience of sitting at the bedside of her thirty-three-year-old brother dying of AIDS "in lonely squalor." Now she is on her way to her beloved snowy garden in Vermont, the home where her husband and children are waiting for her.

Torn between two worlds, Kincaid is tormented by the ambivalence of her memories and conflicting emotions: "I love the people I'm from, and I do not love the people I'm from," she admitted, stating that only through writing could she unravel such contradictions. "I couldn't have become a writer while there among the people I knew best . . . I couldn't have become myself, yet I was one of them, from them. I became a writer out of desperation."

In the late 1970s, her luminous writing talent won her the support of William Shawn, the editor of The New Yorker. "M. Shawn," as Kincaid addressed him, was her ideal reader. "I wrote for him, and whether he liked it or not, it was not important. I just wanted to imagine him reading it. I kept writing for him."[13]

Given this persistence, in her adopted country she grew into a recognizable writer with a unique style, often cited as equally magical and real and yet resisting all canons. A staff member of

The New Yorker, Kincaid was in charge of its "Talk of the Town" for nine years. In 1996, four years after William Shawn's death, she resigned. For her, as for Mavis Gallant, another self-exiled woman and lifetime contributor to this famous weekly, his disappearance marked the end of an era as they had known it.

Dinaw Mengestu

> "We have all those stories that flutter on,
> part of the construction of our identity."
> —MENGESTU,
> Village Voice reading, February 2, 2011.

Dinaw Mengestu was born in Ethiopia during a time of political repression, and only two years old when his family was reunited in the United States. He lived in Paris during the early 2000s, but with the dispersion of the Third Wave of American expatriates, the city had lost its attraction to writers and artists. "The rest of the world turned into Paris, and Paris became more like everywhere else," he despondently wrote in an article for the *Wall Street Journal*[14] in 2008.

Mengestu was at the Village Voice on February 10, 2011, to launch his recent novel *How to Read the Air*,[15] a title as poetic and enigmatic as that of his debut fiction *The Beautiful Things That Heaven Bears*,[16] both critically acclaimed. The novel he presented that night was a story about immigrant lives, but not your usual one: "I find disturbing the ethnic immigration pattern," he stated at his reading. "We become numb to the immigrant narratives; they are known, the journey has already been told."

His next admission was even more surprising: "a couple's narrative," he said, "is another story that needs to be told over and over again." He had in mind the two couples in his new fiction, and particularly the parents of his protagonist Jonas, Ethiopian immigrants who had survived two different perilous journeys to reach America. Aliens in their host country, floating between two languages, they progressively become strangers to each other.

Facing a disintegrating marriage himself with a woman named Angela, Jonas is anxious to understand why and how the marriage of his own parents had dissolved. He remembers "the bursts of violence of his father, his mother, a lost soul, and their lingering, stifling silence" that poisoned his childhood. He recalls the trip they all took to Nashville in an attempt to better know the country where they now live. This, too, turns into a fiasco that marks the end of their marriage. "To understand who they were," Mengestu explained, "could only be done by trying to reconstruct their journey and recreate their lives, a task their son Jonas can only accomplish as a work of imagination he sees as an act of active love toward his parents."

Q: "Why this choice of Nashville?"

Mengestu: "By taking this trip to Nashville, the emblematic place of American folk music, they had wanted to get to the heart of deep America, its history and its popular cultures, so as to strengthen their connection with the US. Instead, it was the irreversible point of non-return of their marriage."

Q: "We never know exactly if we are in a real story or an invented one."

Mengestu: "The boundaries of fiction are incredibly expansive. I want the reader to struggle with the notion of reality. What's reality and what's not? Once you're deeply invested in the story, it becomes the reality, as true to me as any daily experience."

Q: "The scene of the couple's heavy silences, repressed screams, and car honking points to an issue of communication in couples rather than immigrants."

Mengestu: "Right, this novel is about the failing of language in both couples: the parents are not Americans, but immigrants who live between two languages while the young couple, Jonas and his wife, are Americans. The latter have access to knowledge, but they don't have the language to say what and how they feel.

In my novels, I'm not so much concerned with the plot as with the emotional depth of the characters. In both cases, there is an empty space between the characters, one that needs to be occupied by a narrative. Even if they are hard and difficult at times, narratives are vital. Whether true or invented, whether they challenge us or disappoint us, without them we are less formed, less complete. The American model of narrative is the road trip. This one about immigrants is an American book, even if it is an Ethiopian driving."

Junot Díaz

"A culture reveals itself in the narratives
nobody ascribes importance to."
—JUNOT DÍAZ,
   Village Voice reading, February 2, 2009.

The globalizing world and its migratory movements have changed the nature of languages, mixing native and foreign words to suit the needs and circumstances of daily life, but generally speaking, hybrid language is considered "impure" and limited to colloquial expression.

Then came *The Brief Wondrous Life of Oscar Wao*,[17] the novel by the Dominican American Junot Díaz. It marked a turning point in the reader's acceptance of such a literary work, boasting no fewer than two hundred and fifty different Spanish words popping up here and there. He was not the first writer to use Spanglish, the vernacular spoken by Latino people in the States, but this narrative was the first of its kind to be honored with two of the most prestigious American literary awards in 2008, the National Book Critics Circle Award and the Pulitzer Prize for Fiction.

Told again and again that "timely jokes quickly become outdated and footnotes slow down the reading, and furthermore, that there were characters nobody cared about," Díaz did not give up. He told us that "I was desperate to tell this story of a Latino in New Jersey and part of its subculture. I stuck to it."

On the dark, freezing evening of February 2, 2009, our guest writer arrived at the Village Voice after a transatlantic flight delayed by a snow storm. Díaz was exhausted, but opened the event with a few jokes. Evelyn Ch'ien, the author of Weird English,[18] then introduced him, describing his novel as a literary portrayal of the Latino diaspora in America. "His prose," she informed the public, "is representative of cross-cultures, part of our global world. A book like this one can be appreciated only in this time of the global village."

Young and handsome, at once concentrated and exuberant, Díaz read an excerpt from his work after briefly describing the context: its protagonist, Oscar Wao, dead at the beginning of the novel, is remembered by his friends, part of the Dominican diaspora of Paterson, New Jersey. They lament the loss of the fat, lonely boy who, feeling he doesn't belong anywhere, took refuge in his own world of sci-fi and nerd culture.

Ch'ien: "You've just read a passage from the chapter starting with the word 'change,' a key word in your novel. Could you tell us what you mean by it?"

Díaz: "Dynamism is part of the world's happening today. It is in its irrepressible course ahead bent on change, driven by the irrevocable, dynamic march of life. But writers and literature are not part of that map of today's dynamism. My book mostly wrestles with the '80s and feels already outdated. Writers and critics piece together events that have already happened. Where I live, I hear far more complicated language, far more nuanced and cooler than anything I cover. It's far more advanced."

Ch'ien: "What about this 'far more advanced' language? Do you find it at MIT where you teach, or in the Latino diaspora of New Jersey?"

Díaz: "I'm just emphasizing this time gap to explain how Spanish and English are working in my novel. I'll give you an example. If you really want to understand the US at this moment, right now, the biggest mistake you would make would be to read literary fiction. All the weird shit of America is left out of the page. A culture reveals itself in the narratives nobody ascribes importance to."

Ch'ien: "What are those narratives we seem to ignore?"

Díaz: "At school, we had lessons about America, but once home, we would turn on the TV set and a really stupid movie such as *The Planet of the Apes* would appear. Immediately, we would point to the screen [gestures]: This is the America we know, we said to ourselves. This is what gets erased from all the great American novels. I don't think that *The Great Gatsby* can fuck with *X-Men*. . . . For me, junk narratives are probably the most important lens to view the culture and not to forget where we come from, giving access to the American self through throwaway narratives which are not valued, but ask to be watched."

Ch'ien: "Your novel with hybrid language is a challenge to translators, and since we have one in the room, we could ask her to let us hear how your novel language sounds in French."

Laurence Viallet read a passage from her translation and was praised for her audacious and inventive language.

"Where were these strange French words coming from?" some-one asked her.

Viallet: "I turned to a diversity of sources: street language, Verlan, hip-hop, rhythms, rap. . . . We have a very rich and diverse subculture in France, and I just tapped into it."

Concluding his talk, Díaz thanked the audience with these memorable words: "In the US where I spend most of my life, this kind of community is a dying tradition. The presence of an artist in a community is an excuse for the community to celebrate itself."

Azar Nafisi

> "I left Iran, but Iran never left me."
> —NAFISI, Village Voice reading, November 20, 2009.

In 1997, Azar Nafisi came to stay in the United States as an adult, leaving her native Iran for the promised freedom of expression. An elegant woman in a fuchsia suit, her wavy auburn hair framing an open, lively face, Nafisi walked into the Village Voice on November 20, 2009, accompanied by her French publisher, Ivan Nabokov. She was the bestselling author of *Reading Lolita in Tehran: A Memoir in Books*,[19] in which she recounts the experience of secretly teaching her female university students the great works of Western literature censored in Iran.

That evening, another Iranian writer, Goli Taraghi, author of a collection of short stories on exile and now living in France,[20] introduced her. Nafisi was to present her recent book *Things I've Been Silent About: Memories*,[21] a family memoir set in the Tehran of her youth. In fact, her talk would not so much be about the place itself as about books and their significance in her life.

Nafisi opened her reading by placing it under the aegis of Vladimir Nabokov, the Russian American author of *Lolita* whose irrevocable principle was that "readers are born free, and they ought to remain free." With some passion, she too announced that "freedom of expression is constantly on my mind. If it is taken away from a writer, they may continue to write as a protest, but what about the millions and millions of readers in my country and other places who don't have the right to read the kind of books they want to read or to create a space where to debate on them and give rise to exchanges? Books die if they are not read and discussed. This is the very question that has been haunting me for twenty-five years."

Her love of books had started with her father reading her bedside stories from Persian and Iranian epics as well as from all around the world. "Like him," she recognized, "I was very 'promiscuous' when it came to authors and never asked myself where they came from. Over the years and through circumstances, they became my home and that home was in my mind."

Q: "There are many kinds of books. What is the first thing you're looking for in a book?"

Nafisi: "The best achievement of man is to exalt what is unique in us and to join the 'society of mankind,' as Primo Levi remarked. America's values start with Huckleberry Finn who refuses to abandon and give away his friend Jim, the runaway slave. He faces hell and knows it, but he chooses hell rather than separate from his friend."

Q: "What's happening in Iran has no equivalent in the US, but what is your take on the politically correct current in America?"

Nafisi: "There are things in America that are very troubling these days. Everything is so politicized that there is no space anymore for discussions and exchanges. Nowadays, it would seem to me that literature ought to be guided by the respect of conventions, but these are reduced to 'don't': Don't touch this—women—don't touch that—Muslims—and when you hear here in the US some people in the academic world calling Austen, Nabokov, or Fitzgerald reactionaries, you know that they do not understand what fiction is about. It's not about moral diktats; it's about curiosity."

Q: "The word 'curiosity' is vague. Could you give us a few examples?"

Nafisi: "What moves us, writers and readers, is curiosity: I do not know, but I want to know. The very first book I always use in my literary discussions is *Alice in Wonderland*, which is all about learning from wanting to go further to discover what's beyond. . . . Literature is the exact opposite of political correctness; it is irreverent, playful, and questioning. It's a protest against cruelty that comes from blindness, the very essence of Austen's and Fielding's novels. The worst people are people who do not see it and do not want to know."

Hoping to corroborate Nafisi's remarks, a man in the room provided this anecdote: "In 1963, William Shirer, the renowned author of *The Rise and Fall of the Third Reich*, was asked in an interview, 'Could America become fascist?' 'Yes, of course,' he replied, 'but it would be done democratically.'"

After a pause and with some thought, Nafisi confessed, "It's a question I often ask myself."

In conclusion, she added this word of caution: "At a time of great loneliness, when we go through dark times, we should remember the values of great literature and how fragile they are. If we don't pay attention and care, they will wither and die. When Czesław Miłosz, Arthur Miller, Saul Bellow, and Susan Sontag died, what did we do? We should have gone out on the streets, met in libraries, and celebrated them by rereading them and discussing them."

Memories of Silenced Lives

THE HOLOCAUST: NAMING THE INEXPRESSIBLE

Gwen Edelman, Gitta Sereny, Cynthia Ozick,
Art Spiegelman, Nicole Krauss, Daniel Mendelsohn

"Who Shall Bear Witness for the Witness?"[1]

Beginning in the late 1800s, European Jews fled pogroms and then Nazi persecutions, often taking refuge in the Americas, more particularly the United States. Even before the Second World War, Jewish American writers were among the greatest voices of American literature, with their works grounded in urban American settings, yet suffused with ancestral Yiddish ambience. Grace Paley famously acknowledged her own strong Yiddish roots, as did Amy Bloom, vividly recalling at the Village Voice her grandparents who had been immersed in the New York Yiddish culture, enhanced by the mythical Goldfaden Theater, as described in her captivating novel *Away*.[2]

The postwar literature of the Holocaust arose from the urgency to fill the void left by the six million annihilated European Jews and its few stunned survivors. In fact, it took two generations of children and grandchildren to rescue these stories from oblivion. They would be read as survivor narratives of an unprecedented historical cataclysm, and equally important, as attempts to reclaim their individual voices from silence. This literature often takes the form of a journey in search of traces, witnesses and/or memories that bring back the singularity of "the unutterable dismal"[3] of these once-buried lives.

Gwen Edelman

A New York editor and writer, Gwen Edelman lived in Paris for many years, playing an active role in the life of the Village Voice by introducing authors and even starting a small literary magazine *Listen*, destined to enlarge the readership and audience of our bookstore.

She is the author of the novels *War Story*[4] and *The Train to Warsaw*,[5] each with two central characters whose lives are marked by the Holocaust. Both works of fiction open with a train journey that transports its passengers physically and mentally back to their pasts. Edelman presented *War Story* at the Village Voice on September 20, 2001. Her protagonist Kitty is on her way to Amsterdam for the funeral of Joseph, the man she was once passionately involved with. Sitting in the train, she goes over the drama of their love affair, beginning with a chance meeting in a New York bookshop.

Kitty, a young writer, had immediately fallen in love with the older and successful European playwright. Yet her deep devotion could not begin to repair the tormented past of Joseph who, as a young man, had been constantly on the run, hiding from the Gestapo in Vienna and then Amsterdam. Carrying inside "the never-healed scars from his youth," his adult life has been one of wandering from place to place, as well as a flight from any kind of emotional attachment.

Through Kitty's explorations of their complex relationship, Edelman draws the searing portrait of a man locked in a deadly past and living in the stories he carries in his head: "They are his house, his four walls, his ark . . . though he wrote his plays in English, the Austrian-born writer claimed that 'he only exists in his own language with its words and sounds,' a way for him to express the raw feeling of having been expelled from his native land and language," Edelman said.

"Fifty, sixty years after the Holocaust, survivors had not forgotten nor gotten over it," Edelman said, "and it changed the way they saw the world: everything was refracted through their own experience of the war. Everything in their lives was turned upside down, inside out."[6]

On April 20, 2007, Edelman invited her London-based friend, the writer **Gitta Sereny**, to come to the Village Voice to discuss her own work, *Into That Darkness: From Mercy Killing to Mass Murder*,* a classic of Holocaust literature. Edelman prefaced this book as "an examination of conscience through a series of historical interviews Sereny had conducted with Franz Stangl, the Austrian SS commandant of the extermination camps of Sobibor and Treblinka, who, in 1970, was tried and found guilty of co-responsibility for the slaughter of nine hundred thousand people."

Spending a total of seventy hours face-to-face with Stangl in his German prison cell, the author explained that she had tried "to probe the mind of this man who prided himself on having been a perfectionist in his job and a good family man, the two spheres of his life hermetically separated." A few days after her last session with him, Stangl died of a heart attack.

Sereny's interviews once again raise the baffling question that has beset generations since this dire time: How can a human being become the instrument of such overwhelming evil?

---

* Gitta Sereny, *Into That Darkness From Mercy Killing to Mass Murder* (London: Pimlico, 1974, 1995). Sereny was a Viennese-born British journalist, historian, and author of *Albert Speer, His Battle with Truth* (1995), a biography that caused some controversy during her presentation: she was taken to task by some people in the audience for her so-called "complacency" towards Speer, Hitler's Minister of Armaments and War Production.

Cynthia Ozick

The name of Cynthia Ozick immediately summons up "The Shawl," her short story published in The New Yorker in 1980, one of the most visually shattering and unforgettable narratives of the Holocaust in American literature. A Nazi guard has just spotted a fifteen-month-old baby who has gotten loose from the shawl pressed against her mother's breast inside a large coat. Snatching the young child, he hurls her against the electrified barbed wire of the camp in full view of the mother, rendered helpless as she obsessively sucks on her now emptied shawl so as not to scream herself.

Cynthia Ozick was at the Village Voice on September 29, 1988, to launch her new book, The Messiah of Stockholm,[7] a novel in memory of the Polish Jewish writer and artist Bruno Schulz shot dead in the street of Drohobycz* in 1942 by a Gestapo officer. His act was not haphazard, but premeditated, also referred to by Philip Roth in his novella The Prague Orgy (1985).

Accompanied by her husband, Ozick entered the bookstore, looking somewhat shy and disoriented, but my first impression soon disappeared, given the alertness and curiosity in her eyes, magnified by a pair of large, round glasses. Her curly, graying hair pointed to middle age, but her voice was young and melodious.

"The idea of this book," she said in her introduction, "came up during a short stay in Sweden, where it was rumored that Bruno Schulz's presumably lost manuscript had surfaced. Nobody had seen it, nobody knew the content, but according to the myth, Schulz had died leaving behind an unpublished document, now seemingly afloat in Stockholm."

Ozick spoke of being "astounded" by the news, but nothing had followed. She was eager to be back home at her desk imagining this

---

* Drohobycz is one of those cities of Mitteleuropa (Galicia-Volhynia) whose borders kept shifting for centuries. Polish during World War II, after the war, Drohobycz became part of Ukraine, then the Soviet Union. It has been independent since 1991. Back in 1942, its ghetto was the site of the massive extermination and deportation of its Jewish population to death camps.

manuscript, though aware that she should not attempt "to recreate it." "Nevertheless, one night," she said, "it came to me that I was going to do it." And to do so, she had to invent a character called Lars, Schulz's alleged son, adopted in his childhood by a Swede.

Ozick read the surreal passage in which Bruno Schulz's manuscript has been recovered and is now in the hands of this imagined boy. Under his scrutiny of "inky markings—infinitely minute drawings and signs of an unknown alphabet," the unreadable book of loose, battered sheets of paper turns into a "phantasmagorical Drohobycz, invaded by a debauchery of tiny monsters and frantic idols pressed around their Messiah."

Suddenly thrust into a vortex of strong winds, the hay-stuffed Messiah collapses, and while disintegrating, hurls into the air a frail bird, a strand of dried hay in its beak that will spark an inferno of destruction: "The human beings are gone; the idols are gone while this small, beating bird born of an organism called 'the Messiah' dies wailing . . ."

Q: "This stunningly visual and spectacular passage you've just read, isn't it a description of the apocalypse?"

Ozick: "I do not know how this story came about with its description of the perfect book and the destruction of the organism, the Messiah. It's strange writing, but it is not automatic writing since the story has a source though I could say that it wrote itself. It just came out. The rationalization afterward of the book, it seems to me, is the Nazi invasion into Galicia and into Europe, the Nazis as the ultimate idols."

Q: "Why did you choose Stockholm as the locus of your novel?"

Ozick: "*The Messiah* is the story of an orphan, Lars, whose parents have disappeared in the Holocaust, but he has been saved by a Swede who adopts him. He has no origins, he is free to invent whatever he likes, and he invents himself a father, and this father is Bruno Schulz. It is a fable with the obsessive theme of the father running throughout the book, a theme familiar to Bruno Schulz himself and, of course, to Kafka.

Now, what about Stockholm? Sweden remains a society that is somehow normal, that is free of the usual troubles of mankind, those of oppressors and oppressed. Lars's family history is a blank page, but he is the carrier of Europe in its dual realities, that of the oppressor and of the oppressed. He is the expression of the true reality of the planet which is hurt, wounding, wounded, a horror. To imagine himself, he has to invent himself. No, his obsession does not make him crazy, but what it reveals is the reality of Europe which is war."

Q: "Speaking of the history of Europe, how do you feel in Paris?"

Ozick: "I am here in Europe, in Paris, and every moment I spend in this city, I'm constantly reminded of and confronted in my mind with what took place here in the 1940s, and I would even say that it's more real to me than today's Paris. This, I know, is quite unpleasant to acknowledge, but I cannot get it out of my head. It's personal."

Q: "When your books come out in German translation, you must be invited to speak about them. How do you feel there?"

Ozick: "I do not go to Germany. I do, however, admit that Germany is a democratic state and that people are filled with goodwill. And I take it at face value, but I don't take every invitation as atonement. I will say that my not going is my personal memorial. I'm not irrational here; it's personal.

My parents were pharmacists, and in the '30s, they refused to buy Bayer aspirin.... The Germans have been inviting me over and over again; they want Jewish writers to come to Germany, to live in Germany. They are truly and deeply interested in Jewish writers. However, I cannot be and will not be a surrogate for the dead writers. You cannot make exchanges."

The South African writer Nadine Gordimer, future Nobel Prize in Literature recipient (1991), was sitting in the second row of the audience, along with Olivier Cohen, Ozick's French publisher, her Franco-American literary agent Michelle Lapautre, American novelist Diane Johnson, and Parisian-Canadian writer Mavis Gallant.

Addressing Gordimer in a voice betraying great emotion, Ozick solemnly declared, "Tonight, here in France in this bookshop, I am speaking in the presence of Nadine Gordimer. I never dreamed that one day I would be talking in her presence. I'm embarrassed. I don't know how you will take it, Nadine Gordimer, and I apologize in advance, but all my life I saw you as the fulfillment of Anne Frank. Had she survived, she would be in some way who you are, accomplishing what you do."

A woman in the audience broke this silence, apologizing for her question. "A letdown, for sure, after your moving declaration to Nadine Gordimer, but I feel much humor in your work, it's almost woven into the drama . . ."

Ozick: "I'm not conscious of having a sense of humor. I notice that sometimes, when I read something which I consider very dry and serious, people laugh, but humor comes out by accident, and therefore, I cannot count it as humor. This being said, I've always dreamed of being a humorous writer, and if I were reincarnated into a writer I particularly love, I certainly would not choose James nor Proust, but Gilbert and Sullivan."[8]

Concluding her talk, Cynthia Ozick wondered who were the people sitting in front of her: "Could someone tell me his or her life story so I would know?" Spontaneous laughter and deafening applause were her only answer.

Almost twenty years later, I received a note from Mavis Gallant who recalled that evening with our renowned guest author whom she described as "so solemn to meet and so funny to read, as if she were twins."[9]

Art Spiegelman

Defying the usual codes of coherence between content and form, Art Spiegelman made a tragic subject, his parents' experience of the Holocaust, into a comic book, a genre considered as entertainment and so not suitable to portray Nazi death camps, let alone its characters symbolized as animals: the mice are Jews, the cats are Germans, and the pigs, Polish collaborators.

Spiegelman was at the Village Voice on June 2, 2009, to speak about his graphic novel, the international bestseller Maus.[10] His project had come into being with the desire to know more about his parents, he told us. During World War II, they had been wandering through Poland, their native country, hiding from the Gestapo. Both were eventually interned in Auschwitz, survived the death camp, and were exiled in Sweden before ending up in the United States with Art, their little boy.

When he was twenty years old, tragedy struck again with his mother's suicide. Art felt that he had to tell their story, but fascinated since childhood by comics, he deemed he had to do so visually. When visiting his father one day, Art showed him a sketch from his drawings. Pointing to a character, his father blurted out, "Well, that guy, I buried that guy."

Spiegelman stayed five days with him, recording his recollections filled with a multitude of such details. "I was astonished," he admitted, "because I remembered how in the past he had reacted with, 'Oh, nobody wants to hear such stories.'" Their talk became the interview that led to Maus.

Q: "Working on Maus, what came first? The narrative or the visual?"

Spiegelman: "I had to find a visual strategy, staying close to raw sketches, but bringing them into high focus. One important source for me was the drawings that survived the camps; some artists had survived while others had been killed, but all their drawings had that urgency in them which is there in the foreground of *Maus*."

Q: "The voice of a writer is his style. Where is yours? In the narrative or in the drawing?"

Spiegelman: "You look at comics, and you're always looking at one's handwriting, a very fine, illuminated handwriting that tells you so much about the voice of the person you're looking at. Comics are a high condensation. They are a writing that may have more to do with poetry than prose."

Françoise Mouly and Art Spiegelman, June 2, 2009. Village Voice Bookshop archive.

Another kind of "condensation" in style is the caricature. Françoise Mouly, the French-native art director of *The New Yorker* and wife of Spiegelman, then talked about the magazine's famous caricatures and the original artwork of its covers. Both had been essential elements in conveying the horror of 9/11. The September 24, 2001 issue, the first one after the attack, was fittingly released with its all-black cover and only the black shadows of the towers in the background.

Three years later, Spiegelman remembered 9/11 with the cover of his new comics *In the Shadow of No Towers*, again all black, highlighted in the middle by a colorful strip of bodies spinning in the air. These comic characters whirl about like unearthed ghosts, haunting the site of the twin towers, riddled by all that had happened before.

Nicole Krauss

> "This is all my writing is about:
> how to recreate what has been destroyed or lost.
> I write to go home."
> —NICOLE KRAUSS, Village Voice reading, April 27, 2011.

Both novels Nicole Krauss presented at the Village Voice are journeys of two different objects invested with the lives and memories of writers and their books, gone astray during World War II. In *The History of Love*,[11] Krauss describes the worldwide peregrinations of a manuscript entrusted by its author to his friend as he abandons his Polish village, a shtetl soon to be destroyed by the Nazis. Migrating from one continent to another and passing through different hands, new languages, and new authors, this manuscript resurfaces and is finally returned to Leo, its original author, now an aged survivor of the Holocaust living in New York, who dies soon after recovering it. However, the very fact of its existence manages to give meaning to his former life and authorship to him as a writer.

Much later, Krauss was at the Village Voice on April 27, 2011, to speak about her most recent novel *Great House*,[12] also a journey across continents, this time of a writing desk allegedly owned by the celebrated Spanish poet Federico García Lorca, shot dead by the supporters of General Franco in August 1936. We follow the desk's wanderings over the years through a number of countries and the lives of the various people who owned it at one time or another; among them are a Chilean poet, disappeared during Pinochet's reign of terror, as well as an author in New York City who writes fourteen of her novels on it.

Half a century later, the desk ends up in storage in the city and is recovered by the surviving son of its original owner, once a historian in Budapest. In 1941 he and his family had been forcefully deported while their home was ransacked and its antique desk stolen too. After looking for it for so many years, this son comes to realize that its value does not lie in its physical existence, but in its rich, albeit tortuous memory.

A beautiful young woman, reserved and composed, Krauss opened her reading by thanking her French translator who was in the audience, highlighting the fact that all the transformative experiences she had had as a reader had come to her thanks to translations.

"When I start a book," she went on, "I never know where it's going, so the book is a continuing surprise. I think of it as a house. First, I need a doorknob, then a door, and then I fill it up from inside to finally bring in my characters."

Someone in the audience remarked that a house was a fixed structure, not leaving much room for the imagination.

Krauss: "Home is a confusing subject. Of course, a house is always imperfect, and when I start writing a novel, I know that it will have failures, like any house. Yet that house is home. It has something hugely liberating, especially given the kind of background I come from with its geography of displacements, accidental events, a home that felt incredibly elusive."

Q: "Your title *Great House* doesn't evoke books at all. Why did you choose it to speak about writing?"

Krauss: "The title *Great House* is an echo of the name of the school of Rabbi ben Zakkai. After the destruction of the Temple in ancient Jerusalem, he exhorted his pupils to transform their sacred loss into prayers consigned in a book they could carry under their arm. That house, the Temple, is moveable. You recreate your lost home not with bricks, but with words. This is all my writing is about: how to recreate what has been destroyed or lost."

Krauss then read the excerpt of the heart-rending interior dialogue that an aging Israeli, Aaron, imagines with his son who has flown from London to Jerusalem to attend his mother's funeral. A retired judge, Aaron is confronting his own death, revisiting in his head the rift between himself and this son and their mutual failings toward each other. More importantly, he is meditating on loss and recovery.

Q: "There are several voices of old people in your writings. You're young. Why this interest in such voices?"

Krauss: "It took many pages for me to understand where that voice came from. It began for me from a place where I felt lost, a place from which I had to create a lot of material to be able to go on. And that material is voices, but it is strange to realize that the voice of this old man is not mine, far from it. Yet it is one that is close and intimate to me. At this stage of my life, at the exact opposite end of the life of this man, I've nevertheless reached an understanding of things that I feel are incredibly personal to me."

Q: "You said at the beginning that, when you start a new book, you never know where you're going, but there must be a spark that sets you to write. What is it?"

Krauss: "I always saw my novels as being the houses for my voices. However, as I said, I write from a place of uncertainty, doubt, from a place where I do not know the answers. I write to go home."[13]

Daniel Mendelsohn

"It is the detail that makes the story."
—MENDELSOHN,
Village Voice reading, January 23, 2007.*

Daniel Mendelsohn's *The Lost: A Search for Six of Six Million*[14] is a personal and unique evocation of the Holocaust through a five-hundred-page breathtaking narrative of his odyssey to Eastern Europe, and, in fact, around the world to find out what happened to six members of his family in Nazi-occupied Poland during World War II. The book made such an impression on me that I immediately set about inviting the author to present it at the Village Voice. Thanks to his American publisher's representative, within an hour Mendelsohn was on the phone, and by pure chance, he was going to be in Paris the following week to visit friends. We decided on the date of January 23, 2007.

A contributor to the *New York Review of Books*, he is also a scholar in the classical studies who teaches at Bard College.[15] An engaging figure whose charismatic presence seemed to come from his eloquence, he opened his reading by stressing that knowingly he was not writing a history book, was not even interested in one: he was not a historian, his book was about how "families tell stories, narratives that they develop over time, becoming for subsequent generations the scripts of their lives . . ."

In fact, Mendelsohn is a born storyteller whose talent runs in the family, perhaps inherited from his maternal grandfather who,

---

* He gave two more readings to present *How Beautiful It Is and How Easily It Can Be Broken: Essays* (New York: HarperCollins, 2008); and the two volumes devoted to the poet C. P. Cavafy's *Collected Poems*.

as an adult, had immigrated to the US from his native Bolechov in Poland, now Bolekhiv in Ukraine. His ingenious tales had enchanted Daniel's childhood, even though, as it turned out, they were completely romanticized.

"He would go to the grocery store for a quart of milk and come back like Odysseus to Ithaca, saying 'Guess what, you'll never know what happened there,' and I would sit completely mesmerized by yet another story. Not until I was fourteen years old did I realize that, of course, there was nothing at all there; he had transformed each minute little thing into a great tale."

The one narrative his grandfather never told him, though, was that of his brother who had been killed by the Nazis, along with his wife Ester and their four daughters. "My grandfather wouldn't talk about it. It was like a 'black hole' in the history of the family. When he died, the mysterious wallet he had carried with him

Daniel Mendelsohn at the Village Voice Bookshop, January 23, 2007.
© Flavio Toma

every day of his life revealed its secrets—letters from this brother Schmiel, dated 1939 and begging for money, help, affidavits, all the stuff that gave a tragic quality to this object."

Mendelsohn was twenty when this discovery took place, and it "lingered in his mind over years," he told us. It was only when the Eastern world opened up that it became possible to go to that part of Europe. "How soon we forget that there was an Iron Curtain! I couldn't have written this book without the help of Mikhail Gorbachev!" [laughter]

Once in Bolechov, Mendelsohn and his brother Matt, a photographer, were able to get in contact with a few survivors who were still alive in 2003. He described the book as "a sort of a crazy travelogue, at least as the main narrative of my tracking down these people who might remember my family." He explained that the book was not about his family alone; its scope was to use "the microcosmic family event as a window to apprehend a much vaster one."

"But the rhetorical problem with the Holocaust was its size: when we say six million, it's both a totally meaningful and totally meaningless expression. I can't even imagine what six thousand would be or even six hundred. This is why the crucial thing for me was getting people's individual stories firsthand, with their immediacy, and this is why I did not read books, did not become a scholar of the Holocaust."

Through a series of uncanny coincidences, this "immediacy" Mendelsohn was looking for came from a woman who recalled a girlhood memory:

"She and her mother lived in that last house leading to the cemetery where people were shot and thrown into mass graves. During one of those roundups, or *aktions*, the sound of the machine guns firing at people went on for so long, hours and hours, that her mother—they knew what was happening—took out of a closet an old sewing machine, the kind you run with a treadle and, of course, the squeaking of the treadle drowned out the sound of those machine guns.

"This is the story I will never forget because it brought it all home. It is the detail that makes the story, the detail all writers are obsessed with. Of course, we understand abstractly all these things, but it is such a detail that lodges events like this one in the mind."

That night, James Lord was part of the audience.* He asked: "I was very impressed by your book and by the passages in which you created a relation between excerpts from the Torah with events during your quest . . . I wonder if you would comment on whether the Garden of Eden before the expulsion has any particular meaning for Jewish literature."

Mendelsohn: "Well, throughout the book, there are texts of analysis of Genesis. I was trying to understand what might have happened between my grandfather and his brother Schmiel who kept sending these desperate letters. We are unable to know since my grandfather's letters to his brother went up in flames. I needed a text that would help me sort out those things between brothers. I just wanted to ponder over something that was painful and Jewish. And, while I was working on this, my search ended with a great discovery: we were actually taken to the place in Bolechov where Uncle Schmiel died with his family, saw exactly what had happened—they had been shot, and where it was. It was an apple tree in a garden.

At that point, I had already taken my decision on these Biblical passages and had been reading the Book of Genesis for six months with a Hebrew dictionary. Now that I had a tree at the end, the Tree of Knowledge, I needed to start with a tree,

---

* A friend of Gertrude Stein and Picasso, James Lord was a well-known American figure in Paris and author of several biographies of artists, including Giacometti, Picasso, and Dora Maar. He spent his adult life in the city among "the great art-makers of the century" (his words).

even symbolized, that would have the resonance of the Tree of
Life at the beginning."

Q: "Abraham is another Biblical figure in your book. What does
he stand for?"

Mendelsohn: "Abraham is this crazy Jew, like me, going all over
places and not even knowing where he is going. The reason I
go back a lot to Abraham is, first of all, because Abraham was
the name of my grandfather who, like him, was a wanderer
and a liar. Also, the Old Testament illuminates the stories of
the six million lost."

Q: "This book *The Lost*—a search for lost time—summons up
Proust who opens your book with an epigraph from a sentence
in *The Captive*."*

Mendelsohn: "There are two things here: first, the book is a
reconstruction of lost time and you think of Proust; even more
important is what Proust tells us all throughout his *In Search of
Lost Time*: the recovery of a memory happens by pure accident.
There are two references hanging over *The Lost*, one verbal and
the other one visual, and they both seem important in a book
that is trying to retrieve the past: Proust's fantasy of a recovery
of the past by accident, and Sebald's photographs which intimate the tragic vision of the past."[16]

---

* Proust's quote: "When we have passed a certain age, the soul of the child we were
and the souls of the dead from whom we have sprung come to lavish on us their
riches and their spells." Marcel Proust, *In Search of Lost Time: Volume 5*, (London:
Chatto & Windus, 1992).

The Twenty-First
Century is Upon Us

As the bookstore entered its third decade, 9/11 threw the whole world into a cataclysmic shock. All of a sudden, shaken to its foundations, the United States faced not only one of the greatest disasters in its history, but also a newly fractured world.

As if to offer a glimmer of hope, *The New Yorker* closed its first post-9/11 issue, dated September 24, 2001, with the poem "Try to Praise the Mutilated World,"[1] in which the Polish poet Adam Zagajewski entreats us to remember the beauty of the living world: "over the earth's scars / . . . / and the gentle light that stays and vanishes / and returns."

Some nine months later, on June 2002, **Adam Zagajewski** was at the Village Voice to launch his new anthology *Without End: New and Selected Poems*. He opened the evening with his *New Yorker* poem, reciting it with a slight Polish intonation in his voice that symbolically seemed to convey his country's and Europe's empathy for America in the throes of her tragedy.

Jacques Derrida, Beverley Bie Brahic, and Hélène Cixous, March 17, 2004. © Laurence Moréchand

Almost two years afterwards, on March 17, 2004, the French philosopher **Jacques Derrida** appeared at our bookstore to speak about his reflections on the World Trade Center attacks recently published in *Philosophy in a Time of Terror: Dialogues with Jürgen Habermas and Jacques Derrida.*[2]

A compelling, even stunning figure in France, Derrida deconstructed 9/11 for his packed bilingual audience, who hung onto every word. He asked the audience to imagine if "such an act—the worst terrorist attack of all times—this spectacular destruction of two towers and the theatrical but invisible deaths of thousands of people in just a few seconds" could be viewed just as "a terrible crime, a pain without measure . . . it won't happen again, it's over." "No, of course, on the contrary, " he insisted, speaking in English, "there is traumatism with no possible work of mourning when the evil comes from the possibility . . . of the worst to come," which he saw as "anonymous forces . . . absolutely unforeseeable and incalculable, bloodless nuclear, chemical, and biological attacks, but also informational networks on which the entire life (social, economic, military, and so on) of a great nation depends."

Six months after his unforgettable three-hour exchange with his Village Voice public, Derrida passed away. Gathered to honor his memory, a group of scholars reappraised the philosopher's deconstruction concept "as a new philosophy of Enlightenment adapted to our contemporary world, groping for a new light to come."[3]

On the opposite side of the planet, the Indian philosopher Nishant Irudayadason viewed Derrida's work as a search to transcend all possible and visible horizons, or as "thinking a world without boundaries."[4]

This title perfectly describes the world literatures that flourished at a time when terrorism seemed to tempt more than one to retreat into oneself. By contrast, these literatures invited the readers to look beyond their own horizons in order to embark on a literary journey that was at once geographical, historical, cultural, and mind-broadening.

PART THREE

Rounding Out Shakespeare's Stage

COMMONWEALTH LITERATURES

A. S. Byatt, September 14, 1993, signing a copy of her novel *Possession*.
© C. Deudon

Expanding Horizons
BRITISH LITERATURE IN PURSUIT OF RENEWAL
David Lodge and A. S. Byatt

From the very start, our bookstore carried as many British works as American ones, but we had fewer readings with authors from Great Britain, who were used to launching their books at the British Council in Paris.[1] After the Council's program closed in the early 2000s, these writers started to appear more frequently at the Village Voice. Among them, two British novelists, David Lodge and A. S. Byatt, captured the influence of literary currents coming their way from American universities at the time.

A visiting professor at the University of Berkeley where he taught creative writing, **David Lodge** agreed to speak at our bookshop on January 4, 1990. He described how he had become the witness of the "professionalization" of the study of literature through a flagrant misuse of new literary theories in vogue on American campuses, i.e., structuralism, deconstruction, and the like.

As a critic, he could recognize their intrinsic value, but "like any other intellectual system, if abused, these tools mystify people, dominating rather than educating them. This trend is becoming so 'institutionalized,'" he admitted with some regret, "that compared to academic works, my novels are not considered serious literature."[2]

And yet his semi-fictional *The Campus Trilogy*[3] deals with a most serious subject—what is to become of literature—in a successfully bold, satirical manner. The three novels of his trilogy, *Changing Places*, *Small World*, and *Nice Work* are comedies of manners set in the small, closed academic world of theories that seem to exist solely to curb literary inventiveness.

The Californian Paris-based novelist Diane Johnson humorously introduced Lodge as "the scourge of American academia, blithely making fun of its current mechanisms." Lodge concluded his own talk on a sober, if not pessimistic note by stating that "we are getting into a tragic situation for literature."

Three years later, **Antonia (A. S.) Byatt** was at the bookstore on September 14, 1993, to discuss *Possession: A Romance*,[4] her well-received work in defense of "the novel as invention." She compared her fictional work in which she had imagined a Victorian poet, Randolph Henry Ash, his life, his loves, and, even more importantly, his entire body of poetry, in happy contrast with the research findings of the two modern protagonists of this same novel.

Roland and Maud are ambitious scholars embarked on a frantic and competitive hunt for spectacular discoveries among the intimate, secret loves of the poet Ash, the subject of their research. Both scholars are even ready to go as far as resorting to the most unethical and reprehensible acts, such as violating his grave to "promote their careers and bring fame to themselves."[5]

In sharp opposition, Byatt shared with us the noble gesture of the nineteenth-century English novelist George Eliot, one of her beloved authors, who "took with her to her grave the letters of her lover George Henry Lewes, clutched to her dead bosom."[6]

On April 24, 2001, Lodge was back at the Village Voice to launch his latest novel *Thinks*.[7] Describing the current state of literature, he acknowledged that "something had changed in British writing" since his last talk at the bookshop: "We are now witnessing a fertile time in literature," he proudly announced.

Living proof of this welcomed renaissance are several British authors who read with us over the years, including Julian Barnes, William Boyd, Jim Crace, Gabriel Josipovici, A. L. Kennedy, Ian McEwan, Tim Parks, and Graham Swift, to name just a few.

Lodge ascribed such an encouraging literary momentum partly to the Booker Prize jury, whose members had continued to bring to the fore outstanding British authors, "but more crucially," he added, "this jury, viewed as conservative at one time, has opened up to the Commonwealth, now getting a large spectrum of works, including all English-language fiction from everywhere, except the United States. This broadly based literature," he stressed, "embraces the world, raising media interest."

In fact, the grand opening up of British literature had started in 1981 when the Booker Prize was awarded to Salman Rushdie, a young author born in India on the eve of its independence in August 1947, the historical subject of his internationally acclaimed Midnight's Children.[8]

This recognition paved the way for the emergence of flourishing Indian and Pakistani literatures, and soon a new literary dynamic ignited a good number of the countries of the former British Empire. First referred to in academic circles as "postcolonial literatures," a term that linked them to a past empire, they now were evolving into "world literatures written in English," reflecting their contemporary importance and broad appeal.

At the start of the twenty-first century, our bookstore became a platform for some of these essential literary voices that continue to resonate today.

In the Footsteps of Salman Rushdie
Hanif Kureishi, Abha Dawesar, Tarun Tejpal

Hanif Kureishi

"New voices: that's what keeps culture alive."
—KUREISHI, Village Voice reading, January 25, 2005.

Unlike Salman Rushdie, Hanif Kureishi was not born in newly independent India, but in a London suburb, the son of an immigrant Pakistani father who inspired his complex family memoir *My Ear at His Heart: Reading My Father*.[1]

Growing up in the Beatles years of the 1960s and 1970s, Kureishi was just thirty when he achieved literary fame with his screenplay *My Beautiful Launderette* (1985). Directed by Stephen Frears, the film is an unusual comedy set in fast-changing, multicultural London suburbia with a colorful cast of characters: groovy youths, immigrants from the far corners of the world, hustlers, hoodlums, and same-sex lovers. The added success of his novel *The Buddha of Suburbia* (1990) soon made him an iconic figure of the British Pakistani community. On the freezing night of January 25, 2005, our nonetheless cheerful author was at the Village Voice to talk about his memoir, just out in French thanks to Christian Bourgois,[2] also the publisher of Rushdie in France.

Inspired by his father's manuscript found after his death, this work is an unordinary piece of writing, a departure from his popular comedies. Here, Kureishi brings to life his father's account of his own journey from Pakistan to outer London and, as an immigrant, his reflections on racism in the 1950s and 1960s. The memoir also stitches together the intricate relationship between father and son, since "all his life," Kureishi explained, "my father's dream had been to be a recognized writer, but he never was and remained an unpublished and frustrated one to the end."

In his introduction, François Gallix, professor of contemporary English literature at the Sorbonne, drew attention to the subtitle, *Reading My Father*, as "the Jamesian seed" of the author's memories. "Actually," Kureishi objected, "it is about my childhood," making it clear that the story of his father was told from the son's point of view.

In fact, reading his father's manuscript made him want to write about these grown-up lives he was now discovering in some detail: "I had to find my father in his stories about his childhood and growing up in India and his journey to England, as well. We children didn't know nor understand our parents' lives. My father was seen as a Paki and myself, being the only Pakistani in school, I was the Paki too and stared at. I wanted to know more about that race phenomenon, about racism."

Q: "What was the impact of the manuscript on your own life?"
Kureishi: "Finding out about my parents' world made me see them differently. There are certain things our parents cannot or won't speak about. 'Why do they live such a life?' we wondered, 'What is the point?' . . . And suddenly, you get access to such material, and you see the family in context, their relations with their own parents and their place in the continuum of family."

Q: "What did your father think of your books?"

Kureishi: "He thought that they were dirty books and that his own books were far better than mine. I write about sex, drugs, that kind of stuff, while his texts are deep, serious philosophical reflections. I was happy to see such a reaction on his part because it would have been worse to see him defeated or humiliated."

Q: "Your memoir does not develop along a straight line, but with comings and goings. Why this choice?"

Kureishi: "The key in this book is randomness. It was written in a random way as I found more material in my mother's writings and in an uncle's autobiography. It's the randomness of the structure that kept my interest in writing this book. Randomness, as I said, is the key: I saw once on the street a skinhead walking with his friend, a young man, and suddenly, they were kissing. It was a shock, and that's what started me writing *My Beautiful Launderette*. You want a shock—in fact, a series of shocks."

Q: "And if the shock you expect is not there, what keeps you writing?"

Kureishi: "There has to be a new difficulty to go there, to write the book. You want to write something new, never seen before. I wanted to write literary books, but I was wondering, questioning myself, worried even about introducing the Beatles, for instance, or long hair, or even jazz and pop. All that stuff was in American novels, but not yet in British literature. Writers of my generation, those I grew up with, Germaine Greer and V. S. Naipaul, were great writers, but not particularly groovy ones. You read Zadie Smith because she understands the contemporary world."

Q: "There is a 'joie de vivre' in your book, lots of humor which, actually, is your signature. Yet from what we understand, your family environment was not particularly fun."

Kureishi: "I always wanted to be a comic writer. I delight in the absurdities of life. The world is amusing and terrorizing at the same time. Humor is part of the way I see the world."

Q: "The book is more about your childhood as you said earlier, yet the title points to your father."

Kureishi: "Writing this memoir, I became the boss, I became the father, which was rather unusual and rather complicated from my point of view, because my father was certainly the boss in the house. Yet, in the process of writing, I felt guilty for becoming so bossy with my father. Were he alive, I'm sure he would be furious with me. He would have wanted this book to be published on his own terms, with his name on it, and not with his son meddling in it." [some emotion in his voice] "The whole thing became traumatic. So much love in it and so much anger, as well. Writing this book was an act of love and an act of murder, or, more exactly, an autopsy."

LIFE STORIES FROM THE INDIAN SUBCONTINENT

The Indian authors who read at the Village Voice came from a wide diversity of geographical, social, and cultural origins. Among our guest writers was the Indian scholar Rajmohan Gandhi who, presenting his biography of Mahatma Gandhi, summoned up riveting childhood memories with his grandfather.[3] There was likewise Fatima Bhutto, the Pakistani author of *Songs of Blood and Sword*,[4] her poignant evocation of tragic family destinies, those of her grandfather Zulfikar Ali Bhutto and her aunt Benazir Bhutto, both major historical figures of their country and both assassinated; Suketu Mehta and his contrasting portrait of Bombay, the *Maximum City*, as he called it; and there were the novelists, including Bangladeshi Monica Ali, Pakistani Kamila Shamsie, Indian Abha Dawesar, and

Tarun Tejpal, several of them brought to us by Marc Parent, a French editor at Buchet-Chastel with a passion for India.

This section introduces Abha Dawesar, a modern Indian woman, not afraid of tackling the controversial issues of gender and sexual taboos in contemporary India, and Tarun Tejpal, author of *The Alchemy of Desire*, an entrancing novel about love. Tejpal was the famous whistleblower of his country, known for his "sting operations."

Through their respective and quite different works, the two authors succeed in conveying a complex and nuanced portrayal of their native land, far beyond the narrow and often stereotyped Western vision of India at the turn of the twenty-first century.

Abha Dawesar

Born and schooled in New Delhi, Abha Dawesar went to the United States, where she graduated from Harvard University. She is a bright young woman, straight out of a Manhattan financial firm; yet, that night with us, her subject was India.

On November 11, 2007, Dawesar presented her second novel *Babyji*,[5] a bold coming-of-age tale of a Delhi schoolgirl who understands empowerment as being freed from the constraints of childhood, family life, and her Brahmin social class, but most of all, from the defining taboos of the society she lives in. Excelling in mathematics, an exact science, she is likewise interested in quantum physics and the theory of chaos. And there is plenty of chaos in her life: three love affairs, conducted secretly and simultaneously with three different women—her servant (not a small detail since Babyji belongs to the superior caste), her girlfriend and school rival, and a divorced, worldly woman she calls India.

Q: "Female homosexuality in India must be a sensitive subject. Did you meet problems when the book came out in your country?"

Dawesar: "I believe my novel *Babyji* was the first book in India to show homosexuality between women quite openly, and it was certainly the first one to do it without apology. I wrote this story in 1991, at a time when the Indian economy was opening up and television programs were beginning to show images of the Western world, which for so long had been a mystery to us. With student demonstrations all around and given the rapid developments and changes, it felt as if we were experiencing a turning point in the history of India."

Q: "Your book was not censored?"

Dawesar: "There is no censorship in India. My first novel about a homosexual in New York, with scenes far more explicit, was published in India.[6] *Babyji* was well received there, and it was a relief because at the time, a film about homosexuality made by an Indian filmmaker had just been banned, not because of government censorship, but because of angry crowd protests turning into riots. I was not only relieved, but pleased that *Babyji* was published without trouble because homosexuality in India is a crime. There was a petition to suppress this clause in the constitution, and this issue was covered by a newspaper listing all the books that spoke of homosexuality, concluding with: '... and then comes along *Babyji*.'"

Q: "If homosexuality is a crime, could it be that female same-sex intimacy is not perceived in India the same way as male homosexuality?"

Dawesar: "The homosexual act, whether between women or men, has a long tradition in India, and there is even a god who is the product of two male gods, with one becoming a woman to give birth. There is a temple honoring this god, visited by many pilgrims, but forbidden to women, except small girls and very old ones."

Q: "Does this mean that, as long as it is limited to the private sphere, homosexuality is permissible?"

Dawesar: "India is a country of paradoxes. There is a small tribal community in the northeast of India, very isolated in the middle of mountains. In this tribe, two women decided to live together, and one was younger than the other. At first, the elders said, 'You cannot do that,' but the women made it clear that they would continue to live together. In that community, the tradition is that the husband's family gives a dowry to the bride's family, the reverse of the ritual practiced in the rest of India. 'Well,' the elders said, 'if you live together, you have to go through marriage, and whoever of you is the boy, his family will have to give the dowry to his wife's family.' This was done, and the elders and the community blessed the couple.

In India, modernity and tradition often find a way to coexist. Aware that they cannot control the forces that have started to change the country, people regain control by adapting their traditions to the new circumstances."

Q: "In your novel, Babyji's women lovers come from different classes and castes. Does the freedom your protagonist enjoys come from the privilege of her caste?"

Dawesar: "The caste system is very much present in Indian society, but it's changing and mutating. The caste used to rule the daily rituals of people's lives, yet now it seems to play an active role essentially at the time of marriage and for cremation. People, including the elite and the educated layers of the population, are still going through arranged marriages within their own caste, but by their own choice."

People are using technology to continue their own tradition, Dawesar told us, and matrimonial websites are categorized in terms of caste, sub-caste, and language. She made it clear that a caste is not the same as class in the economic sense of the term: "A person of lower caste may well be rich and have power. This is an even more complex system when it comes to elections and is hard to explain to a Westerner because it appears in many ways as anti-democratic, yet initially thought up as a division of power."

Q: "Do you have as many readers in India as in the Western world?"

Dawesar: "Your question is about the same as the one I'm often asked: 'Are you writing for India or for the West?' Actually, few people read in India; they mostly read newspapers and partly because there is no tradition of being alone in India. You're constantly surrounded by family, and if you don't sit alone in a room, how can you read?"

Q: "One of Babyji's lovers is named India. Why did you give her this name?"

Dawesar: "I wanted my book to explore what it is to be an Indian woman today. I wanted to speak directly about India, the country, only through female characters."[7]

Tarun Tejpal

Remembering the success of Tarun Tejpal's launch of his first novel *The Alchemy of Desire*[8] at the Village Voice in 2005, our public was eagerly awaiting the presentation of his second work, *The Story of My Assassins*.[9]

On June 6, 2009, wearing an outfit with a touch of Indian elegance, Tejpal arrived at the bookstore accompanied by his French publisher Marc Parent who, introducing him, proudly announced that Tejpal's first novel had sold a record number of copies of the French translation alone: "whereas *The Alchemy of Desire* was inspired by love and desire," he continued, "this new work shows the reverse side of a 'shining' India. As a matter of fact, *The Story of My Assassins* depicts a world of millions of desperate, miserable people in the face of Indian billionaires, the richest on the planet today."

Tejpal's stark portrayal of this abyss of misery is an insider's view, not meant to be a sensational revelation, but rather to bring to light some obvious truths. What is "sensational" are his

Tarun Tejpal, June 6, 2009, at the Village Voice Bookshop. © Flavio Toma

numerous and daring journalistic investigations as founder and head of *Tehelka*, the most famous investigative magazine in India (the word "tehelka" meaning "sensational" in Hindi). "*Tehelka* is my duty, and my primary commitment is to journalism," he insisted.

One of his cases had led to the disclosure of a widespread corruption scandal with ramifications at the highest governmental levels. In retaliation, his journal was shut down, and he was informed of a plot to assassinate him. Though Tejpal was told that his killers had been arrested, he wondered just who they were. What were their motivations? Who had paid them? His ultimate goal was, as he had said, "to tell the stories of people whose stories do not get told, certainly not in English or in any other languages. In India, my class of people can almost not see them, those two million people living borderline. By writing this story, I was trying to give back dignity to them and show that they also have complex lives."

Q: "Being part of the elite, how did you manage to get close to or be accepted by this 'invisible' population?"

Tejpal: "The challenge with this novel was to sort out the enormous amount of material we receive at *Tehelka*, which, I believe, is not available to another writer. The core of our job is to choose from the extraordinary mass of information washing up at our door day after day and bring it to the reader."

Q: "Why did you choose to turn the material at your disposal into a novel and not a journalistic investigation?"

Tejpal: "When it comes to literature, I want to do something that journalism cannot do. As a fiction writer, I have two principles: subversion and illumination. I want to push the boundaries of seeing. I look for a new way of seeing and that is the voyage. Looking at the material is to look at the soil and see what can come out of it, what it may bring out. As a journalist, I always know what's right and what's wrong, and I always know what

I have to do. As a fiction writer, I'm always in doubt. I try to explore things. I try to understand my world, the world around me. Fiction writing has more to do with myself."

Q: "Storytelling is part of the Indian tradition. Is this story in line with that tradition?"

Tejpal: "There is definitely a tradition of Indian storytelling, stories within stories, stories embedded in other stories, but I was not aware of it until I had finished this second novel. I feel that I belong to such a tradition, and when it comes to traditional Indian writing, you have to think of the Mahābhārata, and my novel The Alchemy of Desire is much structured the way the Mahābhārata is. And this comes from Hinduism."

Q: "Hinduism? Could you elaborate?"

Tejpal: "Deeply in this book is a commentary on Hinduism, an ambiguously modern religion. Unlike Christianity and Islam which are very prescriptive and clear-cut between right and wrong, Hinduism is not, and that is its strength and its weakness. It can validate almost any position: ten different people using the same text can each defend their own interpretation and be right. Ambiguity is at the heart of Hinduism."

Q: "You mentioned at the beginning of your talk that you grew up in a privileged environment, among the English-speaking elite. Isn't English the official language understood and spoken, if not written by all?"

Tejpal: "India has many languages, castes, religions, and I remember in my school days how some boys would have difficulty coping with English. There is a class in India who lives in the English language, apart from the rest of the Indian population. India has at least thirty languages and ancient literatures that go back two thousand years. These are languages as important as Sanskrit, but English has so totally eclipsed them that people who practice only their own language are at a great disadvantage."

Q. "Can English language render the complexities, the specificities of India that traditional languages would convey with their words forged over millennia to express specific local realities?"

Tejpal: "Actually, Indian writers who write in English mean nothing in India; I can tell you that. We'll sell a few thousand copies and that's it. Indian literature in English is driven by the commercial empires of publishing houses in the West sitting in New York or London and deciding what kind of books they want from India, something that readers in the West can easily digest and absorb. So, most of the Indian writers the West loves and reads have zero relevance for the people in India. To them, they are non-authentic."

Q: "Who are they, those writers today you would consider authentic?"

Tejpal: "It's Bollywood that best represents India. It's colorful and idiosyncratic. English language reflects the people who created it: cool, one of understatement, of irony. India is the opposite of the English people. India is color, melodrama, histrionics, and writing in English, one needs to push the language to carry the story of India, and this is a real task."

Reshaping South Africa

MOVING FORWARD AND OUT OF APARTHEID

Denis Hirson, Breyten Breytenbach, Mandla Langa, Damon Galgut

espite censorship and persecutions against the opponents of apartheid rule, including the writers who were forced into silence, exile, or seclusion at home or in prison cells, their voices rose above the heavy exactions. Throughout the 1980s, South African writers were being heard and read all over the world. Among them are novelists André Brink; Nadine Gordimer (Nobel Prize 1991); Es'kia Mphahlele (nominated for the Nobel Prize in 1984); and J. M. Coetzee (Nobel Prize 2003); poet and essayist Breyten Breytenbach; the playwright Athol Fugard; and many more. Their gift to the writing generations that came after them is an extraordinary legacy of courage and original literary bravura.

In 1994, the year Nelson Mandela was democratically elected to lead the country, Denis Hirson, a young South African author living in Paris, celebrated the end of apartheid with the publication of *The Heinemann Book of South African Short Stories*,[1] which was launched at the Village Voice on July 8 of that year.

To open his reading, he imagined the different paths now being cleared for the emerging and impressive array of South African writers: "The high dam-walls of apartheid have contained and given shape to much South African writing up to now. As these walls crack and alter, which new currents will flow through? What of the all too neglected sources of memory and ancestry? Will the power of traditional tales and praise poetry enter contemporary prose? Will new hybrid forms emerge out of what Nelson Mandela has termed 'a rainbow nation'? Perhaps these are some of the questions to ask of writers working in South Africa today."

Denis Hirson

Born in the UK and raised in South Africa, Denis Hirson followed his family into exile in London before moving to Paris in 1975, where he settled permanently. A prolific author of essays, poetry, one novel, and several memoirs, he came to play a vital role in the life of the Village Voice, introducing authors and organizing various literary events, among them our tributes to Ted Hughes and Grace Paley. Perhaps his greatest contribution to our bookstore was allowing us to discover the up-and-coming South African voices he knew, showcasing these fiction writers, essayists, and poets, including himself, whose works reveal the multiple facets of a country in the throes of dramatic change.

Hirson gave his debut reading at the Village Voice on April 24, 1988, with the launch of *The House Next Door to Africa*,[2] a memoir of his early childhood and family life that embraced his grandparents, who had left their native Tsarist Russia for exile in South Africa.

Two more reminiscences of his youth followed: *I Remember King Kong (The Boxer)*[3] and *We Walk Straight So You Better Get Out the Way*,[4] completing the triptych of his early life in Johannesburg, all written in the form of prose poems. A friend of mine who had also spent her own girlhood in South Africa described these two memoirs as "little jewels of books of memories written in unconnected sentences, like little bits of poems, deliciously humorous, sad, and silly, bringing back to me things I had completely forgotten."[5] In them are flashbacks of Denis as a boy, his keen observations of the world around him, and his hidden thoughts trying to penetrate the resounding silence of a father jailed for his opposition to the apartheid regime.

An evening with Denis Hirson (Denis on far right), October 8, 2011.
© Flavio Toma.

Then again, there are also typical boyhood memories and, like any other boy in the world, he was going to school, playing with friends, listening to the latest hits, locking himself in his room, and diving into his own fantasy world, he fondly remembered, stressing that "under apartheid, as in all parts of the world, people were living their lives as best they could under circumstances which were getting worse and worse in the townships while the whites lived in a kind of a bubble of security."[6]

His first "life-shaping memory" was the Sharpeville massacre on March 21, 1960, that the photos in a book on his father's shelves revealed to him: "I was eight at the time, and like all children, I absorbed what was going on, not knowing exactly what it was. The shock of bodies fallen, clothes blotting up blood, a litter of shoes, bags, hats, bicycles . . ."[7] was soon followed by a police search in the family house, leading to the arrest of "the person I felt closest to in the world."[8]

The two incidents were to become one and the same in the mind of the child. "How many events in one's life are there really that are utterly unavoidable in our memories, those we always think back to . . . In my mind I constantly return to the moment my father was arrested, before our relationship was arrested, before he came to sit at the center of gravity of my life, locked in a prison cell.[9]

The following exchanges between Denis Hirson and his audience come from several of his book presentations over the years at the Village Voice Bookshop.

Q: "Had you written your childhood memories soon after leaving South Africa, would they have been the same?"

Hirson: "Memory is the primary material for many of us writers, and while I was writing this book *We Walk Straight* . . . , my father was right there, very much present. Now, about thirty years later, something else is at work: a letting go which involves multilayered images, the way you get the waves coming in and going out, and in between, all those layers of water. So, there are those layers of past and present entering each other, and this is wonderful to me in terms of emotions."[10]

Q: "The reader feels those emotions in your writing. Is there a difference in intensity between recalling your memories and seeing them now on the page?"

Hirson: "A poet, whose name I don't remember, explained that if 'you want to see clearly, your eyes have to be dry.' There is a constant interplay between the emotions you want to keep and the emotions you work out."[11]

Q: "Philip Roth said that all exiles tend to go back to their native countries after a while. You've been back to South Africa. How did it feel revisiting a country that had radically changed since your childhood?"

Hirson: "In my case, my childhood memory is just one of the aspects of South African reality. When I wrote my first book, *The House Next Door to Africa*, it was an experience familiar to many people around me, including my grandparents: they wait seven, eight years and want to go back and repossess their country. Past and present are crossing each other. Yet I wonder if it is possible to go back to the past when it was not possible to write, as if the past could be awoken and be present?"[12]

Q: "Reading your memories, one is astonished at the amount of minute details remembered. What is your secret?"

Hirson: "I have no idea, but being by myself in our garden was a constant treasure for me, with insects and all the other things. Yet there was something else. When I was twelve, I knew I was going to leave South Africa once my father would come out of jail. I wonder if there was not something inside myself that made me take in everything around a tiny bit stronger. But also, memory, the minute something happens, you transform it; memory is doing its work all the time."[13]

Q: "When you now visit your country and having survived, do you feel some kind of guilt?"

Hirson: "I know that many whites in South Africa feel guilty; In fact, all of us have reasons to feel guilty, but this is a position from which I cannot write. One of my mentors is Athol Fugard, the greatest playwright South Africa has had. He really had his hand in the guts of the place, working with it. He had been denied a passport and therefore couldn't leave the country. He invited me to his home when I was seventeen, and years later, when I went back to South Africa, I visited him. I remember we were sitting at the dining room table, just after coming out of his garden shed, and looking at me, he announced, 'Today, I've found something to celebrate.'"[14]

Q: "If you do not feel guilty, did you ever feel you were a victim?"

Hirson: "For South African writers there are two traps: the one of feeling guilty for the white writers and the one of feeling victims for the Black writers. These two traps have infested South African writing to death. For any writer, in any time and place, to acknowledge that there is darkness is to acknowledge that you can go beyond. I want something to take me beyond these feelings of guilt or victimization. And that's what my father gave me. He went to jail, and as incredible as it may sound, I feel that it's his gift to me. Of course, I would have much rather had him bringing me up, but he didn't; he was there in prison, absent to us. At the same time, as the Egyptian Jewish French poet Edmond Jabès said, 'Chaque blessure est une source.' You let go, you transform the wound into something else."[15]

Q: "Mandela's release from prison was a historical moment. Would such major writers as Brink, Gordimer, or Coetzee have written their masterpieces outside the inhuman circumstances of apartheid?"

Hirson: "After Mandela was released from prison, it was, I thought, a turning point for South Africans living in South Africa, a wake-up call. Mandela was out, he was going to come to power, and the people went out on the streets to support him. If this was going to be the future, where had we been in the past? Because, when we grew up, Blacks were only laborers—that's what they were. They were not recognized as full people at all: every single Black was a body and a soul demeaned, not only in political, but also in personal terms.

"So much was wrapped in silence; so much was unspoken. One major problem for an author writing a novel about South Africa, particularly one taking place under apartheid, is how to deal with Blacks and whites on the same page. The question for me now, as a writer, is not to write only from a child's perspective. Trying to juxtapose the innocence of a fine childhood and this darkness of political negation is something to be wondered about, to be pondered over for a lifetime. This is why in my novel *The Dancing and the Death on Lemon Street*, introducing the character of Rosy, the Black maid of a white employer under apartheid, is a major switch for me."[16]

At each of his readings, Denis had friends from South Africa in the audience, those living in Paris and others passing through the city. At the close of events, they would often sing South African songs accompanied on the guitar or evoke personal memories. At one such moment, he concluded, "I don't feel that my books are my own only, they are filled with memories of other people."[17]

Breyten Breytenbach

In 1975, the South African poet and painter, essayist, and activist Breyten Breytenbach was living in Paris. On an illegal visit to South Africa, he was arrested and sentenced to nine years in prison for his political views. It was also about that time that Denis Hirson discovered this poet's writings, "a turning point in my own life," and translated his collection of Afrikaans poems *In Africa Even the Flies Are Happy*, published in London in 1978.[18] "The high dam-walls of apartheid," quoted earlier, were those of the prisons where Hirson's father spent nine years, and the poet Breyten Breytenbach, seven, as he was released in 1982 due to the impact of massive international protests.

On July 1, 2008, Breytenbach came to the Village Voice for the launch of his latest book of poetry, *Windcatcher: New and Selected Poems 1964-2006*.[19] He focused his talk on his writer's experience in prison, one shared by a multitude of other authors, but varying with each passing tyrant. In fact, the conditions of his solitary confinement were especially horrendous as he was not allowed to write. Yet writing was "the only way to keep sense and some kind of sanity, but it could be done only in my mind, recreating the world I knew before, and particularly Paris, trying to hold on to it."[20]

After his second trial and more intense international pressure on the government, Breytenbach was now allowed to write, but under very strict conditions: "I was given a certain number of sheets in the morning, and in the evening, they were taken away from me, and I wouldn't see them again. In other words, if I were to write a story which I couldn't complete in the given time, I couldn't go back to where I had left it the day before, so I had to keep it in mind . . . which, by the way, is an interesting way of writing and has to do with stream of consciousness. You had to hang on to the mood you were in the day before in order to continue the story the next day. Plot and characters were secondary; more important was to keep the feel of the story."

Those sheets of paper were, of course, scrutinized by the prison's security officials and the psychologist as well, "and this," Breytenbach said with an ironic grin, "was a small, bright upbeat to the situation. I had an audience." [laughter] "These people were reading my sheets because it was their job to read them. And so, I was absolutely sure that there would be people to read me." [more laughter]

Mandla Langa

Mandla Langa is the South African author who was assigned the honorable task of editing and completing the sequel to Nelson Mandela's first volume of memoirs, *A Long Walk to Freedom*. This second volume was to stress the urgency of Mandela's mission as president of the country, but was interrupted by his death in 2013. Thanks to Langa, these completed memoirs were published under the title *Dare Not Linger: The Presidential Years*.[21]

On March 17, 2011, Denis Hirson introduced Mandla Langa at the Village Voice. Sentenced to prison for his political activities within the African National Congress (ANC)[22] during his student years, Langa fled the country and lived twenty years in exile as his party's delegate in Africa and Europe.

In 1994, the year of Mandela's election, Langa returned home, but not to the promised land he had envisaged. In the preface to his reading, Hirson had rightly identified Langa as "one of today's South African writers who do not flinch before the new difficulties and unpleasant truths of their fledging country, able to grasp in their writings such issues as exile, betrayal, and power."

A poised and austere presence, Mandla Langa opened the presentation of his novel *The Lost Colours of the Chameleon*[23] by speaking of the lasting effects of political banishment: "We are all now feeling the pain that comes almost thirty years after being away in exile, something vicious on the part of the power of the time, something that left us stunned for life. Exile was not so much a geographic dislocation as something that consumed and branded one for life. People coming back from exile had to face how to deal with whites, something that had never been approached in South Africa before. While we were in exile, small communities were created in the country, and the political situation was characterized by infighting, splits, and betrayals."[24]

Betrayal is, in fact, one the themes of his work. In the passage the author chose, the protagonist suffers from a loss of speech or "mute hysteria" as the result of the betrayal that led to the death of someone dear to him. "This book," he explained in further detail, "is an act of exorcism to come to terms with my brother shot dead in 1994, and how to change, say, what has taken place instead of the promised land. It's all the more problematical as we are all very intimate, knowing each other, killing each other."

The title of his *The Lost Colours of the Chameleon* is an allusion to Mandela's vision of his country as the 'Rainbow Nation,' but also to the speed with which power can change people. "The political reality, like quicksilver, is rapidly changeable," Langa told us, adding that "anyone who thinks a nanosecond that a person in politics is there for altruistic reasons and ideals is deluded. Beyond the chameleon," he went on, "I will opt for Baldwin's 'The Price of the Ticket,' by which he meant 'opting' for human life rather than power."* On this somber note Langa concluded his reading, stressing that "these things needed to be said."

Damon Galgut

Damon Galgut was the youngest of the South African authors to read at the Village Voice and part of the rising generation of writers for whom the central question was to become free from the literature of protest and embrace the complex issues of history and identity. He was not quite twenty years old when he published his first novel and thirty when Nelson Mandela was elected President of their country newly freed from apartheid.

Galgut was invited to our bookstore on April 4, 2005, to talk about his fifth book *The Good Doctor*,[25] a novel representative of its time as

---

* James Baldwin reflects on the value of life in his essay "The Price of the Ticket" (1985). Baldwin further elaborated his stance in a video interview, in which he states: "From my point of view, no label, no slogan, no party, no skin color, and, indeed, no religion is more important than a human being." (Daniel B. Wood, "Celebration of James Baldwin as Writer and Civil Rights Activist," *Christian Science Monitor*, August 1989).

it wavers between the dark apartheid mood that continued to linger, invisibly haunting people's lives, and the hope of a newly united world, albeit pervaded by uncertainties, ambivalences, and betrayals.

This work summons up these two worlds through the characters of two doctors posted to a small provincial hospital in post-apartheid South Africa. One represents the old guard while the younger doctor contemplates setting up some kind of ideal community. The story unfolds against the backdrop of an overhanging mansion, a kind of fort perched on a hill high above the town, formerly the place of the "brigadier," the local official known for his brutally cruel rule over its inhabitants. Believed to have been abandoned at the end of apartheid, in reality, it is still inhabited by this officer, biding his time before a return to power.

Denis Hirson in conversation with Damon Galgut, April 4, 2005.
© Flavio Toma

Introducing Damon Galgut, Denis Hirson recalled this uneasy climate of growing up "in deafened silence at a time when the political opposition was gagged and buried underground, and the artists and churchmen were called to take sides. What Galgut set to do in his writings was precisely not that," he claimed.

Referring to a conference at which our author had taken unorthodox positions opposed to the ideologies of the moment, Denis asked him where he stood in his novel on the question of hope.

Galgut: [a long pause] "You seem to make a connection between ideology and hope. I'm not sure such a connection exists, and, as time goes on, I tend to think that disavowing any kind of ideology is ideology itself. You're kind of never free from that. . . . As far as hope regarding South Africa, I'm very hopeful, to be honest. Where we are, what we've achieved in a very short time is remarkable. I don't like the term 'miracle' often used when speaking about South Africa since it somehow would imply God's intervention. I certainly don't believe that. The arrangement we've come to in South Africa is very pragmatic, and though very imperfect, my personal feeling is that we're right now [2005] in a period of grace."

Hirson: "My question was not about hope in South Africa, but about writing. It seems to me that many South African writers under apartheid drew their central energy from the hope of some sort of human survival. Even in Coetzee's *Waiting for the Barbarians*, there is a touch of hope. However, this doesn't seem to be where you're drawing your energy from as a writer. Where would you say is your center of energy?"

Galgut: [thinking] . . . "The fact that this little hospital exists, continues to function, no matter what the desperation of the people is, speaks of hope. This quality of endurance, doggedness, and insistence is in itself a form of hope. There is also in human situations something kind of amusing, nutty, ridiculous which makes you laugh and this also contains hope."

"Your characters are interesting and complex; they try to make sense of a reality they don't always understand, the new reality of the country. Could you talk about their ambivalence?" someone in the audience asked.

Galgut: "The South African literature most of us know is one clearly centered morally, and the situation was such in the novels under apartheid that there was always a character, an individual that stood against the system. By the time you finished the book, you were feeling okay. It comforted you on your moral status because you identified with the right person. The moral issue clicked. My feeling is that South Africa today is in a complete different place, and all those clear issues are not clear anymore."

Q: "How could it be worse than under apartheid?"

Galgut: "We have all those head figures from the times of the struggle who are now in government, and they behave like ordinary politicians, which is to say that, at times, they are quite morally compromised, given the corruption, scandals, and money. There is a character in my book, a nurse partly damaged by his past, who behaves badly, stealing things from the hospital. It's very hard to know what attitude to take towards a character like that. Is he a victim or is he a villain? The feeling of ambivalence is something new for South African literature, I think. I wanted the reader to be morally disturbed."

Q: "Under apartheid, the majority of South African writers were white liberals. What about Black South African literature today?"

Galgut: "I don't think that many Black writers are taking up the issue of corruption yet. There is a kind of searching for new themes and beyond politics, social ones. What does it mean

to be poor in South Africa as opposed to being politically dis-
possessed? We're in a kind of a searching period. I don't think
that anyone in South Africa knows what the themes really are.
Authors like Denis here are writing about memory and how
this works. There is a feeling that South African literature is
an opened territory, but what exactly the defining themes of
the new South African literature are have still to be found,
and it is quite hard. I should add that for white South African
writers to write anything about corruption is immediately seen
as criticism of the fledgling government and read as a kind of
implicit nostalgia for the old one, which nobody likes to have
hanging around the neck."

Hirson: "There are Black poets today who do not hesitate to be
critical, yet without reducing their writings to slogans. They
are able to weave their present-day critical glance into very
powerful lyrics."

This informative and stirring back and forth between our two
authors concluded with a statement from yet another South
African writer who was at the reading. "In this novel," he said,
"the author has managed to convey at once the despair and hopelessness of a country in the grip of resentment and crime and the
determination and singlemindedness of a nation on the verge of
its existence."[26]

Australian Narratives

AS WIDE AND VARIED AS THE COUNTRY

Peter Carey, Tim Winton, Julia Leigh

Under British and Dutch rules respectively, the ancient lands of India and South Africa were forced to conform to the newly dominant cultures and languages even though, within their multiple ethnic groups, some peoples managed to preserve their native tongues and social identities. It was more complicated with Australia and English-speaking Canada: their immense territories of forests, deserts of sand, and expanses of ice being more sparsely populated, they attracted waves of settlers from Great Britain and other European countries.

Naturally, the development of these two seemingly inhospitable territories did not take place overnight. The clearing of the land and exploitation of its peoples and resources required more than a century to yield prosperity for a growing ruling class, which gradually became powerful enough to impose its own economic and social norms. Mostly emanating from similar English roots, both countries advanced their own literatures with their distinct singularities, maintaining British English as a common linguistic base.

On May 18, 1990, and for the first time in France, the Ministry of Culture invited eleven Australian writers to present their works in several cities under the umbrella program of Les Belles Etrangères. Only one writer was of Aboriginal origin: Colin

Johnson, or Mudrooroo Nyoongah by his native name. This absence of Indigenous Australian literature was all the more surprising as Native American literatures were flourishing in North America, and Bruce Chatwin's travel essay *The Songlines* was enjoying great popularity in the Anglophone world.

In *The Songlines*, the author investigates the millennial and mysterious ritual "walkabout" consisting of a network of "lines" or paths opened tens of thousands of years ago by its Aboriginal ancestors. These tracks were marked by direction signs invisible to the eyes of strangers, but inscribed in the sacred songs that accompanied the Indigenous peoples in their nomadic journeys across the continent. As Chatwin's work had aroused immense curiosity, in turn, we had expected native Australian writers to further explore this ancestral vein.

However, even after the continent's independence in 1901, British literary traditions continued their hold on all Australian literature, and Aborigines were obliquely portrayed as unformed shadows and/or ominous presences. Nonetheless, their integration into the historical process of the nation was becoming increasingly noticeable in the writings of the arising younger generation. For example, in Tim Winton's novel *Cloudstreet* (1991), a ghost-haunted house in Perth is a former orphanage, an unmistakable reference to the stolen generation of children forcefully removed from their Aboriginal families in the name of assimilation. Sadly, no Aboriginal Australian writer read at the Village Voice, but, fortunately, their literatures were starting to fill the literary corpus of their land.

The night of the "Belles Etrangères" three Australian authors were programmed to speak of their works: Peter Carey, Rodney Hall, and Tim Winton. Their narratives were different in content and style, but each one of them summoned the foreboding power of nature, revered for its splendor, but just as endangering in its very essence.

Peter Carey

Among these three Australian writers, we chose to bring to life Peter Carey's narrative through a performance that combined the three excerpts he read from his recent work *Oscar and Lucinda*, an engrossing and subtly ironical novel set in the mid-nineteenth century. Given the circumstances, there was no time left for discussion or exchanges with the audience.

The work unfolds between Great Britain at the peak of its industrial boom, symbolized by the Crystal Palace (Hyde Park Great Exhibition, 1851), and Australia, the new and immense, unmapped continent, a promising arena for an expanding empire. The story depicts Oscar, who breaks away from his father, a fundamentalist

Peter Carey at the Village Voice Bookshop, May 13, 1993. Village Voice archive.

Anglican preacher, and Lucinda, a young Australian heiress and great admirer of the aforementioned Palace. The rebellious Oscar and ambitious Lucinda meet on the ship taking them to her homeland. He is determined to found his own Anglican mission in the hinterland, while Lucinda is bent on enlarging the glass factory she had bought on a previous trip. Their journey at sea is spent gambling, a passion the two adventurers share, creating a complicity between them that includes a strange, mutual attachment.

Upon their arrival, they collaborate on the building of the glass church, combining Lucinda's search for commercial success and Oscar's spiritual aspirations, two fundamental values of their estranged country. He is soon in charge of transporting this architectural miracle from Sydney to the backcountry. Sitting inside the church that is balanced on a barge floating down the river, Oscar begins to reflect on the extravagance and sheer vanity of an endeavor that his fantasy of a romance with Lucinda has rendered imaginable.

All of a sudden, under the pressure of extreme heat, this church explodes into thousands of glass shards, bringing on an apocalyptical sinking of the long boat that takes the nascent wonder and Oscar along with it.

Symbolically, the founding principles of the mother country are gone too, buried deep in these waters by the force of this continent's natural elements.

Tim Winton

Known as the "wunderkind of Australian letters," Tim Winton looked like an easygoing young man in jeans and turtleneck sweater, his long black hair pulled back into a braided ponytail. Born on the wild West Coast of Australia, "the conservative wrong side of Australia," he said, Winton grew up in the sixties and was influenced by American youth culture, its music, and the taut language of Hemingway. He confirmed that this generation "resists the language inherited from Britain and feels closer to Americans who write as they talk, an easy language which people can understand," comparing "the surge of energy" in contemporary Australian literature to American letters in the mid-nineteenth century "when authors, such as Melville, discovered that they were Americans, becoming aware that their works were rooted in their national experience."

His own literary playground embraces big lands, the vast ocean, and the Outback with its immense desert of red sand that stretches to the very edge of the ocean. When he presented his recent novel Dirt Music[1] at our bookshop on March 30, 2004, we learned that it was his ninth work, hailed by some as the quintessential Australian fiction of the early twenty-first century.

The story starts in the invented White Point, once a shanty harbor on the West Coast, but over the years becoming a fashionable resort due to a fast-growing lobster industry. The basic action revolves around three of its characters. First, there is Jim, the successful fisherman, the all-powerful "uncrowned prince" of this place. Then comes his partner Georgie, a former nurse who has roamed the world and left her children to live with him in this promising community. However, dreaming of yet another life, she soon starts to feel out of place. The real outsider is Cambridge-educated Lu Fox, who is trying to deal with the loss of his family in a freak car crash. A loner seeking to break with this trauma, he survives by poaching lobster traps, considered "the worst crime in this community." In time, Georgie and Lu begin to seek solace in each other's embrace, but their secret is soon discovered and only points to trouble coming their way. When his dog is murdered, Lu decides that it's time for him to pull up stakes and leave.

His disappearance is the driving force of Winton's story, turning two failed romances and a Robinson Crusoe adventure into a road novel with a chase across land and sea. Fleeing White Point,

Lu drives two thousand miles up north where "red-blood sand meets the Ocean." He has reached a place where no one will find him, in a mangrove on an island, two hours off the coast by local plane, where only Indigenous people can survive.

Struggling to make his way in this stunning but indomitable wilderness, he lives precariously, seemingly forgetting that "Aborigines always move in groups and with food supplies and that living alone turns into a death in paradise."[2] These words foreshadow the dramatic end of the novel during which the three characters are reunited in a cataclysmic crash, plunging them into a desperate underwater race for survival.

Someone in the audience wondered about the author's involvement in environmental issues in Australia.

Winton: "I joined a defense committee for the protection of the northern West Coast and its coral barrier against the implantation of a kind of Club Med project. I reluctantly got my neck into the fight against it. My involvement prevented me from writing—my daily routine, but the defense committee needed a celebrity, a prominent personality to stop the plan. There were huge demonstrations, and against all odds, we won, and to such an extent that the internet messages and social networks crashed my computer."

Another person asked about the title Dirt Music and what he meant by it.

Winton: "I wrote this book as a tribute to music. We had gathered musicians together from all over and produced a record. Alone on his island, Lu stretches fishing lines between two trees, creating a primitive instrument, but there is also the music in the landscape, the multiple sounds of nature. Dirt Music is about Lu, the musician who used to play on his guitar all kinds of music, anything you could play on the verandah, you know, with no electricity for the guitar. It evokes trash, which is also the earth, the home country."

Julia Leigh

To conclude this reenactment of our Australian readings, I would be remiss to omit another major author, Julia Leigh, also a film director and screenwriter. In Paris on a short visit, Leigh heard about a reading at our bookshop with the American writer Claire Messud.[3] Having already met the author, she offered to introduce her. At the close of the evening, the audience pressed Julia Leigh to say a few words about her own critically acclaimed novel *The Hunter*.[4]

While in *Oscar and Lucinda* and *Dirt Music* implacable natural forces vanquish man, in Leigh's original and powerful work of fiction, the natural world is transmuted into the victim. In this case, it is a female tiger of a rare species that is killed by a hunter, an anonymous M, a man without a home or any emotional attachment for that matter. A biotech multinational has commissioned him to acquire the DNA of a tiger believed to be extinct, last spotted in 1936 on the Haut Plateau of Tasmania, an island state of Australia. The reader closely follows in the footsteps of the hunter tracking for days and nights the elusive animal which, both smart and insolent, initially thwarts numerous traps and failed gunshots.

Phantasmagorical Tasmanian nature is revealed close up through the sharp eye of this predator on the outlook for rock hollows, nooks, and bushes where the tiger may be hiding. At the same time, Leigh's own camera eye closely observes the hunter stalking this majestic animal. He finally manages to locate and kill her in cold blood, then meticulously skins her, now prepared to bring his precious booty back to the lab.

Never moralistic, Leigh intuits in this male hunter a faint sign of reverence for the dead body of his victim, the sacred female tiger: "She is more than an animal to him and observes her body as he would the body of a friend laid out in the morgue." Yet the quiver of emotion he may feel is suddenly reduced to the comment that "she looks nothing like the creature he knew before. . . . Now, her stillness is obscene."

With this chilling metaphor of the solitary tiger and its obsessive predator, Julia Leigh provides a doomed vision of contemporary man's blind obstinacy in targeting and gradually eradicating the resplendence of the natural world in one of its last sanctuaries.

Multilayered English Canadian Voices
LINGERING MEMORIES OF EUROPE
Margaret Atwood, Janet Urquhart, Michael Ondaatje,
and a tribute to Marian Engel

"Canadian Authors Find Paris Can Be a Closed Shop."[1] This compelling title of a 1985 article in a Montreal Anglophone paper confirmed the reality: English-language Canadian literature was more or less unknown at the time in France. The writer Mavis Gallant, who lived in Paris, was a case in point.[2] She was not alone: Margaret Atwood, the author of *Surfacing* (1972), a bestseller in the US and UK, had scant readership here. In fact, the sales of *Surfacing*'s French translation were so low that her publisher most unwillingly had to "let her go."[3]

In the same article, the French editor of a major publishing house in Paris wondered how she could appraise English Canadian literature when she "could not differentiate English Canadians from Americans." For her, "someone writing about rural Ontario was not much different from someone writing about Ohio."

Among other considerations, these sharp observations must have incited the Canadian Cultural Center to initiate a long-term program for the promotion of English Canadian literature primarily through translations and book launches of its writers' works. Our first major Canadian event at the Village Voice was a tribute to Marian Engel in February 1985, organized by Adrienne Clarkson, a Canadian diplomat in Paris and the future governor general of Canada. Clarkson praised Marian Engel's novel *Bear* as a work that holds a special place in Anglophone Canadian literature. Decried by some as "the most controversial novel ever written" in the country, it is regarded by others as "its quintessential book."

Margaret Atwood

Grande dame of English Canadian literature, Margaret Atwood is internationally known for her bestseller *The Handmaid's Tale*,[4] a dystopian depiction of a totalitarian state that subjects its young female civilians to coercive use of their bodies for reproductive purposes. Published in 1985, the novel introduces the constant themes of Atwood's fiction: patriarchal society and its exploitation of women.

These two motifs are likewise at the heart of Atwood's later *Alias Grace*,[5] presented at the Village Voice on April 5, 1998. The work is based on the 1843 headline news of the double murder of a man and his housekeeper by Grace Marks, an immigrant Irish servant of sixteen, known to be of a gentle disposition. Her trial and the ongoing investigation into her motives bring to light her master's pressing advances and the fate of Mary, her best friend, also a servant who, raped by the family's son, has died from a botched abortion.

Yet the doctors and judges who are called in prefer to base their expertise on seemingly invisible mechanisms at work in real life, though often expressed in dreams, a theory much in vogue at the time. Alerted to one of Grace's dreams that, from beyond the grave, Mary is the killing avenger, they conclude that the defendant is possessed by another persona, "alias Grace."

Accordingly, they declare that her crime has no relation to her social condition as a poor, young orphan. The Industrial Revolution in mid-century England had been advocating the rapid development of Canada, and it was most untimely to champion a destitute girl against employers who embody a rising bourgeoisie contributing to the expansion of this fledging province.

Atwood's talk was part of a joint reading with the American novelist Richard Ford, also in Paris for the French publication of his recent collection of three novellas *Women with Men*.[6] Excited by this opportunity to honor such consecrated writers, we planned the big event for a Sunday afternoon with beverages and cakes to be served after the reading.

In my naivete, I had brought together three literary stars: Margaret Atwood, with Mavis Gallant introducing her, and Richard Ford.

As it turned out, Mavis was too tired to attend the reading and would come only to preface Atwood's work, now reprogrammed to close the gala. However, Ford could not be reached and was not informed of this last-minute change. In truth, I had never imagined that he would not be with us from the start.

Given our prestigious guests, the bookshop was filled to overflowing, but our idyllic afternoon was to turn into a burlesque game of musical chairs. Only Atwood was on time, stoically sitting in her seat, graciously chatting with people in the front row.

We decided to start with her alone, but hardly had she begun when she was interrupted by Mavis who, urgently fetched by cab, had arrived and was gingerly making her way through the crowd. Her belated introduction was witty as usual, but soon broken up by the appearance of Ford who, cool, calm, and collected, confessed, "I lost my way." There was a huge burst of laughter in the bookstore, whereupon he took full control of his public, captivating the audience and relegating Atwood and Gallant to second and third fiddles.

Later that night, going over this comedy of errors in my mind, I realized the irony of the French titles on the printed invitation: *Alias Grace* had become *Captive*, and Ford's *Women with Men*, *Une situation difficile*.

I had to laugh as the translated titles appeared to have jinxed the reading. To top it all, our recording of the event had failed its own mission as the tapes proved to be irrevocably inaudible.

Jane Urquhart

This author's novel *The Stone Carvers*[7] is another example of the presence of Europe in Canadian literature at the close of the twentieth century. The author of poetry and fiction about women's destinies, Irish settlers, and immigrants, Jane Urquhart was at the Village Voice on April 7, 2005, to introduce her new work highlighting the role Canadian women played in the historical development of their country.

In her preface to the reading, Nancy Huston[8] spoke of departures, "aplenty in this novel and something very Canadian," she said. Indeed, there's lots of back and forth between the two continents, starting with the journey of a Bavarian priest migrating from old Europe to Ontario to start a mission in the country's wilderness and build a church for the local settlers, his future parishioners. Some years later, young Canadians were to make the opposite journey, crossing the ocean to actively participate in the First World War effort to defend France in the heart of Europe.

The main plot here revolves around Klara, a luminous woman whose brother Tilman and fiancé Eamon fall victim to this war. Tilman returns home crippled while Eamon disappears without a trace. A decade later, hearing of the project to erect a memorial to honor the sixty thousand Canadians fallen on the battlefield of Vimy in the North of France, Klara and her brother leave their Canadian village to participate in this project.

Disguised in male clothes, Klara works at stone carving, the "métier" she has learned from her grandfather, the original builder of the church. Entrusted with the task of shaping faces that symbolize the Canadian victims of this battle, she chisels features of

VILLAGE VOICE BOOKSHOP

We have the great pleasure of inviting you to

An Exceptional Literary Sunday Afternoon

Sunday, April 5th from 4pm to 7pm

with

MARGARET ATWOOD

The author will read excerpts from her latest novel

ALIAS GRACE

CAPTIVE
Traduit de l'anglais par Michèle Albaret-Maatsch
Publié aux éditions Robert Laffont
The author will be introduced by the Canadian writer **Mavis Gallant**

&

RICHARD FORD

The author will read excerpts from his latest work

WOMEN WITH MEN

UNE SITUATION DIFFICILE
Traduit de l'américain par Suzanne V.Mayoux
Publié aux éditions de l'Olivier
The author will be introduced by the American poet **Kathleen Spivack**

Refreshments
With the collaboration of the Cultural Services of the Canadian Embassy

Village Voice Bookshop 6 rue Princesse 75006 tel: 01 46 33 36 47

Invitation card to the joint reading of Margaret Atwood and Richard Ford, April 5, 1998.

Eamon on the countenance of the torchbearer, breathing into him new life while "giving, so to speak, a soul to the monument."

"Vimy," Urquhart stressed, is a historical monument, a symbol of a slice of the history of Canada. When these young men who had contributed to this historical turn of events for Europe, the country of their forbears, returned home to Canada, their experiences and memories became part of the history of their own country."

A woman in the audience wondered why Klara had thought it necessary to disguise herself in men's clothes to work on the monument.

Urquhart: "I see her choice as undergoing a transformation as a sculptor, freeing herself from the past as a 'spinster,' a condition associated with needlework then. Her case reminds me of the story of these two ladies in a Canadian town who were 'seamstresses,' but strongly rejecting such a term, they required their customers to call them 'tailors,' a word that evoked power and called for respect."[9]

As Jane Urquhart had indicated, Canada's participation in global affairs was fundamental in the construction of its identity. When the Second World War broke out, once more, along with the Allies, Canadians crossed the Atlantic Ocean, this time to fight Nazism in Europe. Their commitment to the old continent did not end with Victory Day, but continued with the opening of their country to European refugees. We remember Linette, the native protagonist of Mavis Gallant's story "Varieties of Exile," filled with wonder and excitement at the sight of those long lines of immigrants from different and distant lands bringing with them a diversity of cultures and languages.

Their new lives in Canada have been told, among others, by the Ontario authors Matt Cohen[10] and Anne Michaels[11] in their respective novels presented at the Village Voice, but another facet of this

recurring presence of European wars in English Canadian literature turns up unexpectedly in the novels of Sri Lankan Canadian
poet and fiction writer Michael Ondaatje.

Michael Ondaatje

Born in Sri Lanka and educated in Great Britain, Michael Ondaatje
was not even twenty when he settled in Toronto, soon describing
himself as "a man of no borders" and "a mongrel of place and race."
Ondaatje was to become one of the internationally renowned
fiction authors of Canada, as well as an essayist, editor, filmmaker,
and poet. Meeting him for the first time in 1972, Mavis Gallant
never forgot her first impression: "Everything about him spoke of
poetry."[12] In time, she saw their growing complicity and friendship
as the expression of their common pursuit for the perfect phrase.

It seemed fitting that Ondaatje's first presentation at the Village
Voice on April 9, 1986, should be devoted to poetry as he read from
his collection *Secular Love*[13] and his memoir *Running in the Family*, a
book of vignettes and poems about the rediscovery of his native
Sri Lanka and large family there, remembered from his childhood
and revisited in the 1970s.

Someone asked him about his main source of imagination:

Q: "Canada or Sri Lanka?"

Ondaatje: "From everywhere. When I first came to Canada it was
an exciting time for me, not a traumatic one. However, for a long
time, I forgot my past. I had come to Canada not with a lot of
baggage as people do, but my return to Sri Lanka twenty years
later, my reunion with my family was intentional: I wanted to
rediscover my past and my country. Sri Lanka was a surreal place."

A poet at heart, Ondaatje is also a novelist with a long list of prestigious literary prizes. Three out of the four fictional works he

launched at our bookstore are set in the context of a war: the First World War in *Divisadero*,[14] the Sri Lankan Civil War in *Anil's Ghost*,[15] and World War II in *The English Patient*,[16] a piece he discussed with us on February 17, 1993.

On this occasion, a member of our audience remarked that war is omnipresent in this novel, but never shown. So, Ondaatje made it clear that "*The English Patient* is not a war novel. If it were to be one, which I did not want it to be, I would have depicted action and facts around the people involved. I don't speak about allies or enemies."

In fact, the reader is never directly confronted with the 1944 war raging in Italy, but in this Florentine Villa San Girolamo, which used to be a field hospital, everything speaks of war: damaged by the bombs of the enemy in their retreat, it is now a ruin open to the winds and beleaguered by a mined garden. All the patients have been evacuated but one, a mysterious man known as the English patient who, burned beyond recognition, has been left behind in the care of Hana, a Canadian nurse who volunteers to stay with him. Few words are exchanged between the two, and yet they communicate through the patient's annotations of Herodotus's *Histories* that Hana reads aloud to him from his personal notebook.

These bits of words, interrogations, and expressive silences progressively reveal who they are and where they come from. Soon and out of nowhere, two strangers appear at the villa: one with his bandaged hands, maimed, we learn, during a torture session, and a Sikh drawn to the place by the sound of a piano heard in the distance. Contracted by the British army to defuse mines and buried bombs, Kip also knows that booby traps may well be hidden inside musical instruments.

These four characters locked in together and isolated from the rest of the world remind us of another Florentine "huis-clos" at the time of the Black Death in medieval days. As in Boccaccio's *Decameron*, where young people keep the plague at a distance by inventing an alternative world of stories, the empty and desolate space of this villa is an invitation to fill it with the freely flowing meditative thoughts silently circulating among this family of sorts.

Q: "Writing this novel of the characters' interiority in poetic prose, did it feel different from writing poetry?"

Ondaatje: "I come from poetry and, as in my poems, I leave space in my prose. I suggest and let the reader fill in the blank spaces."

Q: "How do you plan your novels? Do you write detailed outlines?"

Ondaatje: "No, I don't. As I write, I discover the story and the place. I had started this novel as a mystery and wrote a four-page outline, but by the end of it I was so bored that I abandoned it. The book begins with the image of a man crashing in the desert. Who was he? What was he doing there? Why had he crashed? With these images, the book started its quest. While I was describing that desert landscape, I knew I was waiting for someone. That's the way, starting with an image or whatever, something calls for a story, but sometimes there is no story."

Q: "And yet you seem to have control over the narrative and your characters."

Ondaatje: "Oh, no, I don't control my characters. Some writers treat the characters like puppets, and finally we get the feeling that they are talking down to them. It ends up as a didactic piece. As I said, I'm waiting for things to happen. I love accidents, unexpected occurrences. In *The English Patient*, Caravaggio appears at the villa out of nowhere. Or what happens with Kip, the sapper? I did not even know that Kip would be in the novel, but I was describing this field of mines, and I knew that I was expecting someone and here he was.

"But I certainly did not expect what came next: He is concentrated on the bomb he is defusing, the third and most dangerous one, when, all of a sudden, he's rushing out of the pit where he is working, screaming. 'What happened?' everyone asks. 'There's a rat down there,' he yells back."

Q: "Kip, whose name evokes Kipling, is a Sikh medical student turned sapper in the British army. In the course of the novel he becomes aware of his own contradictions between his allegiance to the British Crown and his disillusionment in Europe with its wars for the sake of power. Is he a character you identify with or feel particularly close to?"

Ondaatje: "I feel very close to my characters; each one is a part of myself, including Kip, but at first, I was not aware of this. As a result, fiction is much more intimate, say, than autobiography. With *Running in the Family*, a memoir of my family, I didn't feel as much bereft of my characters as I felt at the end of this novel."[17]

In June 2012, on hearing of the closing of our bookstore, Michael called us from Toronto. His new book was not coming out in France until the fall, but he was nevertheless coming: "I want to read from my new novel as my personal farewell to the Village Voice," he told me. I was moved beyond words, and one of his admissions during one of his interviews crossed my mind: "I've loved the readings at the Village Voice, as an audience member and as a reader."[18] So a date was set for his reading of *The Cat's Table* for June 28, three weeks away.

That night, the bookstore looked like a "crowded pigeon coop" (his own words), but there was also a strong whiff of nostalgia in the air. Fortunately, Ondaatje's playful title *The Cat's Table*[19] seemed to refer to a children's adventure which it is, at least partly.

Before starting to read, Ondaatje warned us that this book was fiction. Yes, he had traveled by sea from Sri Lanka to London as a young boy, but he said, "Luckily, I had no recollection of that trip and I had to invent it all." *The Cat's Table* is the story of that picaresque sea journey told by the narrator as the eleven-year-old Minah who travels from his birthplace of Sri Lanka, Ceylon at the time, to London to be reunited with his long-absent mother.

On the boat he meets two other boys his age, and together they throw themselves into reckless and fun adventures. We follow them in their exploration of the depths of the ship with the marvels of its engine room and their discovery of a magical garden, not unlike the one in Alice's Wonderland. We are seized with awe and terror as the liner is caught in a spectacular gale, and we share their excitement as they pass through the Suez Canal with its intense, colorful life of exotic hustle and bustle on its quays.

But most interesting of all is what's happening at the "Cat's Table," the table farthest away from the Captain and his distinguished guests. Seated in that lowly place with its strange cast of eccentric adult characters, the youngsters pick up fragments of conversations that hint at secret lives and extravagant ways that will continue to fire up their imagination, making their sea passage into a unique coming-of-age experience, a life passage.

Q: "In this novel, like in others, you have people living at the margins of society. Is this a political stand on your part, a class issue?"

Ondaatje: "I'm simply not interested in people with power. There is no intimacy in their conversations or interactions. As I was finishing the book, I thought it would be good to go through the experience of a voyage at sea, and I traveled from Canada to England, seven days at sea. I had a seat reserved at a table of six people. I didn't know them, and they were not my people. I ended up going to the cafeteria every day."

Q: "Two historical figures, Buddy Bolden and Billy the Kid, are the subjects of two of your earlier books. Do you have any other historical figure you would like to write about?"

Ondaatje: "I'm interested in people who are interesting personalities."[20]

Closing our thirty years of readings with Michael Ondaatje was particularly significant to me. I remembered the words he had told us at one time: "There's always a story ahead of us." Indeed, there would be many more stories written by the author in the years to come, but this one—the narrative of a boy on his way to his destiny—was still a blank page waiting to be filled. This thought that the end of this wondrous voyage at sea meant the beginning of a new adventure for the protagonist suddenly brightened up my mood: the end of a story is always the beginning of a new one and the closing of the bookstore would not be our last Village Voice journey.

Michael Ondaatje at the Village Voice with French publisher Olivier Cohen, literary agent Michèle Lapautre, and Edmund White, February 17, 1993. © C. Deudon

PART FOUR

Closing Ceremonies

"Poetry contains the possibility of perfection."
—NICOLE KRAUSS,
   Village Voice reading, April 27, 2011.

"Writing a poem is an affirmation of a voice,
the poet's unique voice."
—C. K. WILLIAMS,
   Village Voice reading, October 14, 2010.

Poetry Festival at the bookstore, 1993. From left to right: Odile, Alice Notley, Mary Jo Salter, Kathleen Spivack, Carolyn Kizer. © C. Deudon

23
The Center Holds
OUR CIRCLE OF POETS

Stephen Spender, Harry Mathews, Marilyn Hacker, Margo Berdeshevsky,
Marie Ponsot, Kathleen Spivack, C. K. Williams, Ellen Hinsey, W. S. Merwin

P oets played a major role in the life of our bookshop, giving regular readings over thirty years. The twentieth century is often referred to as the golden age of poetry in the United States, so it makes sense that many prominent poets of its postwar generation launched their works with us. Though their number is impressive in every sense of the term, it is impossible to recount the three decades of their continued presence in one chapter. Should we include their readings on the basis of personal taste, their individual fame, or the intrinsic literary quality of their works? We finally decided to choose the poets who permanently resided or lived on and off in Paris, in recognition of the importance of our opening pages in that they are dedicated to the Third Wave of expatriate writers coming from the States.

Stephen Spender
One illustrious exception is Stephen Spender, born in Britain but a continental writer at heart, fully engaged in the century's upheavals. At seventy-nine, he was the oldest poet to read at the Village Voice and a rare survivor of the Lost Generation. Essayist and novelist as well,

like a number of British writers of his generation, Stephen Spender lived in Paris in the thirties, contributing to the literary effervescence of this bold literary movement. To my knowledge, he was the last living poet to have presented his work at Sylvia Beach's Shakespeare and Company in a 1937 joint reading with Ernest Hemingway.*

More than fifty years later, Stephen Spender was at the Village Voice on April 16, 1988, to inaugurate his novel The Temple,[1] a fictionalized memoir of three young friends, none other than himself, W. H. Auden, and Christopher Isherwood. In 1929, freshly out of Oxford (for the first two) and Cambridge (for the latter), they went to Germany to enjoy celebrated free speech and free love, away from Britain's crippling censorship laws and amidst scenic landscapes of forests, rivers, and lakes, disturbed only by sporadic gunshots in the distance. In 1932, they decided to leave their paradise as increasing waves of hatred and violence made them fear the worst for their adopted country.

When it first came out, The Temple was immediately banned on the grounds of its homosexuality, and it was only after a long slumber in a Texan archive that a young researcher plucked it from oblivion. Those youthful years were so ingrained in Spender's mind that, working on a newly restored edition in 1988, he was still able to set down all the dialogue and telling details from memory.

As he entered the bookshop, Spender appeared as an imposing, noble figure radiating a full rich life, his solemn expression somewhat softened by a puff of curly white hair. François Xavier Jaujard, prominent French translator and publisher of poetry, introduced him, emphasizing the role of W. H. Auden in Spender's life and poetry and regretting that Spender was little known in France. "It was a shame," he told us, "that Spender had not been translated by

---

* Both writers participated in the Spanish Civil War and both wrote about their own experiences of it: Hemingway in his novel For Whom the Bell Tolls (1940) and Spender in several of his journals and essays.

French poets of his stature, such as Stéphane Mallarmé or Michel Leiris, who had superbly translated T. S. Eliot."

In the crowded room, Stephen Spender opened his talk by acknowledging friends sitting in the audience, including novelist Mary McCarthy, and then refuting Jaujard's remark that he had been influenced by W. H. Auden: "If I understood you well, you spoke of some kind of leadership of Auden and of his influence on our Oxford and later Berlin group. It is puzzling to me that one should use the word 'influence' to describe our relationship. Auden could teach you, immediately discerning 'a marvelous line from absolute trash,' but there is a net difference between teaching and influencing."

He admitted that coming from a more cultivated milieu, Auden was the most sophisticated of the three, and "being the son of a psychoanalyst, he analyzed each of us, his close friends." There was another disparity between the two of them in their respective tastes in poetry, as Auden had hated Romanticism, including the poems of Shelley and Keats, two spirits who had nourished Spender since childhood. "In the mid- and late twenties," he reminded us, "these Romantic poets were the very climax of poetry, whether English, French, or German."

He insisted that he had published this memoir not just out of a desire to see the novel of his youth come out, but equally because "I felt like writing for them, these friends now dead. Their deaths had created a vacuum which, in turn, set me free." To him, The Temple was a personal testament to the generation they had once shared through their works.

After his reading, I approached Mary McCarthy, who was wrapped in a fur coat, a bit odd on that mild April afternoon. She was the center of a crowd of admirers eavesdropping on her conversation with Mavis Gallant.

I asked Mary McCarthy if she would consider presenting her fictional works at the Village Voice. She agreed to do this but only in the fall, after her return from the States. She was never to be back in Paris again, sadly passing away in New York in 1989.

The eighties were certainly not a decade of Romantic poetry. Coinciding with innovative theories of deconstruction in vogue at this time, new currents of poetry were developing, known as Language poetry. Soon after the bookshop opened, a couple of French customers came by looking for a collection of "American Language poets." They were French poets putting together an anthology of this avant-garde movement that called attention to the use of language.

As it turned out, in the spring of 1986, these two French poets—Emmanuel Hocquard and Claude Royet-Journoud—would

Stephen Spender, April 16, 1998. © Roberta Fineberg

present 21+1 *Poètes Américains d'aujourd'hui*. Among other poets, it featured Michael Palmer, Lyn Hejinian, Rae Armantrout, Charles Bernstein, Clark Coolidge, and Keith and Rosmarie Waldrop, all of whom would later give individual readings at the Village Voice.

To my great surprise and disappointment, this collection was not bilingual, but only published in French translation, an aberration, given that the music of the original language would be definitively lost in this work. In his defense, Hocquard explained that one could only understand these new American poets in France through translation. He further maintained that "a poem translated into French is a French poem. It must stand on its own without the crutches of the original text. The American poem need not be present, considering that translation is a writing practice of its own, and it was up to the translator to take full responsibility for his text in French."[2]

This group of French Language poets was joined by two American poets living in Paris: Joseph Simas, founder of the magazine *Moving Letters*, dedicated to experimental poetry, and Cole Swensen, who in her own prose and poetry explored exciting ways to invent language. Both of them translated these French poets into English.[3]

In 1987, a sign of the times was the launching of the first Paris International Poetry Festival at the Place Saint-Sulpice, just around the corner. The Anglophone poets invited to participate in this unprecedented public event were all actively involved in the life and the readings of our bookshop: David Applefield, Pierre Joris, Carol Pratl, Joseph Simas, Cole Swensen, Alice Notley, British poet Douglas Oliver, and American novelist and poet Harry Mathews.

Harry Mathews

As it happens, by the time Harry Mathews gave his first reading at the Village Voice in 1986, he had lived on and off in Paris for more than thirty years. Bilingual and likewise steeped in French literature and culture, he had arrived in the city in 1952, the year his friends Peter Matthiessen and George Plimpton were preparing the launch of the *Paris Review* (1953).

In turn, Mathews founded his own review, *Locus Solus*, the title of a novel by the French writer Raymond Roussel,[4] an irreverent innovator of the language in a surrealist vein who, Mathews said, had enabled him to write fiction "with constraints and sustained intensity coming from the form, the structure of language."[5]

His friend, the American poet John Ashbery, another pioneer who experimented with language, also a member of the *Paris Review* group in the fifties, was back in Paris in 1992 for a retrospective of his poetry and art works at the Pompidou Center. He gave a reading of *Flow Chart*[6] at the Village Voice on June 26, 1992, an event that members of the French intelligentsia from the Cultural Affairs Ministry attended.

Mathews's own prose and poetry are feats of inventiveness, with words stretched to their infinite possibilities as seen in his cult novel *The Sinking of the Odradek Stadium*,[7] and his short story "The Dialect of the Tribe,"[8] which he discussed at our bookstore on May 13, 1986. Written in the form of a fictitious letter to Georges Perec, French author and close friend of his, this extravagant and comical story recounts the daunting task of translating an invented tribal tongue into English.

Wondering how to make a tribal idiom intelligible in another language, Mathews addresses the question of the writing act: the transformative process at work in translation equally concerns creative writing which, he explains, "is an infinitely arduous translation which every writer has to struggle with."[9] Here is one more acrobatic exercise in language, familiar to Mathews who had translated part of *La disparition*, Perec's three-hundred-page experimental novel without the vowel *e*, an extraordinary challenge deftly met by both the author and his translator.[10] Mathews' audacious forays into language challenge the reader, but they are also games for the author, who admitted "I write to entertain myself."[11]

Not surprisingly, he was the first American writer to be accepted as a member of the Oulipo, the experimental Atelier for Potential Literature that aimed at renewing French poetry through language. Besides Mathews, this exclusive club included Georges Perec, Raymond Queneau, Italo Calvino, and the mathematician and poet Jacques Roubaud. They regularly met to invent creative ways of combining new words into sentences and to manipulate language by introducing esoteric terms, puns, mathematical permutations, and "hidden forms," all tossed together like ingredients in a caldron for *Country Cooking*, the title of Mathews's own collection of stories that includes "The Dialect of the Tribe."

Introducing Harry Mathews's first reading at the Village Voice, Edmund White mentioned that before embarking for France, his New York friends had recommended he look Mathews up in Paris, "a great artist," they insisted. Upon his arrival, Edmund went directly to the Pompidou Center to get his address, but "there was no artist listed by that name. "[12] [laughter] This humorous quid pro quo was in line with Mathews's playful games of mirror and "hide and seek," characteristic of the Oulipian spirit but also of his own arcane narrative inventions.

Asked by the audience how he would qualify his experience as an experimental writer in France, Mathews replied: "Nobody in France makes a fuss about being a writer," adding that "readers in this country were used to a bigger range of words. French readers understand what I mean in my writings and support them. In the US, when my first works came out, people couldn't understand my motives for writing such books."

First published in the *Paris Review* in 1962, Harry Mathews remained associated with this literary magazine all his life. In 1973, its headquarters moved from Paris to New York, but maintained an influential presence in France through its editors in the capital. Mathews was one of them from 1989 to 2003, the year of the commemoration of its fiftieth anniversary.

However, with the passing of its founder George Plimpton, the celebration was postponed. In 2006, Philip Gourevitch, Plimpton's successor and the *Paris Review*'s new editor-in-chief, chose Paris, the cradle of the review, to organize belated festivities. On March 3, at the Village Voice, he presided over a number of readings of fiction, essays, and poems that highlighted the broad range of literary contents and styles published in the *Paris Review* over five decades.

The most compelling story we heard that evening involved William Faulkner's humorous account of his quarrel with Hollywood's MGM studio that turned into a comedy of errors.[13] In fact, it ended with the studio firing Faulkner. Olivia de Havilland,

Harry Mathews,
October 10, 1994.
© C. Deudon

the poignant young Melanie in *Gone with the Wind*, marvelously read this hilarious and absurdist exchange at cross-purposes. At the age of ninety, still a most impressive and elegant woman, she had lost none of her dramatic talent as she graciously reached out to the audience crowded in the bookshop.

Marilyn Hacker

> Paris, elegant gray
> godmother, consolation,
> heartbroken lullaby,
> smell of the metro station,
> you won't abandon me.[14]
>
> —MARILYN HACKER

Marilyn Hacker is probably the most Parisian of all the American poets who have read at the Village Voice, not because she has lived in the city since the early 1980s, but in her ceaseless work to capture Paris in all its states: from its bright street corners and hidden back alleys to the fugitive changes of light in the city. Of course, she is not the only poet to use all the possibilities of the language to convey impressions of its classical beauty, its capricious skies and sometimes cruel paradoxes, but she is the poet who always chooses the right word for the subtlest detail of a scene or the nuance of a feeling. Referencing Gertrude Stein, Susan Sontag reminds us that "the distinctive genius of poetry is naming."[15]

Hacker perceives her daily Parisian surroundings not only through her eyes, but through all her senses, the prism of a particular light or a sudden memory metamorphosing the most ordinary sight into a layered vision, as seen in "White voile in open windows, sudden green / and scarlet window-box geraniums / back-lit in cloud-encouraged clarity / against the century-patinaed gray / is such a gift of the quotidian."[16]

She also knows the history of her neighborhood, le Marais, nearly invisible as it is, concealed in its stones and stored in the memory of its people. In her poem "Street Scene V" the quiet evening is suddenly disturbed by the loud popular songs of a group of German tourists in a café under her window, bawdy refrains perhaps heard during the Nazi occupation. Across the street, people are "pulling their curtains," trying to stifle the sounds and perhaps

Marilyn Hacker,
April 9, 1997.
© C. Deudon

the painful memories of those in the building who were wrested away and never seen again.*

Marilyn's Paris is a woven texture of surprises and contrasts, of silvered dreams and raw realities, of more nooks and crannies to be discovered. Two streets away from her "tourist-infested neighborhood," the poet stumbles upon a hidden country scene, frozen in the past: "Behind a shop front, two gray women were/turning clay on wheels that softly whined / . . . / on a clothesline / two work shirts flapped above a cobbled yard . . . ," and just around the corner, "the Cyber Bar,/and, in the rue du Temple, Monoprix."[17]

Another theme of predilection from her rich repertoire is friendship, particularly among women. In fact, many of her poems are snapshots of intimate moments, of longing and mind-wandering through memories of love and separations written down in the privacy of her Parisian home: "I have a reading lamp and an open book. / Last glass of wine, last morsel of Saint André / . . . / What will I say to you when I write to you?/ I'm home, I've cleaned the kitchen, taken/charge of my solitude / . . . What do I tell myself . . . ? / Life's not forever, love is precarious. / Wherever I live, let me come home to you / . . . where you/meet me and walk with me to the river."[18]

One day, I received a note from Mavis Gallant[19] with a faded copy of one of Marilyn's poems. It read: "This is the poem I told you about, which I find haunting . . . It seems to me a fine example of deep emotion transfigured by art." Sent by fax, what is left of it is one miserable blank page of now-invisible words erased by time. I do not remember which poem Mavis was referring to, but such a tribute from a writer regularly compared to Chekhov was a lofty acknowledgement of Marilyn's art.

Speaking of her poetry at a reading on April 9, 1987, Marilyn admitted that "metric poetry was not part of our generation," yet

---

* Marilyn lives in le Marais, the Jewish quarter of the 1930s and 1940s where, starting in 1942, French Vichy policemen deported inhabitants to detention and extermination camps.

her seemingly free-flowing verse is an elaborate architecture of words arranged according to the "strict constraints of the classical poetic forms,"[20] as Edmund White pointed out in his introduction to one of her readings. He then praised her as "a formidable poet, combining in her craft Elizabethan wordplay, the classical precision of the sonnet, the villanelle, or the rondo, together with contemporary narratives and slang."

A prolific and award-winning writer, Marilyn Hacker delves into a wide range of themes and realms, but Paris remains the vital source of her inspiration and the distinctive core of many of her poems. At a number of her talks at the bookshop, someone in the audience would invariably thank her for making them rediscover a Paris they did not see anymore.

Margo Berdeshevsky is another poet inhabited by her adopted city. She finds her distinct poetic voice in her immediate surroundings as she experiments with different forms of writing, mixing words and collages of photos, graffiti, and artworks that complement and enhance the original imagery of her metaphors. On January 10, 2008, at the launch of her recent collection of poems *But a Passage in Wilderness*,[21] Berdeshevsky was introduced by Marilyn Hacker who described her insights as "a perception of existence at its most tragic, yet as a chain of blossoming possibilities."

In the poem "Whom Beggars Call," the poet summons up a typical Parisian scene. On a Christmas Eve, browsing through her local market overflowing with rich, abundant food, she spots a homeless man crouched against the wall of a church, "drowning in plastic, and bottles, and bread, and blood. I watch my coins, how they slip his loose claw. It's because I have purposely eluded making a skin contact . . ."

On her way home, haunted by the man, "his lips, his water-eyes," her hand and his claw "skin to skin," she realizes the boundaries of her own life: "Your tall and educated walls—Break them . . . Your all that is the wound, unhealed." Remembering the words of Saint Augustine, "a heart that understands cuts like rust in the bones,"[22] her experience of a seemingly ordinary encounter becomes an existential revelation on a holy day.

Marie Ponsot happened to be in Paris the weekend of our Poetry Festival at the Village Voice in 1993 and accepted our invitation to read. Now in the city where she had lived for many years, she returned to places once important to her and fittingly chose to read "For My Old Self, at Notre-Dame de Paris: *fluctuat nec mergitur*"[23] a poem suffused with nostalgic emotions from memories of her former Paris life.

Years later, on the fateful night of April 15, 2019, awestruck by the sudden apparition on my computer screen of flames darting out of the cathedral towers, her poem came back to me. Wanting to read it right then, I went to get it down from my shelves. Indeed, the poet's description of "the dark madonna cut from a knot of wood" was truly heartbreaking. At that very minute, the centuries-old Madonna was being consumed into ashes.

Incredulous and longing to hold on to what had been, I recited the poem out loud in an effort to drown out any and all reporter voices and take solace in her invocation: "I call to thank her, loud above / the joy she raised me for, this softfall. Sweet time."

Perhaps hoping to keep this memory of the "sweet time" of her Paris years, Ponsot subtitled her poem "*fluctuat nec mergitur*"("tossed by the waves, but does not sink"). Poets are said to be visionaries.

Kathleen Spivack, another unconditional lover of Paris, had sat in the same classroom as Sylvia Plath in the poetry workshops of their renowned mentor, poet Robert Lowell, in the late 1950s. In her compelling memoir *With Robert Lowell and His Circle*,[24] Spivack recalls her formative years as a young poet and her friendship with some of the major poetic voices of the twentieth century, including Robert Lowell and Sylvia Plath, of course, but also Elizabeth Bishop, Anne Sexton, and Stanley Kunitz, among others.

The daughter of Viennese parents who had left their country in the early '40s for the United States, Kathleen remains emotionally attached to Europe and particularly to France where she has lived part-time over the years as a teacher of American literature and creative writing at a number of universities.

A poet of impressionistic scenes of seemingly simple domestic life, as in *The Beds We Lie In* and *Moments of Past Happiness*, she is also highly sensitive to the history of Europe, its wars, and their aftermath. From *A History of Yearning*, presented at the Village Voice on March 15, 2011, Kathleen read her triptych of "Photographs Already Fading."[25]

In the first poem, "Grandcamp. February 2003," she hauntingly depicts the young soldiers mowed down on the Normandy beaches in World War II: "we breathed the sharp air, the night prickled with stars / and the young men froze where they fell . . ."

Her second poem "Paris. March 2003, Sur le pont, le pont de la déportation" revives the Parisian (and worldwide) demonstrations against the imminent threat of a second war in Iraq. As the protesters slowly progress through city streets and squares, they prod passersby to remember the victims of the Nazi occupation and the Vichy laws: "We filed with the Americans and French . . . / past the Jewish Memorial to the Deportees, / the bridges, the skeletons, the polished plaques / to fallen heroes . . ."

And the poet's triptych ends with "Anthem for Doomed Youth exhibit,"[26] her sublime tribute to the sacrificed generation of British poets, some of whom survived the trenches, including Siegfried Sassoon and Robert Graves, and others who fell on the battlefields of the First World War: "The scholar-warriors made more luminous by time . . ."

In other sections of this anthology, Kathleen reminds us that alongside its horrors, the twentieth century gave rise to the prospect of transcendence through its immense artists. Among these masters, she summons up Gustav Klimt, the painter of *Vienna Before History* and its "lost world" of "jeweled and doe-eyed women," Edward Hopper's "blazing streak of bold yellow," and Claude Monet's "pastel cloudy scrim of swirling pink." These visual references are shafts of light amidst darkness that, in the poet's words, open "endless vestibules of possibility."

C. K. Williams. June 20, 1995. © C. Deudon

C. K. Williams

For C. K. Williams, imbued with the animus of Walt Whitman, poetry cannot exist without the consciousness of the spiritual world. A Pulitzer Prize–winning poet, critic, and translator of international stature, Williams was a central figure of the American writing community in Paris and a great favorite at the Village Voice. During one of his book launches, Charlie, as he was known to his friends, took a long look at the public and good-humoredly compared his readings at our bookstore to his bar mitzvah: "Everyone knows me and I know everyone," he quipped.[27] It was hardly a surprise, as for almost thirty years he and his French wife Catherine had lived on and off in Paris, and it stood to reason that his French and American friends rarely missed one of his readings with us.

Between 1991 and 2010 he launched eight of his poetry collections at the Village Voice. Among them are *Flesh and Blood*,[28] *Repair*,[29] *The Singing*,[30] and *Wait*. He likewise introduced a memoir, *Misgivings, My Mother, My Father, Myself*,[31] and his essay *On Whitman*.[32] Outstanding poets such as Carolyn Kizer, Adam Zagajewski, Jeffrey Greene, and Michael Blumenthal, as well as famed novelist Diane Johnson, prefaced his readings. At the launch of *The Singing* on November 6, 2003, Blumenthal recalled a memorable moment in his youth when a friend pressed into his hands a book by C. K. Williams, urging him to read it. "Immediately, I knew I had stumbled upon someone like no one else ... I sensed in this poet an incredible intelligence, a ravenous hunger for the world. I also sensed someone terribly attentive to his own torments, sufferings and pains and his own longings. It's no accident," he added, "that C. K. Williams shows up on the shelves between Whitman and the other Williams,[33] as I call him, because he combines so many of their virtues, provoking through creative, anxiety-propelled intelligence the beautiful grounded in the human."

A charismatic presence, standing tall but slightly bent over the microphone as he read his poems, Charlie liked to open the evening with a witty remark, loosening up that initially suspended, tense moment and hoping to forge complicity with his audience. After a short pause, he would start reciting his work, slowly articulating the long lines of free verse that characterize the incantatory rhythm of his poetry, bringing on a meditative mood. Then, suddenly, he would crack a joke, breaking the spell and making everyone laugh. I was always amazed by the contrast between this discreet and pensive person and the poet who staged each of his readings as a live performance.

Most of his poems begin with a down-to-earth event, a factual detail or personal memory which he calls an "incident": "My notebooks are filled with them," he said, "incidents I have witnessed, experienced, or were reported to me. [Yet] in order to become a poem, an incident has to impose itself on me; it has to go around in my head for a while and be ruminated, before coming to maturity and ready to come down onto the page."[34]

Williams spent many years in France, but wrote relatively few poems about Paris or Normandy where he later moved. One poem, though, called "Marina,"[35] about Marina Tsvetaeva, one of the greatest Russian poets of the twentieth century, takes place in Clamart where she lived, on the southwestern edge of Paris. After the death of her small child from hunger in the aftermath of the Soviet revolution, she went into exile, first wandering through Europe to finally settle down in this suburb where she lived for twenty years, isolated and impoverished, unpublished and snubbed, even by the community of the Russian diaspora. She returned home on the eve of World War II with two children to face the execution of her husband and the disappearance of her elder daughter and sister in Stalinist camps. Ostracized in her own country and driven "beyond a person's endurance,"[36] Tsvetaeva hanged herself in 1941 in the desolate town of Yelabuga, in deep Russian country.

However, Marina Tsvetaeva's tragic end, emblematic of millions of lives crushed by Stalin's iron fist, is not the focus of Williams's poem, only its starting point. When he presented his collection *Wait* in the fall of 2010, his last reading at the Village Voice, he talked at length about his writing process: "Starting from a factual or incidental element, a poem is to evolve toward a higher point or moral argument,"[37] an objective he shared with Tsvetaeva in her essay "Art in the Light of Conscience."[38] Both poets arrive at the same conclusion: the artist is responsible for his own creation, implying a higher consciousness of the world and the necessity for the artist to elevate art to the spiritual realm. Resonating also with Whitman's embrace of the world, Williams adheres to Tsvetaeva's higher calling for art which is or ought to be "a kind of physical world / of the spiritual . . . a spiritual world / of the physical . . . almost flesh."[39]

The first question from the audience that evening concerned the central notion of ethics in his poetry: "Does this mean, in your view, that there cannot be true poetry without 'the moral argument,' as you call it? And can political or social poems change the world?"

Williams: "Not all of my poems are concerned with the question of morality. I don't write all the time about my political and social convictions. At times I treat them in a poem, but not always, and if not, they go underground into the unconscious of the verses. And I will add that most of the great art works speak about the world of their time, but not necessarily in moral ways.

However, these times are darker than what I've known: the war in Iraq, fundamentalists in power controlling things, and the idea that a Yale student might graduate while not believing in evolution. All that makes me feel an urgency to express all the things that are articulating our world. I even wondered at one point if I should write political essays or political verses that might have more impact. But no, political poems do not change the world, but that doesn't make it less urgent to write them, to write the experience of our time, and whether or not they have an impact is incidental."

Q: "As you read your poems, not only do you go through them, but you also put your listeners through them. Does the act of reading your poems before an audience bring on a relief of emotion?"

Williams: "There is a moral relief when I know how the poem is going to be resolved, and, especially, when it is finished. I noticed that emotion is greater on my first public reading of a poem. There are even poems like 'Marina' when, at my first public reading, my voice broke down and tears came to my eyes, very embarrassing. But then, when I happen to read them again in public, that emotion is not there anymore. It has been evacuated, and now placed in a context, the poem has become an object, and the emotional impact lies in the language."

Q: "Some of the poems you read are quite dark and leave the reader bereft of hope. 'At my age,' you said, 'all I'm doing is confirming my sadness,' but in that sea of darkness, is there a skylight?"

Williams: "Darkness is to yield to authority, its public acquiescence. Skylight is when people communicate directly with others. And writing could be seen as a skylight. Writing a poem is an affirmation of a voice—the poet's unique voice."

Williams closed his reading with the poem "The Foundation,"[40] a tribute to the poets who had been his life's mental companions, and who, like him, viewed poetry as an art above "philosophizing and theories": "I'm with my poets, my Rilke, my Yeats / we're leaping together through the debris, a jumble of wrack, / but my Keats floats across it, my Herbert and Donne . . ." What made poetry? "It was the singing, the choiring, the cadence / the lull of the vowels, the chromatic consonant clatter . . ."

At an earlier event at the bookshop in 1987, in her introduction to Williams's presentation of *Flesh and Blood*, Carolyn Kizer had sensed the true essence of his poetry: "It can wring you out like a rag and exhilarate you at the same time, but then, that's among the oldest descriptions of true art that we have."[41]

In December 2015, just after his passing, a tribute to C. K. Williams was organized by the poet Jeffrey Greene* at the American University of Paris where he taught literature. A community of writers from the Village Voice—Ellen Hinsey, Denis Hirson, Nancy Huston, Jeffrey Greene, Jake Lamar, and I—evoked memories of "Charlie" and read his poems aloud to a large gathering of his grieving Parisian friends.

---

* Jeffrey Greene is the author of a collection of poetry, *American Spirituals*, and prose narratives inspired by his adopted province Burgundy. At the Village Voice, he introduced some of the greater American and other poetic voices of the twentieth century, including Ellen Hinsey, W. S. Merwin, Mark Strand, Lithuanian Tomas Venclova, and C. K. Williams.

Ellen Hinsey and French poet Claire Malroux, November 21, 2002. © Mark Carlson.

Ellen Hinsey

Just back from a conference on contemporary American poetry, C. K. Williams expressed his dismay at the stack of poetry he had read for the occasion in these terms: "unpardonably trivial, unambitious and patently disposable." "Those poems," he told us, "lacked a sense of history, vision of imagination, and moral reflection," but "in stark contrast, these are the very qualities that distinguish the poetry of Ellen Hinsey, one of the handful of poets today who are always worth studying."

Introducing her at the launch of her second collection of poetry, *The White Fire of Time*,[42] written after a family tragedy, Williams went on to describe her as a "a poet who has found the way to be both truthful and original, writing poems absorbing, enlightening, and historically pertinent, as well as philosophically urgent and precise." His words captured the essence of her volume of poems that invoked spiritual forces at the time "when courage is lost in the wild dark hours, when chaos swirls, and face-to-face with the abyss, you near the white fire of time."[43]

Ellen Hinsey arrived in Paris from Boston in 1987 at the height of the Third Wave of American expatriates, "a time," she explained, "coinciding with momentous changes that would overtake Eastern Europe." During the Village Voice years, she wrote three volumes of poetry that she launched at our bookshop: *Cities of Memory*,[44] *The White Fire of Time*, and *Update on the Descent*.[45]

Likewise, Ellen introduced the Village Voice readings of such prestigious poets as Adrienne Rich and the Irish poet Harry Clifton, as we've seen earlier. Thanks to her, we had the immense privilege of discovering and hearing Tomas Venclova,[46] a prominent Lithuanian poet and iconic literary figure of twentieth-century Mitteleuropa. Ellen was also one the few women writers with Carol Pratl[47] who, defying a roster of bureaucratic rules, successfully set up the earlier mentioned First International Women Writers Conference in Paris, featuring major women poets, novelists, and essayists from France, the United States, and, miraculously, the Soviet Union.

On June 6, 1996, Ellen Hinsey launched *Cities of Memory*, a collection of poems reflecting her fascination with Europe—the caldron of ideas, art invention, and ... of repeated wars. Over time, Central Europe would become one of her primary topics of reflection and writing. In his introduction that evening, Denis Hirson saw the source of "her quest for other places, other times and other people in her personal exile, an ocean away from her native country, but one chosen as a way of investigating the world around her and her own self in it."[48] Written after witnessing firsthand the fall of the Berlin Wall, and eager to grasp the meaning of the transformation of post-1989 Germany into the epicenter of Europe in its multiple lights and shadows, Hinsey embarked on a personal odyssey, "moving through time and history, preferably by train, the most potent space for contemplation":[49] "Here, do we dream of the intricate nature / of seasons, or of loss ..."[50]

Cities of Memory opens with the poem "March 26, 1827," the date of Beethoven's death that closed a period of enlightenment, setting a tonality of twilight throughout the collection. Even Paris, La Ville Lumière, is portrayed at sunset through an arc of light descending over the Seine River to disappear behind the horizon, where "only shadows lie."[51] Each city's memory is a piece of the jigsaw puzzle of the continent, the vessel of dreams of empires and disasters of wars, the mastermind of humanistic ideals and Faustian pacts, but also the birthplace of universal thinkers and once-lauded artists forced into exile or even decimated.

Her poem "Lebensraum" sounds the death knell of Europe with the failure of the Polish cavalry to curb Hitler's military expansionism in 1939. Nothing could resist the surge of dark forces that befell Sigmund Freud, the symbol of enlightened Europe. In the poem "The Stairwell, Berggasse 19, Vienna," the grand staircase that used to lead the way up to the master's consulting room and his patients striving for self-knowledge, now takes him down to his inexorable end: "Compelled to exodus / . . . down [Freud] went, following / the balustrade's ebony path . . ." foreshadowing the soon-to-come enforced disappearance of Europe's once-celebrated intellectual and artistic avant-garde.

Ellen presented her third collection of poetry, *Update on the Descent*, on June 4, 2009. In his introduction, the poet Jeffrey Greene pointed out that after *The White Fire of Time*, this new collection "marked the author's return to the physical world, this time to descend into the dark abysses of the abuse and violation of human lives." This was a daunting question that continued to haunt her, and she wanted to find out how it was possible for people to carry out violence against those they had once been intimate with, now imagined to be an enemy or "other." "Who is that other?" and "How does one construct this idea of the other?" were fundamental interrogations she sought to investigate.

Attending witness sessions at the International Criminal Tribunal for the former Yugoslavia in The Hague, she heard eye-witness accounts of torture and executions. Among these was a witness testimony that became a poem titled "Testimony on What is Important." The poem addresses a scene where a victim knew the torturer who was carrying out the acts of violence. While he was doing this, the victim said he had asked him: "Do you know what you are doing?" The court interrupted him with the order: "Stick to the facts." The witness reiterated the same question that was met with the same silence. Addressing the court, he stood firm: "This, I have to say, is what is important."[52]

"I was overwhelmed by the fact that in the middle of it all, someone would have the courage to challenge the conscience of the man carrying out the act of torture," Ellen recalled with emotion in her voice. "I felt this ethical question was immensely moving."[53]

This poignant testimony also reveals the importance of words to name facts or acts, a concern Hinsey raised in a poem titled "Interdiction," in which she addresses the burning question of language in our contemporary world: "It is said that we can no longer use the old words."[54] To cite an example, Hinsey recalled how in the late 1990s, when she was teaching in a Paris suburb, and after a wave of protests and riots, she asked her students to reflect on the word "democracy." "They categorically refused," she said.

It was the first time this had happened to her, and she was very unsettled. She then asked the students to explain their decision. They retorted that it was "banal." Such a reaction made her think: Was it democracy that was "banal," or this big word? Had "the old words become taboos?" Yet ". . . there are things, in the trammeled, / The ruined, the old words, which must still be said . . ."[55]

As a conclusion to her reading, Ellen mentioned that often authors write books in tribute to other authors: "While writing *Update on the Descent*, the French philosopher Simone Weil has been very much on my mind," she said, "but there is another inspiring presence in my work: the Russian poet Marina Tsvetaeva who wrote against the darkness of her century, and whose language endures as a source of elevated inspiration."

William S. Merwin and Odile, May 27, 2002. © Village Voice Bookshop archive

W. S. Merwin

"Poetry is always about hearing, and if you hear it,
    you feel it.
Poetry is rooted in oral language, not the language
    of the written page."
—MERWIN, Village Voice reading, October 10, 2004.

The first time I heard of William S. Merwin was through a friend, the French poet and novelist Michèle Laforest[56] who knew him from Lacan, a small medieval village perched on a haut plateau overlooking the valley of la Garonne in the southwest of France. They were neighbors who became closer through their devotion to poetry. Although life had scattered them to the four corners of the earth—Merwin to Hawaii* and Laforest to Africa in 2000—now in Paris Michèle heard from him, as he was back in their beloved village and spending summers in his former house there. She urged me to invite "this extraordinary person and poet" to read at the Village Voice.

So, I immediately ordered *The Vixen*,[57] his anthology of poetry, and a book of prose, *The Lost Upland, Stories of Southwest France*,[58] with an epigraph in French that read "Là bas il n'y a que des pierres. C'est le causse perdu."[59] I was enthralled by his languag that conjured up a land of austere beauty and mystery that concealed in its bosom the memory of prehistoric times through its rock paintings, as well as traces of the troubadours who, in the twelfth century, had traveled from village to village singing their ballads. I was also won over by his attention to animals, in fact, his genuine love for them.

The author of more than forty volumes of poetry, essays, and translations, awarded numerous national and international prestigious prizes (including two Pulitzer Prizes), William S.

---

* Haiku, Hawaii, was Merwin's permanent residence until his death in 2019.
During the Village Voice years, he used to spend the summer months in Lacan.

Merwin gave his first reading at the Village Voice on May 27, 2002. He presented his recent collection of poems *The Pupil*[60] and *The Mays of Ventadorn*,[61] an evocation of the history and culture of twelfth-century Languedoc through the life and poetry of the troubadour Bernart de Ventadorn. A jewel of a book.

Merwin was impressive, but also gentle and reserved. Most striking was the enigmatic smile on his face, beautifully framed by a mane of wavy white hair.

In his introduction, the American poet Jeffrey Greene pointed out some of the major themes explored in his works: "the dual motifs of light and darkness, of presence and absence and of the poet's continued concern with nature and animals." In reference to the great poetry movement of the 1950s in the States, he also wondered if writers such as Robert Lowell, Stanley Kunitz, or Carolyn Kizer had influenced Merwin in any way. Merwin replied that he didn't think that there was any influence there. "If there was one," he continued, "it came from Spanish and South American Surrealism, and, above all, Neruda."

In fact, perhaps more decisive for Merwin was his encounter with Ezra Pound. During his Princeton years, he had been fortunate enough to meet him as a student. He happened to be in Washington, D.C., and realized that the world-famous poet was interned in nearby Saint Elizabeth's Hospital, a center for psychiatric treatment. Merwin called on him there and, to his surprise, was told that Pound "was willing to see him." Unaware of the exact circumstances of the poet's confinement,[62] he admitted that "I was not too keen to scratch the surface of what I knew."

Once inside, "Pound welcomed me with an open mouth smile," but "the distance between us was beyond calculation."[63] During the encounter, the older man recalled many names of people and things unfamiliar to the eighteen-year-old Merwin, but it was also the seasoned poet who told him that "the troubadours' Provençal language (Occitan or langue d'oc) was the real source of poetry." "He revered them," Merwin confided, "they were his ancestral figures." It is true that Pound's long narrative *Cantos* resonates with Dante's *Divine Comedy*, imbued with the Occitan poetry of the troubadours.

Merwin admitted that Pound did all the talking, but the latter's next two sentences turned out to be extremely valuable to him: "Translating forces you to say in English something that did not happen in English, and it forces you to go where you would not have gone otherwise. Moreover, by translating, you're learning very important things about your own language."[64]

"If he loved to give advice, it was obvious that poetry was more important than his own ego," our author added. Whether influenced by Pound or not, the young man would eventually devote a large part of his writing life to translation. One case in point: Merwin's *Selected Translations*,[65] in which poems from more than twenty different languages fill up eight pages of its table of contents.

His second Village Voice reading on June 4, 2003, was entirely dedicated to this literary art and introduced by the poet and art critic Serge Fauchereau. Merwin recited from *Transparence of the World*, his translations of poems by another French poet, Jean Follain, a friend from his Paris days, who was tragically killed in an accident in 1971. They both shared a fascination for the intriguing power of memory.

"What is translation?" Merwin asked his audience. "We are concerned here with the art of the impossible. What we want is the translation to be like the original, but translation is not and cannot be the original. This is a wonderful situation to be faced with because it implies great freedom." Sensing that his notion of freedom in this process was causing some uneasiness among his listeners, he added with a bit of humor, "I have to be careful here, for I see quite a few eminent French and Anglophone translators in this audience, including Carolyn Kizer and the Irish poet John Montague."

He brought up as an example his desire to translate the poems of the Russian poet Ossip Mandelstam. To do so, he approached Clarence Brown, the distinguished professor of Russian language and literature at Princeton. The latter had managed to get the poems of Mandelstam out of the country, which Mandelstam's widow Nadezhda had learned by heart and secretly transcribed. At the time of the Cold War, smuggling out those transcriptions meant risking not only the second disappearance of these poems, but his own disappearance. "This being said, Brown agreed to collaborate with me on the one condition that I would not try to learn Russian. This was not a problem as for me—the whole matter of translation is to conjure up that sound and vitality of the voice of the original poem and not just relay its meaning."[66]

Renowned for his translations in the States, Merwin was seen as an accomplished and award-winning poet, but unheard of in France at the turn of the twenty-first century. His first book translated and published in France was The Vixen, under the title La renarde, a long narrative poem grounded in the Causse, his home in Southwest France.

He launched this anthology at the Village Voice on October 7, 2004, accompanied by his French translator and friend Luc de Goustine,[67] his French publisher Fanlac, and the American poet Michael Taylor[68] who also lived in that region and was to introduce him. Taylor began by describing Merwin "as a great poet writing at a particularly rich time for American poetry. He is a man of that generation that emerged from Ezra Pound's cloth, the way Russian literature had emerged from Gogol's The Overcoat. As for his translator, Luc de Goustine, he has risen to this challenge by not only managing to convey Merwin's style, but also carrying over the actual texture of his poetry. A mark of achievement," he concluded.

The poet opened his talk by recalling that moment when, in the 1960s, he had discovered the Upland or Causse, which no one knew existed. He felt, he told us, as if he had discovered the other side of the moon: "Then I could walk for a whole day over the stony / ridges . . . and out onto open / hillsides overlooking valleys adrift in the distance" ("Walker"). Lured by the beauty of the place, the restless traveler settled on an old farm that had stood "empty for half a lifetime and been abandoned" ("Old Sound"), but he felt an immediate and "irrational attachment" to it.

I had the privilege of visiting with William and Paula Merwin in Lacan in the early spring of 2003 and again in June 2009 with mutual friends Steven Barclay and his partner Garth. The house that welcomed us bore little resemblance to the half-ruin "shrouded in brambles," with its wall half-fallen and "the gaping holes in the floorboards, piles of rubble and bird droppings." The near-wreck had been restored in keeping the spirit of the place and was now a welcoming old farmhouse of limestone, its walls covered with climbing honeysuckle vines.

Amidst woods and fields, it was flanked on one side by a garden of irises and roses William tended with great care, and, on the other, by two traditional old stone barns with slightly curved roofs of faded red tiles, common in this region.

One morning, he invited us into the barn that was his writing retreat. It was a small shepherd's hut with thick stone walls and a dirt floor. A faint light entered through a tiny window framed by trees outside. Just below it was a table made of rough wood, William's desk, upon which lay sparsely written sheets of paper, perhaps the draft of a poem in progress. Against the opposite wall stood a workbench with some old tools, a reminder that the barn was originally used to store hay for the animals in winter. Little had changed since the sheep had slept here. Even the spiders had been left alone to their labor, spinning numerous webs that hung in corners, veiling the upper part of the graying window panes.

On our way out, crossing the doorsill, what came to my mind was the snakeskin which William had once stumbled upon as he was stepping out of his barn: "I stood up from the writings unfinished on the table / in the echoless stone room looking over the valley / I opened the door and on the stone doorsill / . . . the empty skin like smoke on the stone / . . . lighter than a single / breath" ("Snake").[69]

I vividly recall that magical moment when William invited us into his secret den where he had written so many inspiring poems and continued to work them out. Bare as it was, the place seemed very much alive with the poet's concentration and writing prowess.

Another memory of a beautiful June night in 2009 stands out in my mind. William, Paula, Steven, his mother Barbara, Garth, and I were sitting in the dark around the table on the terrace overlooking the valley. Dinner was over, and we remained there, spellbound by the songs of crickets and the sight of the starry sky. Not used to such brightness in the city, I stared at the immensity of the summer night above us, hypnotized by its radiance while, like an ancient mariner, William named and described the constellations, folding in stories and folklore heard from local farmers.

Stars are a recurring theme in Merwin's poetry, fading away at dawn to vanish into the vast unknown. Though invisible in daylight, these same stars have kept watch over us imperturbably so since time immemorial. In an interview with Bill Moyers in 2009, the poet referred to the image of the "fading star" in his poem "The Nomad Flute"[70] as a metaphor for the great unknown inside us, that dark part of ourselves we are mostly unaware of, but which nonetheless guides our lives. "It is life's great mystery, and it is what gives it its dimension and its depth." Asked what makes a poem, Merwin answered: "following what we don't know."[71]

Similar to the star, invisible but ever-present, this land of stone remains alive through continued human activity made evident in the shepherd huts built with those same stones. The ruins of the Ventadorn Castle welcome the visitor with a poem of the troubadour Bernart de Ventadorn: "Those stones saw them alive. In these lines they live again." Not far, red scriptures list the names and dates of birth and death of the men, women, and children who, one day in 1944, "had been / ordered in German to that spot where they were shot/then the Germans set fire to the buildings / with the animals inside" ("The Red").

The thirty-year ritual "verre de l'amitié" that always followed our readings.
© C. Deudon

Animals occupy a special place in Merwin's life and work, and he stresses "the importance of animals at a time and age when man—our species—sees himself so separate from the animal, which is also a part of himself." In the poem "Substance," "It was / the animals themselves that were the weight and place/ of the hour . . . / . . . bearing the sense of it . . ."

His anthology *The Vixen* opens with the poem "Fox Asleep," in which the creature is waiting to be awakened to life; the collection closes with "Vixen." The famously swift animal has now frozen into the hieratic figure of a dark fairytale, "the Princess of what is over." The last lines of "Vixen" are a haunting and poignant plea: "let me catch sight of you again going over the wall / and before the garden is extinct and the woods are figures / guttering on a screen let my words find their own / places in the silence after the animals."

The Vixen is also an elegy. The poet told us that "language begins with elegy, [expressing] grief with its consonants, interrupting the undulations, trying to break it. Poetry is really about what can't be said; it is about absence . . ." "Language is a paradox," he continued, "because it is language that allows us to remember and express what has been lost."

Asked by a young poet in the audience about his lack of punctuation, Merwin set down a difference between prose that requires punctuation for rational discourse and poetry, "which is always about hearing . . . The moment the punctuation is taken out, you have to pay attention to the rhythm of the poem."

Cultivating language and cultivating the earth are both creative acts that are part and parcel of a long tradition. While the gardener helps the soil sprout and renew itself, the poet uses language to turn absence into presence, as Merwin writes in his poem "Place":

> On the last day of the world
> I would want to plant a tree.[72]

EPILOGUE

When I opened the Village Voice Bookshop in 1982, I could not foresee that the nascent digital world would take over our lives, let alone imagine that thirty years later, it would force us to close.

The cause was not the fading away of the "glorious tradition of Americans in France"[1] as we feared at one time, but Amazon, the first online bookstore that began to be a serious threat to our existence after 2000, when its discounts to individual internet consumers started to match or even exceed those granted to independent bookstores. Gradually, competitive pressure and margin erosion worsened with the general adoption of the smartphone that accelerated the popularity of online book-buying. Ironically, if technology was our bookstore's undoing, it is likewise technology, albeit in its most primitive form, that allowed this record of our writers' voices to survive and thus be woven into this memoir.

As we have seen throughout these pages, our archive of author readings covers a specific time in the history of postwar Anglophone literatures. On the one hand, it testifies to the flourishing of a wide variety of American voices with their own specificity, and, on the other hand, the emergence of world literatures in English that opened up new and exciting literary horizons at the turn of the twenty-first century.

What brought these voices together in this recollection are the
city of Paris and the Village Voice Bookshop, the stage of all our
readings and the "home" of the Third Wave of American expatriates. For these expatriates, as for their predecessors in the First
and Second Waves, Paris continued to hold a special place in their
imagination. We did not reference the Lost Generation of the
interwar years by lengthily citing Ernest Hemingway, its usual
emblematic writer. Rather, we have tried to shift this historical
focus to a revival of the women writers and artists of the Left
Bank who, through their creative accomplishments, allowed the
bookshop of Sylvia Beach and the salons of Natalie Barney and
Gertrude Stein to become the deep wellspring of the literary and
artistic vanguard movements of the time.

Opening this memoir with the felicitously named chapter "Paris
Was a Woman,"[2] we have decided to come full circle with three
exemplary American women of the postwar era whose time in
France, particularly in Paris, transformed their adult lives.

By an extraordinary coincidence, on June 7, 2012, just days
before the closing of the bookstore, Alice Kaplan came to the
Village Voice to present *Dreaming in French: The Paris Years of
Jacqueline Bouvier Kennedy, Susan Sontag and Angela Davis*,[3] just released
in the States. In it, she shows how their student years abroad in
Paris played a decisive role in their destinies, but more importantly, how that experience was crucial in their mature achievements and commitments to their country. Jackie Kennedy is
portrayed as a unique figure whose political and social stances
and late career as a literary editor raised her above the fashion
icon she was often reduced to; Susan Sontag, as the influential
intellectual whose stunning, provocative essays and theoretical
studies were to be hailed in Europe and beyond; and Angela
Davis who, having observed the value of political commitment
in France, became a writer and philosopher with a strong sense

of justice and a fearless political activist who put her life on the line in her dedication to fighting for liberation.*

Presenting her book that evening, Kaplan pointed out what these women owed to their time abroad and how their fame in America reverberated back to France, revealing another facet of the traditional cultural exchanges between the two countries. In their own way, the authors and public of the Village Voice Bookshop have contributed to this ongoing historical dialogue.

On the last day of June 2012, our shop went dark with its windows cloaked, "its voices stilled."** It is my hope that, now awakened, these "village voices" fully resonate inside the pages of this memoir, at once highly collective and strongly personal.

What was still is

There are still Voices

There's just no longer a Village.***

* Unlike Susan Sontag, Angela Davis did not read at our bookshop, but one day she dropped by to invite everyone in the store to the talk she was to give outside Paris on the topic of US prisons and the imprisonment of African American people. Her brilliant, informative speech and her charismatic personality galvanized the crowd, the majority of which were women.
** Kathleen Spivack's "Books You Speak," a poem dedicated to the Village Voice on the Farewell Day, June 16, 2012.
*** Nancy Huston's inscription in the Farewell Guest Book, June 16, 2012.

"A Chair, a book, and some imagination provide a heaven
for dreaming and creation / for all true artists are makers of the revolution."*

---

* In June 2004, Carol Allen, an active member of the expatriate community, came
up with the original idea of having our public inscribe lines from famous English
works on the chairs we used for our readings. Here is a drawing of one of these
chairs by artist Katia Gerasimov.

ACKNOWLEDGMENTS

Remembering Michael Neal

Among our colleagues, no one was more important to the life of the Village Voice bookstore than Michael Neal, an eccentric man in an "eccentric place," to borrow the expression Susan Sontag used for our bookshop. Easygoing and extroverted by nature, Michael felt at home in Paris and knew its history as no one else did, but he also remained British to the core with his sharp sense of humor and large stock of anecdotes that never missed bringing on "good laughs" (as he would say) from his listeners.

It is difficult to imagine him without a book in his hands or a pile of books precariously balancing on his shoulder—an image that has stayed with me since he first walked into the bookshop. Writer Edmund White once drove home this point. When author Alice Kaplan was looking for information on Vichy collaborator Robert Brasillach, he quickly informed her that "Michael is a remarkable bibliophile to consult." In turn, Michael preferred to call himself a "bibliomaniac," a term that brought to mind his sheer passion and frenzied hunting after rare historical documents. Relentlessly he would track them down through his personal network of collectors and booksellers. Among them was his good friend Martin Stone, one of the world's experts on the antiquarian book business.

A voracious reader, always on the lookout for new finds dug out of some dark corner of history, Michael was the only one I've known to have gone through the forty volumes of the Nuremberg trial archives and the twenty volumes of the complete works of George Orwell, his great literary hero whom he would quote at the snap of a finger, to the astonishment of just about everyone. While most of his favorite authors were British literati now forgotten, relegated to the "oubliettes," as he would say, Michael was also an inveterate admirer of Bob Dylan, often welcoming customers by singing lyrics of the popular American bard and future Nobel Prize winner.

In fact, he was very eclectic in his literary tastes, boasting, just a few days before he died, of his night table crowded with the complete poetic works of William Blake alongside the novels of Marcel Proust in French and English translation. I will never forget the expression of surprise on the face of travel writer and essayist Pico Iyer when Michael produced the out-of-print edition of George Painter's famous biography of Proust he had promised him the day before. "A gift," he chuckled, handing it to him. Years later, in an interview, Iyer described Michael as a "man of trust." I too recognize that "trust" is the word that defined our working relationship for more than twenty years: we shared not only a love for books, but the same basic values, and "trust" was certainly at the top of our priorities. More than a

Michael Neal, Village Voice Bookshop, 2004. © Alison Harris

highly principled associate, Michael was a true friend and remained a dear one well after our Village Voice years. He is sorely missed by everyone who knew him—former colleagues, customers, and friends who speak of him with deep fondness.

*   *   *

The Village Voice was a collective venture that included authors, publishers, collaborators, and customers, as well as a close circle of friends and family. I wish to express my gratitude to each and every one of them for making it a fulfilling journey in every sense of the word.

First, I am beholden to all the authors who read at the Village Voice, and particularly those presented here. Each one is a unique voice in the chorus of this memoir. I owe a particular debt to the writers of the Third Wave of American expatriates who built up the reputation of the bookstore. Among them are Jeffrey Greene, Ellen Hinsey, Denis Hirson, Nancy Huston, Diane Johnson, Jake Lamar, and of course, Edmund White, not forgetting the late Mavis Gallant and C. K. Williams, and as well David Applefield, Jim Haynes, Carol Pratl, and John Strand. I cannot thank Steven Barclay enough for inviting some of the most prestigious writers from his San Francisco agency to read with us.

Bookshops are much more than shelves of books, and their prestige relies heavily on their booksellers—discriminating book lovers committed to making these books known and read. Over the years, apart from our Michael Neal, we had a number of knowledgeable and highly valued collaborators: the very first ones were Susan Hermann,[1] Friederike Holl, and Yann Hellier, whose enthusiasm and commitment set just the right tone, making our fledging bookstore-cum-café a welcoming and friendly place; Aude Samarut and Mariana Czarniecka always recommended the right book to the right customer, while Vincent Pierrot, a devotee of the seventh art, created a new momentum in our shop by adding a section of import DVDs and inviting prestigious film directors, such as Budd Schulberg, Jonas Mekas, and Frederick Wiseman to talk about their films. And thank you to Marc Fairbrother, our cool digital geek who revamped our initial internet site, making it a lively and attractive window on our bookstore events.

I learned a great deal from American and British publisher representatives who regularly visited the Village Voice to present their seasonal catalogues. Rebecca Byers was among the first ones to push open our door, bringing with her the art of choosing the most suitable titles for our shop that, much later on, Michael Ondaatje was to describe as a "carefully edited bookstore."

Needless to say, French publishers played an important role in our bilingual offerings. Among them, I owe special thanks to Francis Geffard, Éditions Albin Michel, and the founder of Festival America who introduced us to some of the great voices of the Native American Renaissance, to Olivier Cohen (Éditions de l'Olivier), and the publishers Christian and Dominique Bourgois, Ivan Nabokov (Plon), Marc Parent (Buchet-Chastel) for inviting their Anglophone authors to take part in joint readings with their French translators. Among the latter were language magicians that included Claro, Brice Matthieussent, Michel Lederer, Paule Guivarch, and the late Jean-Pierre Carasso, Bernard Hoepffner, and François Lasquin, all of whom enchanted us with their linguistic prowess and inventiveness.

In the last two years of the bookstore, a time of great uncertainty for us, Vera Michalski, the head of the Editorial Group Libella, commissioned the Village Voice to provide the multilingual library of her Foundation Jan Michalski with American books. Her commitment prolonged the life of our bookshop, a gesture for which I am most grateful. In her work with American and French publishers, American-born literary agent Michèle Lapautre facilitated many of our bilingual events, attending every single reading of the authors she represented, always with a beaming smile on her face.

Our bookstore was part of a Paris network of Anglophone cultural institutions, and we enjoyed working with Simone Suchet of the Canadian Cultural Center; Charles Trueheart, the head of the American Library in Paris; as well as the librarians of the British Council, Irish Cultural Center, American School of Paris, and Marymount International School, who invited us to participate in their own book events. I would also like to acknowledge the mutual support that existed among the various Anglophone bookstores in the city, and thank in particular Susan Rosenberg, the senior manager of Brentano's, Sylvia Whitman of Shakespeare and Company, and Penelope Fletcher of the Red Wheelbarrow.

My warmest thanks to Mary Eleanor Gawronski who, as the Cultural Attaché at the American Embassy in the 1990s, enhanced the visibility of American authors in France, and who, as a friend, showed unwavering support for our bookstore by attending our events whenever possible.

Scholars and professors of American and British literatures regularly took part in our readings. I want to express my appreciation to Noëlle Batt, Marc Chénetier, Isabelle de Courtivron, Nelcya Delanoë, Marta Dvorak, Larry Dewaele, Françoise Palleau, and Joëlle Rostkowski for sharing with us their singular insights into the works of the authors they introduced. I would be remiss if I did not acknowledge the literary critic Livia Manera Sambuy, who presented the documentary film about her visit with Philip Roth in the States, giving us a rare opportunity to meet this icon of American letters in the privacy of his home. Greatly appreciated by everyone who had been close to the bookshop, her New Yorker piece on its closing was a token of her friendly support over the years.

Our regular audience holds a special place in the story of the Village Voice. Their pertinent questions enriched the debates with our authors; in this regard, Jeanette Demeestère, Diane Murez, and Carol Allen come to mind. The latter organized special readings and other activities, including her memorable "Chair Party," a playful and poetic celebration of our community.

Books have a way of creating special bonds among people, and indeed, they sparked my friendship with Adine Sagalyn, taking her back to her childhood and me to my days in Amherst, Mariette Job, Mira Rogulski, Sylvain Laroze, Polina Livchitz, and the artist Kathy Toma who, on several occasions, made our window displays into original works of art that attracted the attention of passersby. Likewise, I was deeply touched by Janet Skeslien's allusion to our bookshop in her fictional work *The Paris Library*, a personal homage to the courage of the librarians of the American Library in Paris during the Nazi occupation.

Active support did not end with the closing of our bookshop, and my fondest gratitude goes to Steven Barclay, Rebecca Byers, Marie-Florence Estimé, Judith Fleiss, Sarah Gaddis, Yann Hellier, Denis Hirson, Friederike Holl, Jake Lamar, Vincent Pierrot, Mira Rogulski, Jean Pierre de Roo, and Kathy and Flavio Toma for reading the manuscript or parts of it. Their constructive criticism and suggestions were of great value to me, and an encouragement.

In today's society, like all business ventures, independent bookstores must keep pace with the irreversible march of a world that requires professional and digital expertise. My warmest thanks to Jacques Guillo and Azad Nadir for their invaluable advice and technical assistance, as well their friendly support over the years.

I am indebted to the photographers and artists who, through their respective works, have kept alive some of the most memorable moments of the Village Voice. They include the photographers Catherine Deudon, Roberta Fineberg, Alison Harris, Leigh Miller, John Minihan, Steve Murez, and Flavio Toma, as well as the artists Kathy Toma, "Le Prince Esspé," Katia Gerasimov, and the graphist Rollin. Finally, a sincere tribute to Ricardo Mosner, whose imposing painting *Serie Tremenda* accompanied us over the years, colorfully framing the staircase to the second-floor readings.

Since our closing in 2012, a number of our authors have passed away. Sadly, we cannot name them individually, but we hope that our own body of recollections will make their voices resonate again in the context of their readings at the Village Voice Bookshop in Paris.

It took several years for this memoir to come into its own, and I want to express my deepest gratitude to my close friend Virginia Larner, who has accompanied me through its latest stages. A regular at our bookshop events and a discriminating reader herself, Virginia spared no time or effort going over the manuscript's different versions with her sharp eye for detail and nuance, always showing implicit respect for the raison d'être of my undertaking. Her critical consideration of each chapter and invaluable suggestions are a matchless token of our friendship, and in a way, her own tribute to the authors remembered and celebrated in this memoir.

I would like to express my deepest thanks and appreciation to Barry Gifford for sending the manuscript of *Village Voices* to his own publisher, Seven Stories Press.

My sincere gratitude goes to Dan Simon, publisher and president of Seven Stories Press. He has generously offered a new home to so many of our Anglophone authors who made our bookshop their port of call in Paris. Thank you, Dan Simon, for daring to take a chance on this memoir of a particular time and a place and for giving its "Voices" a fuller and lasting resonance among the narrative works of your highly respected anthology of publications.

For closely reading my manuscript, my deep gratitude goes to Noa Mendoza, who patiently and graciously accompanied me through the editing process. Always attentive to my own views, she likewise continued to enlarge the range of other, often-promising alternatives. Thank you, Noa, for making our written exchanges over thousands of miles an ongoing and enriching conversation. It has been a most gratifying experience working with you.

Discreet but always there when needed, the deeply felt presence of my family has made all the difference to me.

The team that made the Village Voice Bookshop

(*top*) ODILE with GLORIA H. TURULLOLS

(*far left*) VIRGINIA LARNER
© V. Larner

(*left*) KATHY TOMA
© Flavio Toma

(*below left*) STEVEN BARCLAY and VINCENT PIERROT
© Alison Harris

(*below right*) YANN HELLIER and MICHAEL NEAL

NOTES

Prologue

1 Erica Warner, "A Quiet Murmur, a Mighty Voice" in *The Times Online*, June 28, 2009.

Introduction

1 Richard Wright, *Twelve Million Black Voices* (New York: Viking, 1941).

2 Saul Alinsky, *Rules for Radicals: A Pragmatic Primer for Realistic Radicals* (New York: Vintage, 1971). Translated into French as *Manuel de l'animateur social* (Paris: Éditions du Seuil, 1976).

Part I

1 "Paris, Paris Above All, Paris!" This quote is from Steve Twomey's "Paris' New Literati Conjure Up Ghosts of a New Generation." *Chicago Tribune*, December 12, 1985.

CHAPTER 1

1 Hazel Rowley, "Beyond Bookkeeping," *The Australian Literary Review*, December 2007, reprinted under the title "It Takes a Village" in Bookforum, February/March 2008.

2 Edmund White, *The Flâneur: A Stroll through the Paradoxes of Paris* (London: Bloomsbury, 2001), 20.

3 Edmund White, *My Lives* (London: Bloomsbury, 2005), 198.

4 James R. Mellow, *Charmed Circle: Gertrude Stein and Company* (New York: Praeger, 1974).

5 *La nuit princesse*, Guy d'Arcangues (Brussels: André de Rache, 1981), dedicated to Jean Castel, the owner of the private club Chez Castel.

6 Barry Gifford, "The Lost and Found Generation: Odile Hellier and the Village Voice Bookstore," Punch magazine, April 23, 1986.

7 *The Village Voice* was brought to us weekly by Stanley Hertzberg, an American broker in the international press.

CHAPTER 2

1 The title "Paris Was a Woman" refers to *Paris Was a Woman: Portraits from the Left Bank*, title borrowed from Andrea Weiss (London: HarperCollins, 1995). The author presented her book at the Village Voice on June 20, 1996.

2 "In the rue Princesse, a few streets away from the rue de L'Odéon . . ."— Barry Gifford, "Lost and Found Generation," *San Francisco Review of Books*, 1985.

3   William Wiser, *Book World*, October 13, 1985; Wiser is the author of *The Great Good Place: American Expatriate Women in Paris* (New York: W.W. Norton, 1991), presented at the Village Voice on November 22, 1991.

4   Noël Riley Fitch, *Sylvia Beach and the Lost Generation: A History of Literary Paris in the Twenties and Thirties* (New York: W.W. Norton, 1983). Riley Fitch launched two more books at the Village Voice: *Anaïs: The Erotic Life of Anaïs Nin* (London: Little, Brown, 1993) and *Appetite for Life: The Biography of Julia Child* (New York: Anchor Doubleday, 1997).

5   Noël Riley Fitch, Village Voice reading, July 31, 1983. Eleanor herself had related this anecdote to Fitch.

6   Fitch, Village Voice reading, July 31, 1983.

7   Fitch, Village Voice reading, 1983.

8   Shari Benstock, *Women of the Left Bank*, University of Texas, 1986.

9   Shari Benstock, Village Voice reading, January 15, 1987.

10   Shari Benstock, *Women of the Left Bank*.

11   Shari Benstock, *Women of the Left Bank*.

12   Shari Benstock, Village Voice reading, January 15, 1987. Some elements in her talk are drawn from the presentation of her biography of Edith Wharton: *No Gifts from Chance* (New York: Scribner's, 1994), which she launched at the Village Voice in 1995.

13   Shari Benstock, Village Voice reading, 1987.

14   Natalie Barney, *Aventures de l'esprit*,

15   Joan Schenkar, Village Voice reading, October 10, 2000.

16   Rémy de Gourmont, *Lettres à l'Amazone* (Paris: Mercure de France, 1927).

17   Joan Schenkar, Village Voice reading, 2000.

18   Barney evokes her life-changing encounter with Oscar Wilde as a small child in *Aventures de l'esprit*.

19   Joan Schenkar, *Truly Wilde: The Unsettling Story of Dolly Wilde, Oscar's Unusual Niece* (London: Virago Press, 2000).

20   Schenkar, *Truly Wilde*, 166. Schenkar is also the author of (among other works) a collection of plays *Signs of Life, Six Comedies of Menace* (Middletown, CT: Wesleyan University Press, 1998) and the biography *The Talented Miss Highsmith* (New York: St. Martin's Press, 2009), all of them presented at the Village Voice.

21   Joan Schenkar, Village Voice reading, 2000.

22   Village Voice reading, quote from *Truly Wilde*, 169.

CHAPTER 3

1   "There can be no innovation without tradition . . ."— John Strand, *Paris Exiles*, Winter 1984.

2   *Paris Passion: The Magazine of Paris*. Its life span (1981-1994) coincides with that of the Third Wave of American expatriates in Paris.

3   Bernard-Henri Lévy, known as BHL, was one leader of the new French intellectual current called "Les Nouveaux Philosophes," much in vogue in the 1980s.

4   The history of the American Center in Paris is told with brio by Nelcya Delanoë in *Le Raspail vert: l'American center à Paris (1934-1994): Une histoire des avant-gardes franco-américaines* (Paris: Seghers, 1994). The author launched her work at the Village Voice (December 8, 1994), introduced by Henry Pillsbury, film director, actor, and a long-time director of the American Center.

5   Editors, *Paris Exiles*.

6   An American expatriate artist, Minick designed the magazines *Paris Exiles* and *Sphinx*. Together with his partner Jiao Ping, they launched their book *Chinese Graphic Design in the Twentieth Century* at the Village Voice on October 26, 1990. Ricardo Mosner had

been living in exile in Paris since the 1970s. Two major exhibits in New York and Paris enhanced his reputation.

7   Andrei Sinyavsky (Abram Tertz), became famous in the Western world in 1966 when he was sentenced to seven years of prison for his anti-Soviet fictional characters. Thereafter, forced to exile, he settled in Fontenay-aux-Roses near Paris where he died in 1997.

8   Nancy Huston, *Lettre Internationale*, N°21, 1989.

9   David Applefield, interview in *Paris Voice*, 2004.

10 Alain Bosquet, of Russian origin, is the author of a large body of work, including poems, essays, novels, and plays.

11 Edouard Roditi, Village Voice reading, July 4, 1985.

12 Among the American writers invited to this International Writers' Conference (1962) were William Burroughs, Norman Mailer, and Mary McCarthy.

13 Lynne Tillman is an American novelist and the author of *Bookstore: The Life and Times of Jeannette Watson and Books & Co.* (New York: Harcourt Brace & Company, 1999).

14 Jim Haynes, *Thanks for Coming* (London: Faber & Faber, 1984). *Meeting Jim* (2018) is a documentary film of Haynes' life and his celebrated dinners "Chez Jim."

CHAPTER 4

1   The title "Black America in Paris: Updating the Myth" references the cover headline of *Paris Passion*, Issue 44, January 1986.

2   Baldwin divided his time between the US and his house in Saint-Paul-de-Vence in Provence.

3   Magdalena J. Zaborowska, *James Baldwin's Turkish Decade: Erotics of Exile* (Durham, NC: Duke University Press, 2009).

4   James Baldwin, "The New Lost Generation" (1961), in *Collected Essays* (New York: Library of America, 1998).

5   Baldwin, "Encounter on the Seine: Black Meets Brown" (1950), in *Collected Essays*.

6   Gordon Heath had not always been a singer of American spirituals and folksongs, but, as Baldwin recalled, he had enjoyed an international career as one of the rare African American actors performing Shakespearian roles on New York and London stages. Together with his American actor friend Lee Payant, he opened the night club The Abbaye in the heart of Saint-Germain-des-Prés, famous for its "caves" and cabarets, to present a repertoire of American jazz and folk music.

7   Ted Joans, *The Truth: Mehr Blitzliebe Poems* (Hamburg: Loose Blätter Press, 1983).

8   Leonard Weinglass, *Mumia Abu-Jamal's Fight against the Death Penalty*, with an introduction by E. L. Doctorow (Monroe, ME: Common Courage Press, 1995).

9   His death sentence was commuted to life imprisonment in 2011.

10 Ernest Gaines, *A Lesson before Dying* (New York: Knopf, 1993).

11 James Emanuel, *Reaching for Mumia: 16 Haikus* (Paris: l'Insomniaque, 1995). He wrote the poems to raise funds for a new trial for Mumia.

12 Emanuel, *Deadly James and Other Poems* (Detroit: Lotus Press, 1987).

13 Richard Wright, *A Father's Law* (New York: Harper Perennial, 2008).

14 Julia Wright, Village Voice reading, May 29, 2008.

15 Ibid.

16 Ibid, also mentioned in her introduction to the novel.

17 Baldwin, "Alas, Poor Richard" (1961), *Collected Essays*.

18 Baldwin, "Everybody's Protest Novel" (1949), *Collected Essays*.

19   Jake Lamar, *Bourgeois Blues* (New York: Plume, 1992). Village Voice reading, January 1, 1995.

20   Lamar, *Rendezvous Eighteenth* (New York: St. Martin's Press, 2003). Village Voice reading, November 20, 2003.

21   Lamar, *Ghosts of Saint-Michel* (New York: St. Martin's Press, 2006). Village Voice reading, June 6, 2006.

22   Lamar, *Rendezvous Eighteenth*, 177.

CHAPTER 5

1   "Emergence of a Literary Force," Title inspired by Elizabeth Venant's article in the *Los Angeles Times*, March 23, 1986.

2   Jeff Greenwald, *San Francisco Examiner*, February 1988.

3   Virginia Larner, "Making Waves: A Letter from Paris," *ALSC Newsletter*, Winter 2003.

4   Edmund White, *The Flâneur: A Stroll through the Paradoxes of Paris* (London: Bloomsbury, 2001).

5   Ibid.

6   Johnson is the author of the Paris trilogy: *Le divorce, Le mariage,* and *l'Affaire,* as well as several nonfiction books and a biography of Dashiell Hammett.

7   "A Conversation with Diane Johnson," *Paris through Expatriate Eyes*, Terrance Gelenter, Paris, December 2010.

8   Diane Johnson, *Into a Paris Quartier* (Washington, DC: National Geographic Directions, 2000).

9   Steven Barclay, *A Place in the World Called Paris*, with a foreword by Susan Sontag (San Francisco: Chronicle Books, 1994).

10   Barclay, *A Place in The World Called Paris*, 24, 87.

11   Steven Barclay, Village Voice reading, June 29, 1995.

12   David Downie, *Paris, Paris: Journey into the City of Light* (Fort Bragg, CA: Transatlantic Press, 2005).

13   The word "bouquiniste" is derived from "bouquin," the familiar French term for a book.

14   David Sedaris: *Me Talk Pretty One Day* (Boston: Little, Brown, 2000). Translated into French by Georges Monny as *Je parler français* (Paris: Éditions J'ai Lu, 2000). Village Voice reading, December 5, 2000.

15   Sedaris, Village Voice reading February 9, 2006, from *Dress Your Family in Corduroy and Denim* (Boston: Little, Brown, 2004).

16   In Baudelaire's *Les Fleurs du mal* (Paris: Édition Gibert Jeune, 1959).

17   Edmund White, *The Flâneur*, 16.

18   White, *The Farewell Symphony* (London: Vintage UK, 1998), 456.

19   White, *The Flâneur*, quotes in order: 52, 46, 47.

20   White, *The Farewell Symphony*, 456.

21   Adam Gopnik, *Paris to the Moon* (New York: Random House, 2000).

22   Gopnik, *Paris to the Moon.*

23   Diane Johnson, *Persian Nights* (London: Chatto & Windus, 1987).

24   Johnson, *Le divorce* (New York: Dutton, 1998), followed by *Le mariage* and, the last, *l'affaire. Le divorce* was translated into French as *Une américaine à Paris* (Paris: Editions Nil, 2000).

25   C. K. Williams, introduction to Diane Johnson, Village Voice reading, October 5, 2000.

26   Johnson, Village Voice reading, October 5, 2000.

27 Alan Riding, "The Writer's Notebook," *New York Times*, April 1997.

28 Edmund White, *A Boy's Own Story* (New York: Dutton, 1983), published in French under the title *Un jeune américain* (Paris: Rivages, 1984). White's other launches at the Village Voice included *Forgetting Elena; Nocturnes for the King of Naples; Caracole; The Beautiful Room Is Empty; The Farewell Symphony; The Married Man; Fanny: A Fiction; Genet: A Biography;* and *The Darker Proof* (with Adam Mars Jones). White also introduced many American authors, both famous and relatively unknown.

29 Susan Sontag's blurb on the back cover of *A Boy's Own Story*.

30 Edmund White, *The Farewell Symphony* (New York: Knopf, 1998), 461; Village Voice reading, September 12, 1998.

31 White, *The Flâneur*, 159.

32 *Vogue* magazine, February 1988.

33 White, *Genet: A Biography*, with a chronology by Albert Dichy (London: Chatto & Windus, 1993). Translated into French by Philippe Delamarre (Paris: Gallimard, 1993). Village Voice reading, October 22, 1993.

34 White, *Genet: A Biography*.

35 Genet's response to Sartre's remark in his biography *Saint Genet, comédien et martyr* (Paris: Gallimard, 1952).

36 White, Village Voice reading, April 24, 1997.

CHAPTER 6

1 All these details on Joyce's stay in Pula come from Ivanjek's typescript of his documentary film, Village Voice Bookshop archive.

2 John Calder, *The Theology of Samuel Beckett* (London: Calder Publications, an imprint of Alma Classics, 2012), and its companion essay *The Philosophy of Samuel Beckett* (London: Calder, 2001).

3 Calder, Village Voice reading, March 29, 2012.

4 Anne Atik, *How It Was: A Memoir of Samuel Beckett* (London: Faber & Faber, 2001).

5 Atik, Village Voice reading, December 4, 2003.

6 Festival Les Belles Etrangères: Irlande, November 27 to December 7, 1989. Reading at the Village Voice, November 27, 1989.

7 Derek Mahon, Village Voice reading, November 27, 1989.

8 Harry Clifton, *The Desert Route: Selected Poems* (Newcastle upon Tyne: Bloodaxe, 1992); *Night Train through the Brenner* (Loughcrew: The Gallery Press, 1994).

9 Deirdre Madden, *Nothing Is Black* (London: Faber & Faber, 1994).

10 Mahon, foreword to *The Desert Route*, by Derek Mahon.

11 Harry Clifton, Village Voice reading, June 21, 2000.

12 Clifton, *On the Spine of Italy: A Year in the Abruzzi* (London: Macmillan, 1999).

13 Clifton, Village Voice reading, June, 21, 2000.

14 Ellen Hinsey, introduction to Harry Clifton, Village Voice reading, June 21, 2000.

15 Clifton, *Night Train through the Brenner*.

16 Madden, *Remembering Light and Stone* (London: Faber & Faber, 1992).

17 Madden, *One by One in the Darkness* (London: Faber & Faber, 1996).

18 Madden, Village Voice reading, September 26, 2002.

19 Madden, from *Nothing Is Black*, Village Voice reading, April 14, 1996.

20 Madden, *Authenticity* (London: Faber & Faber, 2002). Village Voice reading, September 26, 2002.

21 Clifton, "To the Fourteenth District" in *Secular Eden: Paris Notebooks 1994-2004* (Winston-Salem, NC: Wake Forest University Press, 2008).

CHAPTER 7

1 "Varieties of Exile": This title references Mavis Gallant's collection *Varieties of Exile*, ed. Russell Banks (New York Review Books, 2003).

2 Nancy Huston, Village Voice reading, December 4, 2002.

3 Nancy Huston, *Nord perdu* (Arles: Actes Sud, 1999). Translated into English in 2002 by the author.

4 Mavis Gallant, afterword to *Paris Stories*, selected with an introduction by Michael Ondaatje (New York: New York Review Books, 2002).

5 Marta Dvorak, a scholar specialized in Canadian literature, wrote an essay on Gallant, *The Eye and the Ear* (Toronto: University of Toronto Press, 2019).

6 Gallant, *Overhead in a Balloon: Stories of Paris* (Toronto: Macmillan, 1985).

7 Gallant, *Paris Notebooks, Essays and Reviews* (Toronto: Macmillan, 1986). Translated into French by Françoise Barret as *Chroniques de mai 68*, (Paris: Deuxtemps Tierce, 1988).

8 Gallant, Village Voice reading, May 17, 1988.

9 "Miss Barricades" in *Évènement du Jeudi*, 1968.

10 Gallant, *Rue de Lille*, trans. Pierre-Edmond Robert (Paris: Deuxtemps Tierce, 1988).

11 Gallant, *Paris Stories* (New York: New York Review Books, 2002).

12 Gallant, letter to me, October 22, 2004.

13 "The Other Paris," one of her first New York stories, later reprinted in *The Collected Stories of Mavis Gallant* (New York: Random House, 1996).

14 Gallant, Village Voice reading of *The Pegnitz Junction*, June 11, 1999.

15 "Varieties of Exile" (1976) reprinted in *Varieties of Exile*, selected with an introduction by Russell Banks (New York: New York Review Books, 2003).

16 Gallant, letter to me, October 22, 2003.

17 Gallant, letter to me, August 6, 1999.

18 Gallant, letter to me, October 22, 2003.

19 Gallant, Village Voice reading, June 11, 1999. *The Pegnitz Junction: A Novella and Five Short Stories* (Port Townsend, WA: Graywolf Press, 1984).

20 Gallant, afterword, *Paris Stories*.

21 Michael Ondaatje, introduction to *Paris Stories*, by Mavis Gallant.

22 Gallant, *The Cost of Living: Early and Uncollected Stories*, with introduction by Jhumpa Lahiri (New York: New York Review Books, 2009).

23 Gallant/Lahiri joint reading at Village Voice, February 19, 2009.

24 Gallant, *What Is to Be Done?* (Ontario: Quadrant Editions, 1983).

25 Gallant, letter to me, March 23, 2009. Allusion to her joint reading with Michael Ondaatje, October 19, 2004.

26 Gallant, Village Voice reading, December 3, 2009.

27 Gallant, letter to me, September 2004.

CHAPTER 8

1 Paul Gilet, *Le Monde des Livres*, February 1973.

2 Raymond Federman, *Smiles on Washington Square* (New York: Thunder's Mouth Press, 1985).

3 Raymond Federman, *The Voice in the Closet*, (Buffalo, NY: Starcherone Books, 1979).

4 Federman, Village Voice reading, March 25, 1986.

5   "Happy fous" meaning "happy foolish."

6   Carmen Callil, *Bad Faith: A Forgotten History of Family and Fatherland* (London: Jonathan Cape, 2006). Translated into French by Françoise Jaouen as *Darquier de Pellepoix, ou la France trahie* (Paris: Buchet-Chastel, 2007). Village Voice reading, April 18, 2006.

7   Marc Parent, editor at Buchet-Chastel, introduced several of his authors at the bookshop, including English-language Indian writers.

8   Carmen Callil, *Bad Faith*, Village Voice reading, April 18, 2006.

9   Callil, Village Voice reading, April 18, 2006.

10 Callil, *Bad Faith*, 104.

11 British by birth, Alan Riding is a journalist and long-time foreign correspondent for the *New York Times*. He is likewise the author of *Essential Shakespeare Handbook* (2004) and *Eyewitness Companions: Opera* (2006).

12 Alan Riding, *And the Show Went On: Cultural Life in Nazi-Occupied Paris* (New York: Knopf, 2010).

13 Simone de Beauvoir, *La force de l'âge* (Paris: Gallimard, 1960).

14 Riding, Village Voice reading. *And the Show Went On*, 240.

15 Censorship imposed on La Bibliothèque nationale de France applied to all libraries, bookstores, and publishing houses. See Janet Skeslien Charles's *The Paris Library*, a semi-fictionalized memoir of the American Library in Paris under Nazi occupation (New York: Atria, Simon & Schuster, 2020).

16 Barbara Will, *Unlikely Collaboration: Gertrude Stein, Bernard Faÿ, and the Vichy Dilemma* (New York: Columbia University Press, 2011). Village Voice reading, November 16, 2011.

17 Simone de Beauvoir quoted by Riding, Village Voice reading, February 3, 2011.

18 Herbert R. Lottman, *The Purge: The Purification of the French Collaborators After World War II* (New York: William Morrow & Co, 1986). The author presented it at the Village Voice on October 15, 1986.

19 This chapter is entirely based on Alan Riding's talk at the Village Voice, February 3, 2011.

20 Alice Kaplan, *The Collaborator: The Trial and Execution of Robert Brasillach* (Chicago: University of Chicago Press, 2000).

21 Guilloux, *OK, Joe* (Paris: Gallimard, 1976). Translated into English by Alice Kaplan as *OK, Joe* (Chicago: University of Chicago Press, 2003).

22 Introduction by Robert Grenier, Village Voice reading, October 6, 2005.

Intermezzo

1   Edmund White, *The Flâneur: A Stroll through the Paradoxes of Paris* (London: Bloomsbury, 2001), 22.

2   Arthur Phillips: *Prague* (New York: Random House, 2002). Village Voice reading, November 26, 2002.

3   White, *The Flâneur*, 22.

4   White, *The Unpunished Vice* (New York: Bloomsbury, 2018), 167.

Part II

CHAPTER 9

1   Quote from Coover's *Paris is Burning* (New York: Viking, 1976). Robert Coover, Village Voice reading, 1986.

2   Jim Haynes, see Part I, Chapter 3.

3   Julian Beck, *The Life of the Theatre* (New York: Limelight Editions, 1972).

4   Judith Malina, *Poems of a Wandering Jewess* (Paris: Handshake Editions, 1982).

5   See Nelcya Delanoë's *Le Raspail vert, l'American center à Paris, 1934-1994, Une histoire des avant-gardes franco-américaines* (Paris: Seghers, 1994).

6   The French publisher of Ginsberg's *Howl and Other Poems* (San Francisco: City Lights Books, 1959), trans. Jean-Jacques Lebel and Robert Cordier (Paris: Christian Bourgois, 1966).

7   As stated by the poet Kenneth Rexroth.

8   Kazuko Shiraishi, *My Floating Mother, City* (New York: New Directions, 2009). Read in 1982 at the Village Voice, this poem does not seem to have been published before 2003.

9   Hubert Selby Jr., *Last Exit to Brooklyn* (London: Calder & Boyars, 1968).

10 Ginsberg's quote is taken from the foreword of a new French translation of *Last Exit to Brooklyn* by Jean-Pierre Carasso and Jacqueline Huet (Paris: Albin Michel, 2014).

11 See John Calder's preface to *Last Exit to Brooklyn* (London: Calder & Boyars, 1968).

12 Philippe Manœuvre, introduction to Hubert Selby Jr., Village Voice reading, October 25, 1988.

13 Two epigraphs open Selby's novel *The Demon* (London: Calder & Boyars, 1977): "Blessed is the man that endureth temptations . . ." James I: 12-15 and "I sought the Lord, and he heard me, and delivered me from all my fears," Psalms 34:4-6.

14 Selby, *Last Exit to Brooklyn* (London: Calder & Boyars, 1968).

15 Selby, *Seeds of Pain, Seeds of Love* was a work in progress, seemingly never published.

16 William H. Gass, *The Tunnel* (New York: Knopf, 1995).

17 Gass, Village Voice reading, February 6, 2007.

18 Gass, *The World within the Word* (Boston: David Godine, 1979).

19 Gass dedicated an essay to Rainer Maria Rilke: *Reading Rilke: Reflections on the Problems of Translation* (New York: Knopf, 1999).

20 Gass, Village Voice reading, February 6, 2007.

21 William Gaddis, *Carpenter's Gothic* (New York: Viking, 1985).

22 Gaddis, *The Recognitions* (New York: Harcourt Brace, 1955). Translated into French by Jean Lambert (Paris: Gallimard, 1973).

23 Chénetier's articles are compiled in *Au-delà du soupçon* (Paris: Seuil, 1989) and *Sgraffites, encres & sanguines* (Paris: Off-Shore Presses de l'École Normale Supérieure, 1994).

24 Gaddis, *J R* (New York: Knopf, 1975).

25 Gaddis, Village Voice reading, December 3, 1985. All Gaddis's quotes and the Q and A session are from this reading.

26 Expression first used in 1817 by the English poet Samuel Taylor Coleridge.

27 Gaddis, *Gothique charpentier*, trans. Marc Cholodenko (Paris: Christian Bourgois, 1988).

28 Sarah Gaddis, *Swallow Hard* (New York: Atheneum, 1990). Village Voice reading, April 23, 1991.

29 Sarah Gaddis, *Swallow Hard*.

30 Don DeLillo, *Mao II* (New York: Viking Penguin, 1991). Translated into French as *Mao II* by Marianne Véron (Arles: Actes Sud, 1992).

31 *The Letters of William Gaddis*, edited by Steven Moore with an afterword by Sarah Gaddis (Champaign, IL: Dalkey Archive Press, 2013). The quote refers to the letter to DeLillo dated July 19, 1988, 451.

32 Hubert Nyssen, introduction to DeLillo, Village Voice reading April 2, 1992.

33 DeLillo, *Mao II*.

34 A reference to the 1989 fatwa or death sentence pronounced by Iran's Ayatollah Khomeini against the Indian-born British-American author Salman Rushdie.

CHAPTER 10

1   This title inspired by Jay McInerney's novel *Bright Lights, Big City* (New York: Vintage, 1984).

2   Jay McInerney, *Brightness Falls* (New York: Knopf, 1992).

3   Not to be confused with Paul Auster's *New York Trilogy* (Los Angeles: Sun & Moon Press, 1986), which includes *City of Glass* (1985), the first of the three novellas.

4   McInerney, *Story of My Life* (New York: Atlantic Monthly Press, 1988). Village Voice reading, November 3, 1993.

5   McInerney, *Trente ans et des poussières*, trans. Jean-Pierre Carasso and Jacqueline Huet (Paris: Éditions de l'Olivier, 1993).

6   McInerney, *Story of My Life*.

7   Nod to neophyte bondsman and narrator Nick Carraway in F. Scott Fitzgerald's *The Great Gatsby* (1925).

8   Jerome Charyn, *El Bronx* (New York: Mysterious Press, 1997). Village Voice reading, May 7, 1997.

9   Charyn, Village Voice reading of *Paradise Men* (New York: Mysterious Press, 1987), October 14, 1988.

10 Charyn, Village Voice reading of *Death of a Tango King* (New York: New York University Press, 1998), January 26, 1999.

11 Charyn, Village Voice reading of *El Bronx*.

12 Richard Price, *Clockers* (New York: Houghton Mifflin, 1992). Nominated for the National Book Award and adapted to the screen in 1995.

13 Price's novel features a fictive city in the north of the Great New York, but, at his reading, the author referred to it as the Bronx.

14 Price, Village Voice reading, October 22, 1993.

15 Charyn, *Movie Land: Hollywood and the Great American Dream Culture* (New York: Putnam and Sons, 1989).

16 James Ellroy, *American Tabloid* (New York: Knopf, 1995).

CHAPTER 11

1   Russell Banks interviewed in *France-Culture*, November 11, 2016.

2   Jack Kerouac, *On the Road* (New York: Viking, 1957).

3   Douglas Kennedy, at the presentation of his novels *The Pursuit of Happiness* and *Leaving the World*, Village Voice readings, May 11, 2001, and September 24, 2009.

4   Barry Gifford and Lawrence Lee, *Jack's Book: An Oral Biography of Jack Kerouac* (New York: St. Martin's Press, 1978).

5   Barry Gifford, *Wild at Heart* (New York: Grove Press, 1990).

6   Gifford, *Landscape with Traveler: The Pillow Book of Francis Reeves* (New York: Dutton, 1980), inspired by Sei Shōnagon, the first-century Japanese author of *The Pillow Book*.

7   Gifford, *Port Tropique* (Berkeley, CA: Black Lizard Press, 1980).

8   Gifford, *The Imagination of the Heart* (New York: Seven Stories Press, 2009). In fact, it was not to be the last sequel. At the request of his readers, in 2015, under the title *The Up-Down*, the author published the final episode, this time focusing on Pace, Sailor and Lula's son.

9   The South and Chicago refer to the places where the author grew up and lived for periods of his life.

10   David Payne, *Gravesend Light* (New York: Knopf, 2000). Translated into French by Delphine Le Chevalier and Jean-Louis Chevalier as *Le phare d'un monde flottant* (Paris: Belfond, 2001).

11   John Biguenet, *Oyster*, HarperCollins US, New York 2002, published in French as *Le Secret du bayou*, tr:trans. France Camus-Pichon, Albin Michel, Paris, 2008.

12   Biguenet's quotes are from his Village Voice reading, July 26, 2010.

13   Terry Tempest Williams, *Refuge: An Unnatural History of Family and Place* (New York: Pantheon, 1991).

14   Williams, *Finding Beauty in a Broken World* (New York: Random House, 2008). Village Voice reading, March 17, 2009.

15   Williams, *The Hour of Land: A Personal Topography of America's National Parks* (New York: Farrar, Straus and Giroux, 2016).

16   Williams, Village Voice reading, December 19, 2009.

CHAPTER 12

1   Raymond Carver interviewed by David Applefield in *Frank*, Winter 1987-1988.

2   Jim Harrison, *Julip* (New York: Houghton Mifflin, 1994).

3   Harrison, Village Voice reading, May 16, 1995.

4   Brice Matthieussent, introduction to Jim Harrison, Village Voice reading, May 16, 1995.

5   Jim Harrison, *Dalva* (New York: Washington Square Press, 1989).

6   Harrison, Village Voice reading, May 16, 1995.

7   Harrison was horrified by the violence escalating in America: "Anyone can buy an AK-47, firing up to 300 shots a second. The people associated with the NRA are mostly right-wingers. You cross the frontier to Toronto, Canada, with more Black people than Detroit; it has thirty killed per year while Detroit [has] up to 800-900. The NRA is all whites, and right-wing neighborhoods are much more dangerous than Black communities."

8   Guillaume Apollinaire, French poet, author of the poetry album *Le bestiaire* (1911).

9   Harrison, Village Voice reading, May 16, 1995.

10   These gardens surround the official residence of the prime minister of France.

11   Raymond Carver, *Will You Please Be Quiet Please?* (New York: McGraw Hill, 1976). Translated into French by François Lasquin as *Tais-toi, je t'en prie* (Paris: Éditions Mazarine, 1987).

12   Peter Taylor, *Summons to Memphis* (New York: Knopf, 1986). 1987 Pulitzer Prize for Fiction.

13   Denis Hirson, Village Voice reading of *White Scars: On Reading and Rites of Passage* (his literary memoirs), March 15, 2007.

14   Carver in *Frank*, Winter 1987–88. The title "Collectors" is a play on words: they are the bailiffs who collect and also the function of the vacuum cleaner. Hence translated in French as "L'aspiration."

15   Richard Ford, "Good Raymond," *New Yorker*, October 5, 1998.

16   Raymond Carver interviewed by David Applefield in *Frank*, Winter 1987-1988.

17   Carver, Village Voice reading, April 9, 1987.

18   Robert Stewart, "Reimagining Raymond Carver on Film: A Talk with Robert Altman and Tess Gallagher," *New York Times Book Review*, September 12, 1993.

19   Richard Ford, *A Piece of My Heart* (London: Collins Harvill, 1987); US date 1976.

20   Edmund White, introduction to Richard Ford, Village Voice reading, June 26, 1987.

21   Jonathan Raban, *Coasting* (London: Collins Harvill, 1987).

22 Raymond Carver, *In a Marine Light: Selected Poems* (London: Collins Harvill, 1987).

23 Tess Gallagher, "Embers" in *Moon Crossing Bridge* (Minneapolis, MN: GraywolfPress, 1992).

24 Richard Ford, *Rock Springs: Stories* (New York: Atlantic Monthly Press, 1987).

25 Ford, "Good Raymond," *New Yorker*, October 5, 1998.

26 Ibid.

27 Gérard de Nerval was an important poetic figure of French Romanticism.

28 Edmund White, introduction to Richard Ford, Village Voice reading, March 29, 1989.

29 Ford, Village Voice reading, March 29, 1989.

30 Ford, Village Voice reading of *The Lay of the Land*, September 16, 2008.

31 Ford, the Bascombe trilogy: *The Sportswriter* (New York: Random House, 1986), *Independence Day* (New York: Knopf, 1995), and *The Lay of the Land* (New York: Knopf, 2006).

32 Ford, Village Voice reading, *Independence Day*, March 7, 1996.

33 Ford's reading from *The Lay of the Land*, September 16, 2008.

34 Russell Banks, *Continental Drift* (New York: Harper & Row, 1985).

35 Interview with Raphael Bourgois, France Culture, October 9, 2016.

36 Banks, *The Darling* (New York: Harper & Row, 2004), translated into French as *American Darling* by Pierre Furlan (Arles: Actes Sud, 2005).

37 Russell Banks, *Cloudsplitter* (New York: HarperCollins, 1998).

38 Banks, *The Reserve* (New York: HarperCollins, 2008).

39 "I am beautiful as a dream of stone," epigraph adapted from Baudelaire's poem "La beauté" in *Les Fleurs du Mal*.

40 Character inspired by the Canadian artist Rockwell Kent, famed painter and illustrator of Melville's *Moby Dick*.

41 Banks, Village Voice reading, March 4, 2008.

CHAPTER 13

1   Hazel Rowley, *Richard Wright: The Life and Times* (New York: Henry Holt, 2001).

2   Hazel Rowley, *Tête-à-Tête: Simone de Beauvoir and Jean-Paul Sartre* (New York: HarperCollins, 2005); the paperback edition: *Tête-à-Tête, The Tumultuous Lives and Loves of Simone de Beauvoir & Jean-Paul Sartre* (New York: HarperPerennial, 2006).

3   All quotes are from Rowley's reading.

4   Bianca Lamblin, *Mémoires d'une jeune fille dérangée* (Paris: Balland, 2006), translated into English by Julie Plovnick as *A Disgraceful Affair* (Boston: Northeastern University Press, 1996).

5   Simone de Beauvoir, *Pour une morale de l'ambiguïté* (Paris: Gallimard, 1947); *The Ethics of Ambiguity*, trans. Bernard Frechtman (New York: Citadel Press, 1948).

6   Beauvoir, *The Second Sex*, trans. Constance Borde and Sheila Malovany-Chevallier (London: Jonathan Cape, 2009), 285.

7   Hazel Rowley, Village Voice reading, January 12, 2006.

8   "My books are voyages, risky voyages, involving a great deal of passion on my part," writes Rowley in "The Ups, the Downs: My Life as a Biographer," *Australian Book Review*, July-August 2007.

9   Kathleen Spivack about her friend Hazel Rowley.

10 *Le Monde*, October 19, 2006.

11 Claude Lanzmann in *The Patagonian Hare: A Memoir* (New York: Farrar, Straus and Giroux, 2012) refers to Rowley's *Tête-à-Tête* as "the umpteenth American biography of

the Sartre/de Beauvoir partnership, made up entirely of petty spite and sordid rumors intended for an ignorant public," 160.

12   Serge Rezvani, *Le testament amoureux* (Paris: Éditions Stock, 1981).

13   Rowley, "Censorship in France" in *The American Scholar*, December 2008. The fate of Rowley's biography is also referenced in *Magnificent Obsessions: Honouring the Lives of Hazel Rowley*, ed. Rosemary Lloyd and Jean Fornasiero (Newcastle upon Tyne: Cambridge Scholars Publishing, 2013).

14   All quotes are from Rowley, Village Voice reading, 2005.

15   Ayaan Hirsi Ali incurred the same risk as her friend, the filmmaker Theo van Gogh, murdered by a Dutch Islamist in 2004, and before him, Salman Rushdie, the victim of a fatwa, his books burned in public places in several countries, survivor of multiple assassination attempts.

16   Constance Borde and Sheila Malovany-Chevallier, *Le deuxième sexe*. A first translation had been published in the United States in 1953, but with cuts and alterations reflecting a decade when the American woman was glorified as homemaker, housewife, and mother.

17   Rowley's long-standing relationship with the Village Voice is cited in an article she wrote, published in *The Australian Literary Review*, December 2007, reproduced in "It Takes a Village" in *Bookforum*, February/March 2008.

18   Rowley, *Franklin and Eleanor: An Extraordinary Marriage* (New York: Farrar, Straus and Giroux, 2010).

19   Rowley, "The Ups, the Downs, My Life as a Biographer," annual lecture, La Trobe University, 2007.

20   James Joyce, "The Dead" in *Dubliners*, annotated edition (New York: Penguin, 1992).

21   Grace Paley, "A Poem about Storytelling," http ://voetica.comVoetica (blog), https:// voetica.com/poem/4864

22   Paley, *Just as I Thought* (New York: Farrar, Straus and Giroux, 1998), translated into French by Suzanne Mayoux as *C'est bien ce que je pensais* (Paris: Rivages, 1999).

23   Noëlle Batt, author of *Grace Paley, Conteuse des destins ordinaires* (Paris: Éditions Belin, 1998).

24   This statement from the Q and A refers to her reading of November 23, 1996, when President Clinton had just been reelected. He had signed the new memo on affirmative action, but there was also the bombing of the Oklahoma Federal Building with 168 people killed (1995); Louis Farrakhan's Million Man March of African American men on Washington, D.C. (1995); and the acquittal of the African American murder suspect O. J. Simpson (1995). These events further exacerbated racial tensions in the US.

25   Rich, *The School among the Ruins: Poems 2000-2004* (New York: W.W. Norton, 2004).

26   Ellen Hinsey, *Cities of Memory* (London & New Haven, CT: Yale University Press, 1996).

27   Ellen Hinsey, introduction to Adrienne Rich, Village Voice reading, July 18, 2006.

28   Rich, "The Art of Translation," *American Poetry Review*, vol. 27, no. 3.

29   The French poet and translator Claire Malroux and translators Maria Luisa Moretti and Marisol Sánchez Gomez who had flown to Paris from Italy and Spain to meet the poet in person for the first time.

30   Adrienne Rich, Village Voice reading, 2006.

31   Ibid. In "Poetry and Experience" (1965), Rich writes "I have to say that what I know I know through making poems," from *Poetry and Prose* (New York: W.W. Norton, 1993).

32   Rich, *The School among the Ruins*, 22.

33   The term "not" is underlined by the author.

34   Sontag, Village Voice reading, March 28, 2002.

35   Sontag, *Illness as Metaphor* (New York: Farrar, Straus and Giroux, 1978).

36   Sontag, *AIDS and Its Metaphors* (New York: Farrar, Straus and Giroux, 1989).

37   Sontag, *Regarding the Pain of Others* (New York: Farrar, Straus and Giroux, 2003).

38   Sontag, *The Volcano Lover* (New York: Farrar, Straus and Giroux, 1992).

39   Sontag, *In America* (New York: Farrar, Straus and Giroux, 2000).

40   Sontag, *Where the Stress Falls* (New York: Farrar, Straus and Giroux, 2001).

41   We had a closed-circuit system that allowed people to follow the reading from everywhere in the bookshop.

42   Chantal Thomas is a prize-winning novelist, playwright, and author of essays on Sade, Casanova, and Thomas Bernhard, among others, and now a member of the Académie Française.

43   Sontag, "Homage to Halliburton" in *Where the Stress Falls* (New York: Farrar, Straus and Giroux, 2001).

44   Elizabeth Bishop, one of the major American poets of the twentieth century, traveled widely and settled in Brazil where she lived for many years.

45   Allusion to Sontag's first novels: *The Benefactor* (1963) and *Death Kit* (1967).

46   In 1993, Sontag staged Beckett's *Waiting for Godot* in Sarajevo during its siege and under heavy shelling.

47   Susan Sontag, "Looking at War," *New Yorker*, December 1, 2002.

48   David Rieff, *Swimming in a Sea of Death: A Son's Memoir* (Simon & Schuster, New York, 2008).

CHAPTER 14

1   *The Clouds Threw This Light: Contemporary Native American Poetry*, ed. Phillip Foss (Santa Fe, NM: Institute of American Indian Arts Press, 1983).

2   See Edouard Roditi, Part I, Chapter 3.

3   William Jay Smith, *The World below the Window: Poems 1937-1997* (Baltimore: John Hopkins University Press, 1998); the author's reading was introduced by Carolyn Kizer, June 4, 1998.

4   N. Scott Momaday, *House Made of Dawn* (New York: Harper & Row, 1968), translated into French by Yves Berger as *La maison de l'aube* (Paris: Gallimard, 1996).

5   Francis Geffard, founder of Terre indienne, an imprint of the publishing house Albin Michel, and of the biennial Festival America in Vincennes that has been showcasing authors from South, Central, and North America since 2002.

6   James Welch, *Winter in the Blood* (New York: Harper & Row, 1974); translated into French by Michel Lederer as *L'hiver dans le sang* (Paris: Terre indienne, Albin Michel, 1992).

7   Welch, *Fools Crow* (New York: Viking, 1986).

8   James Welch's Q and A session, Village Voice reading, May 10, 1992.

9   Erdrich, *Love Medicine* (New York: Holt, Rhinehart and Winston, 1984).

10   Joëlle Rostkowski, *Le renouveau indien aux Etats-Unis, un siècle de reconquêtes* (Paris: L'Harmattan, 1986).

11   Marc Chénetier, professor of American literature at Université de Paris 7-Denis Diderot.

12   Louise Erdrich, *The Beet Queen* (New York: Henry Holt, 1986).

13   Michael Dorris, *A Yellow Raft in Blue Water* (New York: Henry Holt, 1987).

14   Peter Nabokov, *Where the Lighting Strikes: The Lives of American Indian Sacred Places* (New York: Viking, 2006). Translated into French by Marie-France Girod as *Là où la foudre frappe, lieux sacrés de l'Amérique indienne* (Paris: Albin Michel, 2008).

15   Erdrich, reading from *The Plague of Doves* (New York: HarperCollins, 2008).

16 David Treuer, *The Hiawatha* (New York: Picador USA, 1999). The title refers to the name of the Chicago Railway Company where the protagonist's younger brother used to work. Translated into French by Marie-Claire Pasquier as *Comme un frère* (Paris: Albin Michel, Terres d'Amérique, 2002). The French title hints at the novel's plot, i.e., a Cain and Abel tragedy.

17 Treuer, *Rez Life: An Indian's Journey through Reservation Life* (New York: Grove Press Atlantic, 2012), 4.

18 David Treuer, *The Hiawatha*.

19 David Treuer's Q and A session, Village Voice reading, May 15, 2002.

CHAPTER 15

1   Morrison was in conversation with theater director Peter Sellars who staged performances of *Desdemona*, based on the libretto by Morrison. This "literary and musical collaboration" premiered at the Théâtre des Amandiers, Nanterre, October 13, 2011.

2   Jake Lamar, Village Voice reading, January 17, 1995.

3   Lamar, *Bourgeois Blues* (New York: Plume, 1992).

4   Lamar, *Close to the Bone* (New York: Crown Publishers, 1999).

5   Bob Swaim taught film studies at the American University of Paris. He is the director of, among others, the documentary film *Lumières noires* (2006), on the Congrès des écrivains et artistes noirs, Paris, 1956, reported by James Baldwin in "Princes and Powers," *Collected Essays* (New York: Library of America, 1998), 143.

6   John Edgar Wideman, *Brothers and Keepers* (New York: Holt, Rinehart and Winston, 1984). Translated into French by Marianne Guénot as *Suis-je le gardien de mon frère?* (Paris: Jacques Bertoin Éditeur, 1992).

7   Wideman, Village Voice reading, February 2, 1992.

8   Wideman, *Philadelphia Fire* (New York: Henry Holt, 1990).

9   Paule Marshall, *Brown Girl, Brownstones*, reprint from Random House Edition (1959) with an afterword by Mary Helen Washington (New York: The Feminist Press, 1981).

10 Marshall, *Fille noire, pierre sombre*, trans. Jean-Pierre Carasso (Paris: Éditions Balland, 1983).

11 Barbara Chase-Riboud, *Sally Hemings* (New York: St. Martin's Press, 1979). This novel was mentioned by the author at her later presentation of *Hottentot Venus* (New York: Doubleday, 2003) at the Village Voice, April 8, 2004.

12 Jayne Cortez, *Firespitter* (New York: Bola Press, 1982). Village Voice reading, November 13, 1984.

13 Sapphire, *Push* (New York: Knopf, 1996). Translated into French by Jean-Pierre Carasso as *Precious*, Sapphire's protagonist (Paris: Éditions de l'Olivier, 1997).

14 Morrison, *Beloved* (New York: Knopf, 1987). Translated into French by Hortense Chabrier and Sylvia Rué (Paris: Christian Bourgois, Éditeur, 1989).

15 Michel Fabre, author of *La rive noire, de Harlem à la Seine* (Paris: Lieu Commun, 1985); Richard Wright, *La quête inachevée* (Paris: Lieu Commun, 1973, 1986); Geneviève Fabre, *Le Théâtre noir aux Etats-Unis* (Paris: CNRS, 1982).

16 Morrison, *Beloved* (New York: Knopf, 1987). Pulitzer Prize 1988.

17 Barbara Hendricks, *Lifting My Voice: A Memoir* (Chicago: Chicago Review Press, 2014), 375.

CHAPTER 16

1   C. P. Cavafy's poem "The City," quoted in Andre Aciman's "Alexandria: The Capital of Memory" in *False Papers* (New York: Farrar, Straus and Giroux, 2000).

2   Aciman, *Eight White Nights* (New York: Farrar, Straus and Giroux, 2010).

3   Aciman, *False Papers*.

4   Renaud Machart, Village Voice reading, November 5, 2010.

5   Aciman, *Eight White Nights*, 33-34.

6   Aciman, *Eight White Nights*, 37.

7   Amy Tan, *The Joy Luck Club* (New York: G.P. Putnam's Sons, 1989).

8   Tan, *The Opposite of Fate: Memories of a Writing Life* (New York: G.P. Putnam's Sons, 2003). Village Voice reading, June 2, 2005.

9   Jamaica Kincaid, *A Small Place* (New York: Farrar, Straus and Giroux, 2000).

10   Kincaid, Village Voice reading, January 14, 2000.

11   Kincaid, *My Brother* (New York: Farrar, Straus and Giroux, 1996). Translated into French by Jean-Pierre Carasso and Jacqueline Huet as *Mon frère* (Paris: Éditions de l'Olivier, 2000).

12   Kincaid, *The Autobiography of My Mother* (New York: Farrar, Straus and Giroux, 1996).

13   Kincaid, Village Voice reading, 2000.

14   Dinaw Mengestu, "Why the Expats Left Paris," *Wall Street Journal*, July 6, 2008.

15   Mengestu, *How to Read the Air* (New York: Riverhead, 2010).

16   Mengestu, *The Beautiful Things That Heaven Bears* (New York: Riverhead, 2007).

17   Díaz, *The Brief Wondrous Life of Oscar Wao* (New York: Riverhead, 2007). Translated into French by Laurence Viallet as *La brève et merveilleuse vie d'Oscar Wao* (Paris: Plon, 2009).

18   Evelyn Ch'ien, *Weird English* (Cambridge, MA: Harvard University Press, 2004).

19   Azar Nafisi, *Reading Lolita in Tehran: A Memoir in Books* (New York: Random House, 2003.

20   Goli Taraghi, *A Mansion in the Sky: Short Stories* (Austin, TX: Center for Middle Eastern Studies, University of Texas at Austin, 2003); French publication: *La Maison de Shemiran* (Arles: Actes Sud, 2003).

21   Nafisi, *Things I've Been Silent About: Memories*, (New York: Random House, 2008). Translated into French by Marie-Hélène Dumas as *Mémoires captives* (Paris: Plon, 2009).

CHAPTER 17

1   Epigraph inspired by "Aschenglorie," Paul Celan, *Selected Poems and Prose*, trans. John Felstiner (New York: W.W. Norton, 2000): "No one / bears witness for the / witness."

2   Amy Bloom, *Away* (London: Granta Books, 2007). Village Voice reading, June 26, 2008.

3   Saul Bellow, *Dangling Man* (New York: Vanguard Press, 1944).

4   Gwen Edelman, *War Story* (New York: Riverhead, 2001). Translated into French by Anne Damour as *Dernier refuge avant la nuit* (Paris: Belfond, 2002).

5   Edelman, *The Train to Warsaw* (New York: Grove Press, 2014).

6   Edelman, Village Voice reading, September 20, 2001.

7   Cynthia Ozick, *The Messiah of Stockholm* (New York: Knopf, 1987).

8   Gilbert and Sullivan, Victorian-era theatrical partnership, Gilbert as dramatist and Sullivan as composer of operas and comic operas.

9   Mavis Gallant, letter to me, July 23, 2005.

10   Art Spiegelman, *The Complete Maus: A Survivor's Tale* (New York: Pantheon, 1996).

11   Nicole Krauss, *The History of Love* (New York: W.W. Norton, 2005).

12   Krauss, *Great House* (New York: W.W. Norton, 2010). Translated into French by Paule Guivarch as *La grande maison* (Paris: Éditions de l'Olivier, 2011).

13   Krauss's Q and A session from her Village Voice reading, April 27, 2011.

14   Mendelsohn, *The Lost: A Search for Six of Six Million* (New York: HarperCollins, 2006).

15   Mendelsohn is the author of two academic works, *Gender and the City in Euripides' Political Plays* (1994) and *The Elusive Embrace: Desire and the Riddle of Identity* (2000).

16   W. G. Sebald's *The Emigrants* (published in German in 1992 and in English in 1996) is remarkable for its innovative use of text with black and white photos.

Intermezzo

1   This poem was later included in Adam Zagajewski's *Without End: New and Selected Poems* (New York: Farrar, Straus and Giroux, 2002). An award-winning Polish poet, Zagajewski divided his time among his native Poland, Paris, and the US where he taught.

2   Giovanna Borradori, *Philosophy in a Time of Terror: Dialogues with Jürgen Habermas and Jacques Derrida* (Chicago: University of Chicago Press, 2003). Entirely devoted to Jacques Derrida, our evening started with a presentation by the French writer Hélène Cixous of her *Portrait of Jacques Derrida as a Young Jewish Saint* (New York: Columbia University Press, 2004). In it, Cixous explores through language the meaning of being Jewish for someone like Derrida, the philosopher who "scoffed at boundaries and fixed identities." The event was moderated by Bie Brahic, Canadian poet and English translator of Cixous's works.

3   "Le Monde des lumières à venir" in *Un Jour Derrida*, Editions de la bibliothèque publique d'information, November 2005.

4   Nishant Irudayadason, "Thinking a World without Boundaries: Derrida and Tirumular, an Endeavour of Comparative Philosophy" (dissertation, Université Paris-Est, 2008), https://www.researchgate.net/publication/278634579_Thinking_a_world_beyond_boundaries_Derrida_and_Tirumular_an_endeavor_of_comparative_philosophy.

Part III

CHAPTER 18

1   An institution with a rich cultural tradition in France since 1944, the British Council organized a series of encounters with British writers. Christine Jordis, author of several books on English literature, was in charge of this program from 1979 to 1991.

2   David Lodge, Village Voice reading, January 8, 1990.

3   Lodge's *Campus Trilogy* includes *Changing Places* (1975), *Small World* (1984), and *Nice Work* (1988), all originally published by Secker and Warburg, London.

4   A. S. Byatt: *Possession: A Romance* (London: Chatto & Windus, 1990). Winner of the Booker Prize that same year.

5   Byatt, Village Voice reading, September 14, 1993.

6   Ibid.

7   David Lodge, *Thinks* (London: Secker & Warburg, 2001).

8   Salman Rushdie, *Midnight's Children* (London: Jonathan Cape, 1981).

CHAPTER 19

1   Hanif Kureishi, *My Ear at His Heart: Reading My Father* (London: Faber & Faber, 2004). His father had immigrated to England in the wake of the partition of Pakistan from India.

2   Kureishi, *Contre son coeur*, trans. Jean Rosenthal (Paris: Éditions Christian Bourgois, 2005).

3   Rajmohan Gandhi, *Mohandas: A True Story of a Man, His People and an Empire* (London: Penguin Books, 2007). Village Voice reading, October 2, 2008.

4   Fatima Bhutto, *Songs of Blood and Sword* (London: Jonathan Cape, 2010). Village Voice reading, January 27, 2011.

5   Abha Dawesar, *Babyji*, (New York: Random House, 2005). Translated into French by Isabelle Reinharez (Paris: Éditions Heloïse d'Ormesson, 2004).

6   Dawesar, *Miniplanner* (Berkeley, CA: Cleis Press, 2000).

7   Dawesar, Village Voice reading, November 11, 2007.

8 Tarun Tejpal, *The Alchemy of Desire* (London: Picador, 2005), translated into French by Annick Le Goyat as *Loin de chandigar* (Paris: Buchet-Chastel, 2005).

9 Tejpal, *The Story of My Assassins* (New Delhi: HarperCollins India, 2009). Translated into French by Annick Le Goyat as *Histoire de mes assassins* (Paris: Buchet-Chastel, 2009).

CHAPTER 20

1 *The Heinemann Book of South African Short Stories*, ed. Denis Hirson and Martin Trump (London: Heinemann, 1994).

2 Denis Hirson, *The House Next Door to Africa* (Manchester: Carcanet, 1987).

3 Hirson, *I Remember King Kong (The Boxer)* (Johannesburg: Jacana Media, 2004).

4 Hirson, *We Walk Straight So You Better Get Out the Way* (Johannesburg: Jacana Media, 2005).

5 Louise Klapisch, letter to me, dated June 12, 2005.

6 Hirson, *The Dancing and the Death on Lemon Street* (Johannesburg: Jacana Media, 2011). Village Voice reading, October 8, 2011.

7 Hirson, *The House Next Door to Africa*. Village Voice reading, April 21, 1988.

8 Hirson, *White Scars: On Reading and Rites of Passage* (Johannesburg: Jacana Media, 2006). Village Voice reading, March 15, 2007.

9 Ibid.

10 Hirson, *We Walk Straight So You Better Get Out the Way* (Johannesburg: Jacana Media, 2005). Village Voice reading, March 23, 2006.

11 Ibid.

12 Hirson, Village Voice reading, October 8, 2011.

13 Ibid.

14 Hirson, Village Voice reading, March 23, 2006.

15 Hirson, Village Voice reading, October 8, 2011.

16 Ibid.

17 Ibid.

18 Breyten Breytenbach, *In Africa Even the Flies Are Happy: Selected Poems*, trans. Denis Hirson (London: Calder Publications, 1978).

19 Breyten Breytenbach, *Windcatcher: New and Selected Poems 1964-2006* (Orlando, FL: Harcourt, 2007).

20 Breytenbach, Village Voice reading, July 1, 2008.

21 Nelson Mandela and Mandla Langa, *Dare Not Linger: The Presidential Years* (London: Macmillan, 2017).

22 ANC: African National Congress, the political party led by Nelson Mandela which carried him to power.

23 Mandla Langa, *The Lost Colours of the Chameleon* (Johannesburg: Picador Africa, 2008, 2011).

24 Langa, Village Voice reading, March 17, 2011.

25 Damon Galgut, *The Good Doctor* (London: Atlantic Books, 2003), launched at the Village Voice on the occasion of its French publication, *Un docteur irréprochable*, trans. Hélène Papot (Paris: Éditions de l'Olivier, 2005). He received the Booker Prize for his novel *The Promise*, (London: Chatto & Windus, 2021.)

26 Galgut in conversation with Denis Hirson, Village Voice reading, April 4, 2005.

CHAPTER 21

1   Tim Winton, *Dirt Music* (London: Picador, 2002). Translated into French by Nadine Gassie as *Par-dessus le bord du monde* (Paris: Rivages, 2004).

2   Tim Winton, Village Voice reading, March 30, 2004.

3   Claire Messud, *The Last Life* (London: Picador, 1999), about a French-Algerian family haunted by having to leave their native country and past life due to the outbreak of the Algerian War.

4   Julia Leigh, *The Hunter* (London: Faber & Faber, 2000), originally published by Penguin Australia in 1999.

CHAPTER 22

1   Anne Tremblay, *The Montreal Gazette*, August 10, 1985.

2   Mavis Gallant, see Part I, Chapter 7.

3   Tremblay, *The Montreal Gazette*, August 10, 1985.

4   Margaret Atwood, *The Handmaid's Tale* (Toronto: McClelland & Stewart, 1985).

5   Atwood, *Alias Grace* (Toronto: McClelland & Stewart, 1996). Translated into French by Michèle Albaret-Maatsch as *Captive* (Paris: Éditions 10/18, 1998). Village Voice joint reading with Richard Ford, April 5, 1998.

6   Richard Ford, *Women with Men*, (New York: Knopf, 1997); In French: *Une situation difficile*, trans. Suzanne Mayoux (Paris: Éditions de l'Olivier, 1998).

7   Jane Urquhart, *The Stone Carvers* (Toronto: McClelland & Stewart, 2001).

8   Nancy Huston, see Part I, Chapter 7.

9   Jane Urquhart, Village Voice reading, April, 7, 2005.

10 Matt Cohen, *Nadine* (Markham, Ontario: Penguin Canada, 1986) and *Emotional Arithmetic* (Toronto: Lester & Orpen Dennys, 1990). Village Voice reading, November 9, 1995.

11 Anne Michaels, *Fugitive Pieces* (Toronto: McLelland & Stewart 1996). Village Voice reading, September 17, 1998.

12 Mavis Gallant, letter to me, October 24, 2004.

13 Michael Ondaatje, *Secular Love* (Toronto: Coach House, 1984) and *Running in the Family* (Toronto: McClelland & Stewart, 1982). Village Voice reading, April 9, 1986.

14 Ondaatje, *Divisadero* (New York: Knopf, 2007). Village Voice reading, September 6, 2007.

15 Ondaatje, *Anil's Ghost* (New York: Knopf, 2000).

16 Ondaatje, *The English Patient* (New York: Knopf, 1992). Translated into French by Marie-Odile Fortier-Masek as *L'homme flambé* (Paris: Éditions de l'Olivier, 1992). Village Voice reading, February 17, 1993. A few years later, Ondaatje was to publish *Warlight*, his fourth novel about war (New York: Knopf, 2018).

17 Ondaatje, Q and A session, Village Voice reading of *The English Patient*, February 17, 1993.

18 Hazel Rowley, "It Takes a Village," in *Bookforum*, February/March 2008.

19 Ondaatje, *The Cat's Table* (New York: Knopf, 2011).

20 Ondaatje, Q and A session, Village Voice reading of *The Cat's Table*, June 28, 2012.

Part IV

CHAPTER 23

1   Stephen Spender, *The Temple* (London: Faber & Faber, 1988).

2   Foreword to the anthology *21+1: Poètes Américains d'aujourd'hui* (Montpellier: Delta, 1986).

3 Village Voice reading, June 13, 1986. Joseph Simas had translated French poet Anne-Marie Albiach's *Mezza voce*, and Cole Swensen, Emmanuel Hocquard's *L'invention du verre*. Conversely, Emmanuel Hocquard had translated Michael Palmer, Pierre Joris, Jerome Rothenberg, Anne-Marie Albiach, and Keith Waldrop.

4 Raymond Roussel (1877-1933), French poet, novelist, and playwright.

5 Harry Mathews, Village Voice reading, May 13, 1986.

6 John Ashbery, *Flow Chart* (New York: Knopf, 1991). Village Voice reading, June 26, 1992.

7 In my copy of *The Sinking of the Odradek Stadium* (Manchester: Carcanet Press, 1985), Mathews inscribed the words "Surprise and inevitability" that convey the spirit of this novel and his work in general.

8 Mathews, "The Dialect of the Tribe," first published in *Country Cooking*, reprinted in *The Human Country: New and Collected Stories* (Normal, IL: Dalkey Archive Press, 2002).

9 Mathews, Village Voice reading, May 13, 1986. For the author, the process of writing is to be compared to the composer's art. Both he and Roussel had pursued studies in music.

10 Georges Perec's novel *La disparition* was to be translated in its entirety by Gilbert Adair under the title *A Void* (London: Harvill Press, 1994).

11 Mathews, Village Voice reading, May 13, 1986.

12 Edmund White's introduction to Harry Mathews, Village Voice reading, May 13, 1986.

13 William Faulkner, interview in the *Paris Review*, Issue 12, Spring 1956.

14 "Paris, elegant gray . . ." Marilyn Hacker, "Explication de Texte" in *Desesperanto: Poems 1999-2000* (New York: W.W. Norton, 2003)

15 Susan Sontag, *Where the Stress Falls* (New York: Farrar, Straus and Giroux, 2001). The author refers to Gertrude Stein's definition of poetry: "Poetry is nouns, prose is verbs," p. 5.

16 Marilyn Hacker, *Squares and Courtyards* (New York: W.W. Norton, 2000).

17 Hacker, "Rêve Champêtre" in *Desesperanto* (New York: Farrar, Straus and Giroux, 2010).

18 Hacker, "Going Back to the River" in *Going Back to the River: Poems* (New York: Random House, 1990). Translated into French by Jean Migrenne as *Fleuves et retours* (Paris: Éditions Amiot-Lenganey, 1993).

19 Mavis Gallant, see Part I, Chapter 7.

20 Hacker, Village Voice reading, April 9, 1987.

21 Margo Berdeshevsky, *But A Passage in Wilderness* (Rhinebeck, NY: Sheep Meadow Press, 2007). Village Voice reading, March 8, 2008.

22 Berdeshevsky, "Whom Beggars Call" in *But A Passage in Wilderness*.

23 Marie Ponsot, "For My Old Self, at Notre Dame de Paris: fluctuat nec mergitur," *Paris Review*, Issue 133, Winter 1994.

24 Kathleen Spivack, *With Robert Lowell and His Circle* (Lebanon, NH: Northeastern University Press, 2012).

25 Kathleen Spivack, *A History of Yearning*, Vol. XX, N° 1, The Sow's Ear Poetry Review, Milwood VA, 2010.

26 *Anthem for Doomed Youth*, an exhibit organized by the Imperial War Museum in London in 2003. The title of her poem refers to Wilfred Owen's "Anthem for Doomed Youth," one of the emblematic British poems of World War I.

27 C. K. Williams, Village Voice reading, October 14, 2010, for the launch of *Wait* (New York: Farrar, Straus and Giroux, 2010).

28 Williams, *Flesh and Blood* (New York: Farrar, Straus and Giroux, 1987); National Book Critics Circle Award for Poetry (1987).

29 Williams, *Repair* (New York: Farrar, Straus and Giroux, 1999); Pulitzer Prize for

Poetry (2000). Village Voice reading, December 5, 1999. Introduced by Adam Zagajewski and attended by John Felstiner, translator and biographer of the poet Paul Celan and others.

30 Williams, *The Singing* (New York: Farrar, Straus and Giroux, 2003); National Book Award (2003).

31 Williams, *Misgivings: My Mother, My Father, Myself* (New York: Farrar, Straus and Giroux, 2000).

32 Williams, *On Whitman* (Princeton, NJ: Princeton University Press, 2000).

33 Blumenthal's reference to the American poet William Carlos Williams.

34 C. K. Williams, Village Voice reading, November 6, 2003.

35 Williams, *Wait* (New York: Farrar, Straus and Giroux, 2010).

36 Williams, *Wait*. Village Voice reading, October 14, 2010.

37 Remark made during his presentation of his essay *On Whitman*, Village Voice reading, October 14, 2010.

38 Marina Tsvetaeva, *Art in the Light of Conscience* (London: Bloodaxe Books, 2010).

39 Williams, "Marina" in *Wait*. Village Voice reading, 2010.

40 Williams, "The Foundation" in *Wait*.

41 Carolyn Kizer, introduction to Williams's presentation of his collection *Flesh and Blood*, Village Voice, 1987.

42 Ellen Hinsey, *The White Fire of Time* (Middletown, CT: Wesleyan University Press, 2002). Village Voice reading, November 21, 2002.

43 Hinsey, Village Voice reading, November 21, 2002.

44 Hinsey, *Cities of Memory* (New Haven, CT: Yale University Press, 1996); Yale Series of Younger Poets Prize (1995).

45 Hinsey, *Update on the Descent* (Hexham, Northumberland, UK: Bloodaxe Books, 2009); Village Voice reading, June 4, 2009.

46 Hinsey conducted a series of interviews with Toma Venclova collected in *Magnetic North* (Rochester, NY: University of Rochester Press, and Suffolk: Boydell and Brewer, 2017).

47 Carol Pratl, see Part I, Chapter 3.

48 Denis Hirson, introduction to Ellen Hinsey, Village Voice reading, June 6, 1996. See Part IV, Chapter 23.

49 Denis Hirson, introduction to Ellen Hinsey, Village Voice reading, June 6, 1996.

50 Hinsey, "Trains at Night" in *Cities of Memory*.

51 Hinsey, "The Art of Measuring Light" in *Cities of Memory*.

52 Hinsey, "Testimony on What is Important" in *Update on the Descent*.

53 Hinsey, Village Voice reading, June 4, 2009.

54 Hinsey, "Interdiction" in *Update on the Descent*.

55 A few years later, Ellen would publish *Mastering the Past: Contemporary Central and Eastern Europe and the Rise of Illiberalism* (New York: Telos Press, 2017).

56 Michèle Laforest, novelist and poet, gave several readings at the Village Voice. The translator of Amos Tutuola in French, she invited the Nigerian author to read at our bookstore from *The Palm-Wine Drinkard* and *My Life in the Bush of Ghosts*. Village Voice reading, May 21, 1985.

57 W. S. Merwin, *The Vixen: Poems* (New York: Knopf, 1996).

58 Merwin, *The Lost Upland: Stories of Southwest France* (New York: Knopf, 1992).

59 Causse perdu: a secluded limestone plateau which sounds like "cause perdue" in French or "lost cause."

60 Merwin, *The Pupil: Poems* (New York: Knopf, 2001). Village Voice reading, May 27, 2002.

61 Merwin, *The Mays of Ventadorn* (Washington, D.C.: National Geographic Society, 2002).

62 After World War II, Ezra Pound was locked in this hospital in Washington, D.C., largely because of his radio broadcasts on Italian public radio in support of Mussolini and fascism.

63 Merwin, *The Mays of Ventadorn* (Washington, D.C.: National Geographic Society, 2002). Village Voice reading, May 27, 2002.

64 Merwin, Village Voice reading, May 27, 2002, recalling the words of Ezra Pound during their conversation at St Elizabeths in Washington, D.C.

65 Merwin, *Selected Translations* (Port Townsend, WA: Copper Canyon Press, 2013).

66 Merwin, Village Voice reading, May 27, 2002.

67 A distinguished and prolific author and translator, Luc de Goustine introduced Merwin to the French public through *La renarde* (Perigueux: Éditions Fanlac, 2004), his luminous translation of *The Vixen*.

68 Michael Taylor, American poet, translator, and editor of a bilingual edition of Merwin's prose and poems, *L'appel du Causse* (Perigueux: Éditions Fanlac, 2013).

69 Merwin, "Walker," "Old Sound," and "Snake" in *The Vixen: Poems* (New York: Knopf, 1996).

70 Merwin, "The Nomad Flute" in *The Shadow of Sirius* (Port Townsend, WA: Copper Canyon Press, 2008).

71 Also quoted by Terry Tempest Williams in *The Hour of Land* (New York: Farrar, Straus and Giroux, 2016), 360.

72 "On the last day of the world I would want to plant a tree . . .", Merwin, "Place" in *The Rain in the Trees* (New York: Knopf, 1988).

Epilogue

1 Edmund White, *The Unpunished Vice: A Life of Reading* (New York: Bloomsbury, 2018).

2 Title borrowed from Andrea Weiss, *Paris Was a Woman: Portraits from the Left Bank* (San Francisco: Harper, 1995). See Part I, Chapter 2.

3 Alice Kaplan, *Dreaming in French: The Paris Years of Jacqueline Bouvier Kennedy, Susan Sontag, and Angela Davis* (Chicago: University of Chicago Press, 2012). See Part I, Chapter 8. Kaplan is also the author of *French Lessons*, a memoir of her own junior year in France (Chicago: University of Chicago Press, 1993).

Acknowledgments

1 Susan Hermann launched our tearoom. See her article "The Renaissance of Salons de thé in Paris," *Paris Passion*, September-October 1982.